Endorsements

"Believing the unseen" requires great courage and conviction. Of a truth, the Christian's walk is not for the fainthearted: very often during the journey does the believer question its purpose, especially when confronted with life's seemingly difficult choices. Such 'crossroads' however, are purely borne out of ignorance – the main platform from which the prey-seeking devil launches his destructive weapons. Therefore, the onus is on every believer to actively seek the truth and be free.

Walking In The Light of His Mysteries exposes the essence of true Christian fellowship with God. This inspirational work draws from the author's extensive experience as a servant of the Lord Jesus Christ, and provides a powerful insight into God's divine agenda for those who choose His path.

-Dr. Supo Olusi
The World Bank, Washington DC,
USA

A real insight into God's timeless truth. This book has great potential to challenge, change, and transform lives. Indeed, a practical demonstration of the dynamics of God's power. An inspirational book with relevant examples that demonstrate the miracle working power of God. In reading, you will discover detail by detail how God's Word has worked for others, and can also work for you. A *must-have* book for all!

-Rev. Julius K. Dake
Bible Life Family Ministries, London,
UK

Another extraordinary book from Pastor Didi breathing with Godly and lively wisdom for having and living quality life by divine design! He wrote about purpose in His first book, but this one in my view helps you fulfil your purpose. It's truly an 'encyclopaedia' of practical wisdom from a bible point of view to help the reader to appreciate the love and grace of Jesus Christ and to help them to walk in God's provision and victory.

The subject of the book in general seriously provokes and introduces new thinking in many areas including fear, life's challenges, God's mysteries, predestination, tongue speaking, honour's rewards, Satan's schemes, and miracles, while also providing and arming readers with proven Godly truths about how to positively tackle and address critical issues affecting believers' walk of faith.

Truly, this book will be remembered as a valuable contribution to the church and Christianity, and I highly recommend it!

-Rev Kau J Dolopei
Church of the Living God, Philadelphia, USA

Pastor Didi is both a trusted colleague and a dear friend.

In this book he has systematically unearthed keys that unlock to us the mysteries of God. Not merely that we would better understand Him, but rather that we could walk into and ultimately live in the fullness of His promise.

A must-read for those who want to understand what it is to "know Him and the power of His resurrection and the fellowship of His sufferings".

-Pastors Phil & Lisa Gibson
Elevate Church, Spennymoor, UK

Walking in the Light of His Mysteries

God's Supernatural Platform
for Creating Miracle Moments,
Change & a Glorious Future

SAYE DIDI DOLOPEI

Published by **Aleph World** Press
www.alephworld.co.uk
Durham, UK

Walking in the Light of His Mysteries:
God's Supernatural Platform for Creating Miracle Moments,
Change and a Glorious Future
by Saye Didi Dolopei

Copyright © Saye Didi Dolopei 2011, 2014
ALL RIGHTS RESERVED

First Published 2011
ISBN: 978-1-60047-607-5

Revised Second Edition 2014
ISBN: 978-0-9926055-1-3

NO PART OF THIS BOOK MAY BE REPRODUCED IN ANY
FORM, BY PHOTOCOPYING OR BY ANY ELECTRONIC OR
MECHANICAL MEANS, INCLUDING INFORMATION
STORAGE OR RETRIEVAL SYSTEMS, WITHOUT PERMISSION IN WRITING
FROM THE COPYRIGHT OWNER/AUTHOR

Unless otherwise indicated, Bible quotations are taken from The New King James
Version. Copyright © 1994 by Thomas Nelson, Inc.

Review does not represent the World Bank's view but is only the opinion of the reviewer.

Printed in the United Kingdom

The names and identifying characteristics of certain individuals referenced in this book might have been altered. This book contains the opinions and ideas of its author. It is sold or distributed with the understanding that neither the author nor the publisher is engaged in rendering specific legal, medical, tax, insurance, financial, investment, accounting, or other professional advice or services. If the reader requires such advice or services, a competent professional should be consulted, and relevant laws vary from country to country. Every individual may not find the strategies and suggestions outlined in this book to be suitable, and there is no guaranteed or warranty that they will produce any particular results in every individual. No warranty is made with respect to the accuracy or completeness of all the information contained herein, and both the author and publisher specifically disclaim any responsibility for any liability, loss, or risk, personal or otherwise, which is incurred as a consequence, directly or indirectly, of the use and application of any of the contents of this book.

0   1   2   3   4   5   6   7   8   9

Dedication

To God, alone wise, be glory through Jesus Christ forever. Amen.
Romans 16:27

Also to our Son, Malachi who is God's special gift to us, conceived and delivered through the faithfulness of God Almighty, and through 'God who cannot lie', for our joy and blessing.

Your Mom and I truly love you, Son. Most of the principles of Godly faith and teachings now penned here as a book, became real to us while we waited for you. We therefore pray they will work for you also as you grow to love, trust and serve the God and the Father of our Lord Jesus Christ!

Key Foundational Bible Texts

(Isaiah 29:11-12) "The whole vision has become to you like the words of a book that is sealed, which men deliver to one who is literate, saying, "Read this, please."And he says, "I cannot, for it is sealed." Then the book is delivered to one who is illiterate, saying, "Read this, please."And he says, "I am not literate.""

(Mark 4:11) "...To you it has been given to know the mystery of the kingdom of God...."

(Psalm 25:14) The secret of the Lord is with those who fear Him, and He will show them His covenant.

(Romans 16:25, 26) "Now to Him who is able to establish you according to my gospel and the preaching of Jesus Christ, according to the revelation of the mystery kept secret since the world began but now made manifest, and by the prophetic Scriptures made known to all nations, according to the commandment of the everlasting God, for obedience to the faith- to God, alone wise, be glory through Jesus Christ forever: Amen."

(Acts 15:18) "Known to God from eternity are all His works."

(Psalm 89:15-17) "... Blessed are the people who know the joyful sound! They walk, O Lord, in the light of Your countenance. In Your name they rejoice all day long, and in Your righteousness they are exalted. For You are the glory of their strength, and in Your favour our horn is exalted".

(Ephesian1:15-19) "That the God of our Lord Jesus Christ, the Father of glory, may give to you the spirit of wisdom and revelation in the knowledge of Him, ...the eyes of your understanding being enlightened; that you may know what is the hope of His calling, what are the riches of the glory of His inheritance in the saints, and what is the exceeding greatness of His power toward us who believe, according to the working of His mighty power".

(Acts 22:14, 15) *"...that you should know His will, and see the Just One, and hear the voice of His mouth. ...be His witness to all men of what you have seen and heard...."*

Contents

Introduction   xiii

Part I

THE REVEALED SECRETS OF THE MYSTERIES OF GOD
[Concepts in the Mysteries of God and How They Relate to You]

Chapter One
Understanding the Mysteries of God: Their Nature, Power,
and Purpose   3

Chapter Two
Unravelling the Mysteries of God: Divine Wisdom, Satan's Lies
and Believers' Walk   31

Chapter Three
The Holy Spirit, Grace, and the Mysteries of God: Believers'
Untold Blessings and Inheritance   45

Chapter Four
The Believer's Secret Weapon: Golden Truth about Glossolalia
in the Mysteries of God   71

Chapter Five
Walking in the Light of His Mysteries: "The Cloud of Witnesses"   81

Part II

LIVING THE REALITIES OF THE MYSTERIES OF GOD
[*The Possibilities and the Price*]

Chapter Six
More than Conquerors: You Must Prevail — 93

Chapter Seven
The Overcomer: You can *Get Up, take Up your Bed and Walk!* — 105

Chapter Eight
The Comeback: Your Faith Has Made You Whole — 115

Chapter Nine
The Faith-*er*: Do Not Be Afraid — 131

Chapter Ten
The Riser: Out of the *Ashes* and into Life — 177

Chapter Eleven
The Spell Breaker: Overcoming Fear and Negativity — 201

Chapter Twelve
The Transformer: Help to Rise and Power for Change and Greatness — 227

Chapter Thirteen
The Breakthrough: Capitalizing on God's Miracle Moment — 255

Chapter Fourteen
The Proof: He's Alive and Miracles Still Happen — 261

Part III

POSITIONING YOURSELF FOR BLESSINGS AND MIRACLES

[More Possibilities in the Mysteries of God: Possessing, Recovering and Enjoying Your Blessing and Inheritance]

Chapter Fifteen
The Giant Killer: God's Secret Wisdom for Attaining Heights — 283

Chapter Sixteen
The Goliath Challenge: Anticipating Your Divine Opportunities — 293

Chapter Seventeen
The Magnetic Nature: Provoking and Possessing Miracles — 305

Chapter Eighteen
The Power of Faith with Perseverance: Resurrecting Lost Miracles — 323

Chapter Nineteen
The Permanence of God's Blessing: How I Recovered My 'Miracle' — 329

Closing
Having and Living the Triumphant Life is a Decision Away! — 337

Epilogue
Having a Nice Day in a 'Nasty World' — 343

Introduction

"that the God of our Lord Jesus Christ, the Father of glory, may give to you the spirit of wisdom and revelation in the knowledge of Him, the eyes of your understanding being enlightened; that you may know what is the hope of His calling, what are the riches of the glory of His inheritance in the saints, and what is the exceeding greatness of His power toward us who believe, according to the working of His mighty power" (Ephesian1:15-19).

If you can *see* it...

Nothing compares with the grace and blessing of being able to precisely *see* from the Word of God, what God is saying, and what He intends, concerning all who truly believe and trust in Him. In truth, He has already made available everything we need, and indeed, all we could potentially become. But, in order to know and to enjoy the things which God has already made available, we need, first of all, to be able to *see* them.

Let me illustrate this with a wonderful miracle that God performed on one *special* Friday night at Church, when a few of us gathered to study and to pray. Without really anticipating what God would do that night, there were just about five of us including my wife and I, seated in a semicircle, conducting our regular Bible study and prayer. The other three included a very young couple in their early thirties and their little son who, remarkably, loved the Word of God.

They had joined the church not very long before this meeting, and had previously explained to us that the lady of the family had major health issues which progressively deteriorated and compounded over time. The most noticeable of those issues were her inability to physically stand for more than a few minutes or to walk any meaningful distance without the aid of a walking stick or her motorised scooter. They always carried her scooter in the back of their car, even when they drove to places including Church. Coupled with those, she also had a really terrible fear of crowds and meeting new people, hence she stayed indoors most of the time.

But, as we read from our Bibles and took turns to share our thoughts that night, suddenly I was inspired to 'build Scriptures upon Scriptures'. We began with the book of Ephesians, learning about believers' inheritance and blessings in Christ, and then finally referred to the ultimate passage for that night, Isaiah 53. At a point in our reading, I deliberately lay emphasis on the key message of the passage, concerning our glorious redemption, the provision for healing and blessing, and the crucial price Christ had to pay as a result.

We read the passage avidly, and line by line, trying to get as much as the Holy Spirit would allow us that night. In the middle of reading and exhortation, I saw the eyes of the lady begin to water, then joy began to build up, and suddenly she exclaimed at the top of her voice, "*I see it!– I see it now, (calling her husband name)! – I see it now!*" At that moment, she was lifted to the ground overwhelmed by the presence of the Spirit of God. That was it! She was thereafter set free from depending on a walking stick, and her scooter, which she later sold. Within a matter of days she could face crowds, was able to stand as long as she wanted, and went on to sing with our worship team.

Why did she get healed the manner in which she did? I believe because she *saw* it! What did she *see?* That her healings were possible, Jesus Christ had already paid for it and taken it upon Himself. She saw that she was forgiven and, through Christ was qualified to receive

God's peace and to live a life of the quality that God intended for her.

So, how do we get to *see*? Simple; the *eyes of our understanding must be quickened* or *enlightened* like Paul desired for believers (including you and me) whom he prayed for in the book of Ephesians. That means *understanding* is connected to *seeing*, and without *understanding* it is impossible to *know* what God has in stock for us, hence we cannot have or take advantage of 'God's stock' to help make our lives conform to the quality of life He intends for us.

What is *understanding*? It is simply being able to *see* and to grasp what God has said, or spoken and provided in His Word. Spiritually speaking, *understanding* is therefore the *eyes* with which we *see*, especially all that God says or has spoken and provided, just as it happened to the lady in our illustration.

Understanding is therefore so extremely crucial that in Proverbs 4:7, after a wise man commended wisdom to be indispensable, he also went ahead to admonish that, *"in all your getting get understanding"*. In another place, he thoughtfully exclaimed, *"Get wisdom! Get understanding!"* (Proverbs. 4:5), presupposing that enjoying a vibrant and victorious life of any kind with God and other human beings was impossible without these two, but especially *understanding* first and foremost in place.

The wisest king ever to walk this earth, King Solomon, asked God Almighty for an 'understanding heart'; literally a hearing and a *seeing* heart, to be able to judge and to discern. God favourably granted him both 'wisdom and understanding', so that there has not been anyone like Solomon before or after him (1Kings 3:9-13; 4:29).

Lack of *understanding* causes colossal damage and is responsible for spiritual blindness and apathy. It also explains why, contrary to God's will for His people, we still suffer the extent of powerlessness presently widespread within the church (cf Hosea 4:6). Because of a lack of *understanding* most of God's will and purposes for believers remain shrouded as great mysteries to us, even though God did not intend it so. Due to lack of *understanding* believers continue to fail to become all that God has already said is possible, because generally we are unable to literally *see* what God has said, and is saying. And for the same reason, believers often fail to *see* and to realise what God has provided and continues to provide.

For a fact, whatever one is able to *see,* they will without fuss believe, and what they can believe, they will ultimately become (cf. John 1:2). That is why the Holy Spirit, who searches all things, including the 'deep things of God', has as His purpose to enlighten or quicken our *understanding* so that we can *see,* even things that *"eye has not seen, nor ear heard, nor have entered into the heart of man."* Yet, these are *"things which God has prepared for those who love Him" (1 Corinth. 2:9-10)*.

So, there's really no mystery to the will and purposes of God for those who love God, people called believers. The only mysteries that exist, are due to our own failure to *see* what God has already prepared and provided; of course things He has made bare in His Word which Paul describes profoundly as the 'Prophetic Scriptures' (Romans 16:26), and Peter calls the 'Prophetic Word', *"which you do well to heed as a light that shines in a dark place, until the day dawns and the morning star rises in your hearts"* (2Peter 1:19).

No doubt, if we can *see* it, then we can have it, but to *see* it, we must have the *understanding* of what has already been done and given by God. This happens when the Holy Spirit causes such understanding to enter our own spirit or heart by shedding His light on the spoken, written or revealed Word of God.

In essence, God's mysteries are really no mysteries for the believer who has the capacity and is able to *see* what God has placed in His Word. Hence, what believers should be doing is learning how to *see,*

Introduction

and developing the capacity to be able to build proper *understanding* and to *rightly divide the word of truth,* according to Apostle Paul's advice in 2Timothy 2:15.

This book, therefore, is an attempt to help people to first of all establish the nature of what has come to be termed as the mysteries of God, or simply the mystery of God's will; trying to 'demystify' what the whole mystery is about, including its main content and how it works in relation to God's plans and purposes for believers. The idea is that once people are able to ascertain what the mystery of the will of God involves, they can begin to pull down some of the false barriers that have been erected over time. Subsequently, they might be able to hopefully pursue and *see,* by the help of the Holy Spirit, things that are possible within the will of God, and then be able to receive them, in order to become all that God intends for their lives.

Following thereafter, some efforts are put into exposing readers to practical ways in which the mystery of God's will has played out in the lives of men and women of faith from Scriptures. The idea behind this approach does not necessarily involve making a specific outline of the mysteries of God, but it is to help readers to see and realise, first of all, that the mysteries of God are already part and parcel of daily living.

Secondly, by this approach, readers are able to observe firsthand from the scriptures, what is possible within the mysteries of God, and how the mysteries of God, or the mystery of God's will, actively plays out through the lives of normal people in real life. Thirdly, by considering the lives of real biblical personalities, lively principles will be drawn, with potentially immense benefits for those who intend to replicate the wisdom and blessings from those lives for contemporary life application and victories.

Throughout this book, readers will come across some relevant personal testimonies, including our own, and those of others, whose names are not disclosed as a matter of expediency. This is intended to help readers appreciate that God's *truths* and mysteries are as accessible and relevant even today as they were then.

You will notice that, we have deliberately divided our presentation in this book into three major parts. This is only for the convenience of presentation as we deem fit for connecting with readers. Also, you will notice our prolific use of Scriptural references. Again, this is deliberate, and intended to allow readers to enjoy the grace, wisdom and timelessness of the Bible (Word of God), and also hopefully be blessed by the extra inspiration the Holy Spirit might bring you from reading the passages.

Part One deals mainly with biblical concepts pertaining to the Mysteries of God, and how they relate to the believer and their faith journey in general. The goal was to attempt to establish the nature, power and purpose of the Mysteries of God in relation to God's plans, Satan's agenda, the believers' inheritance, and of course the finished and triumphant works of Jesus Christ.

Part Two focuses on 'the Possibilities and the Price' regarding the Mysteries of God, especially for those who intend to 'pursue and to practise' the tenets and principles of the Mysteries of God. In principle there is a whole new 'world' of blessing, victories and a beautiful future awaiting all who will endeavour to *"put on the Winning Spirit"* through their 'pursuit and practice' of the tenets and principles relating to the Mysteries of God. To such, the Mysteries of God manifest as *God's Revealed Secret Wisdom for a Glorious Life and Future*.

In *Part Three*, there are still 'More Possibilities in the Mysteries of God' for believers to explore in terms of possessing their possessions, recovering what the devil stole and the power and grace for enjoying their blessings and inheritance. It is always true that *"giant problems require giant solutions"*; however, in the mysteries of God, *giant killers are not always muscular* in physique. It takes more than a 'giant' to overcome a 'giant' or a frightening opposition. Secondly, 'giants' are unavoidably necessary for promotion; and the bigger the giant the better your chances, and the bigger your miracles. Hence, it is important to learn how to deal effectively with your 'giants', and learn significant qualities for literally creating your miracle moments and for maintaining your miracles without losing them to the 'Thief', or your adversaries.

We pray that, by the grace of God, this book will be of tremendous blessing; helping you to discover, in most instances, how to walk in God's divine plans, helping you to access His strategies for attaining your God-given purpose, and for living a victorious Christian life. It is our prayer that your study in the Mysteries of God will lead you into God's revealed wisdom, and will then filter through your decisions and choices at the spiritual, emotional and physical levels, thereby resulting in the quality of life only God has in mind especially for you.

We hope you find the *closing* which we entitled "*Having and Living the Triumphant Life is a Decision Away!*" most helpful. You might like to contact us after reading it and we will be very glad to hear from you regarding your questions.

We have also included an *epilogue* or what is often referred to as an *afterword* for further encouragement to those of you who might need it. It is entitled *Having a Nice Day in a 'Nasty World'*. We understand that sometimes, times and things get too difficult to cope, but we have an all-loving, all-giving, and Almighty God who cares about us.

May God Almighty richly bless you as you read!

- **Pastors Didi and Dorothy**
Good Word Ministries, Durham UK

Part I

THE REVEALED SECRETS OF THE MYSTERIES OF GOD
[*Concepts in the Mysteries of God and How They Relate to You*]

Chapter One

UNDERSTANDING THE MYSTERIES OF GOD: THEIR NATURE, POWER AND PURPOSE

"...To you it has been given to know the mystery of the kingdom of God...." (Mark 4:11)

"Knowledge is power." You might have already heard this said a dozen times along with similar claims like, 'having the right kind of knowledge is even more powerful'.

Well, despite the controversy that surrounds the claims and principles of "knowledge is power", it is clear that the notion behind this, and other derivatives, hold some truths in them, especially when they are brought into line with what the Bible teaches.

Let's take for example Hosea 4:6, which says, *"My people are destroyed for lack of knowledge..."*. Although this statement in its original context stands as the basis and purpose behind what would be an unwelcomed situation in Israel, it also assumes that, if people seize and pursue the right kind of knowledge, it will help to avert being destroyed (cf Isa. 53:11). Likewise, by pursuing and possessing the right kind of knowledge, people can gain, or are able to place themselves at an advantage in a given circumstance; thus are like the righteous who 'through knowledge are delivered' (Proverbs 11:9).

In such a case, knowledge is truly power and powerful. Hence, the lack of knowledge would mean powerlessness and might leave people, especially believers, at a disadvantage with untold outcome. Sadly, where such a situation exists, the lack of knowledge might start and perpetuate a vicious circle of a 'low' life of defeat as opposed to a 'high' life of triumph. In some cases, the situation is inclined to encourage an "unsound mind" and unhealthy fear, which ultimately haunts and hurts the physical health and future of their victims. On the other hand, *"God has not given us a spirit of fear, but of power and of love and of a sound mind"* (2 Timothy 1:7).

As a pastor, my experience in dealing with diverse people, including Christians, has taught me that, even with recent technological advancement, there still is a great need today to address the problem of "lack of knowledge" as the Bible sees it. From the Bible's point of view, many people lack the relevant knowledge of God's truth and revelations, to be able to make the right changes and adjustments that they desperately need. Similarly, without first appreciating the knowledge and wisdom of God, it is virtually impossible for anyone to adequately transition, or to reposition themselves for a life and a future of the blessed quality which God promises. That is why; God in His unlimited wisdom released such knowledge and wisdom beforehand. But, clearly many have not availed themselves to seeking or pursuing the knowledge and wisdom that God has already made available. This of course explains why, regrettably, there still are increasingly among believers at all levels, a huge struggle in the areas of faith, commitment to God and to other believers; spiritual indifference, and indeed a barrage of "unsound mindedness", which sadly continue to haunt and hurt many within various churches.

Surely, true change through Christ is possible, and yes, anyone can be truly transformed, but only through God's prescription – *"and do not be conformed to this world, but be transformed by the renewing of your mind"* (Romans 12:2). If we will do it God's way, we will definitely and ultimately attain God's result.

And You Shall Know the Truth

Very often people are told, and rightly so, *"you shall know the truth, and the truth shall make you free"* (John 8:32). However, just like the 'devout' Jews to whom Jesus gave this candid advice, so many believers today falsely assume to know the *truth* and to already be *free;* when in fact they are not. The Jews who were then in the company of Jesus, as devout as they seemed, only assumed they were already *free;* being the descendants of Abraham and having never been in bondage to anyone. But, Jesus' hint to them was a wake-up call about their need for more than what they assumed. To begin to pay more attention to their spiritual state of bondage and hopelessness; and to stop assuming that some privileged connections or involvement with Abraham, *the father of faith*, would save them any more than neglecting the *truth* and failing to hold to the words and teachings of Jesus, and being His disciples (John 8:30-35).

Such failings and neglect, especially regarding the relevant knowledge in God or of the *truth,* whose consequence is the lack of true *freedom* among believers and unbelievers alike, paralyzes, in many ways, the most sincere person from attaining the quality of life and future God intends for them. Simply because they can't make the necessary changes and adjustments to reposition and transition into that which God has prepared and already granted.

As a result, so many people become paralyzed by unwarranted fear, powerlessness through discouragement, and the biggest concern being the '*lack of sound mind*', which allows worries, anxieties, and stress to dominate, and to shred the lives of believers, contrary to the truth and promises of the Word of God *(see 2Tim.1:7)*. This is so because, to many people, God's will for His children, His wisdom and power are still a great mystery; something exoteric, distant, impossible, or even too hard to come by, and too difficult to comprehend. Hence, in most cases, many people never get the relevant knowledge in God, or the knowledge of the *truth,* and neglect the *truth* which only sets people free. In some cases, as Paul suggests, they are *"always learning and never able to come to the knowledge of the truth"* (2Tim. 3:7).

Obviously, any mindset that regards God's will or His *truth* that frees as a mystery and hard or impossible to comprehend, does no good for a believer. It only raises a huge hurdle and is always a crippling liability to anyone who seeks to know God and to live for Him. Sooner or later, it starts a spiral of failure of personal *faith*, then failure in life and of course failure in any attempt to maximise our God given potential, and to live up to God's expectation for our lives. The reason being; if I find it impossible to know God's will or His *truth*, I'll have no possible *road map* for the quality of life God expects from me, and in fact no *blue-print* to life's purpose and how to overcome when life's challenges emerge.

Again, if I don't have a 'sound mind' as part of the paralyses leading from my lack of the knowledge of the *truth*, it is basically because I failed to grasp the will of God through the knowledge of the *truth* or His Word of power (Heb. 1:3); which builds power which generates 'sound mind' which the Holy Spirit mediates (2 Tim. 1:7; Acts 1:4, 8) by quickening or enlightening my understanding (Eph. 1:18). Remember, God says, *"my people are destroyed for lack of knowledge…"* (Hosea 4:6).

Anyone who cares to know the truth will recognise immediately that God is not at all a mystery, nor are His ways, wisdom or will. God is our Father who desires us to know and have everything available that He has released for our victory. As the Scriptures say, *"His divine power has given to us all things that pertain to life and godliness, through the knowledge of Him who called us by glory and virtue"* (2 Peter 1:3). This is even more powerful when we consider the reason why God reveals Himself and gives us all things that pertain to life and godliness, including *exceedingly great and precious promises*. It is the demonstration of His uncapped generosity to believers *"that we might* even be partakers of His divine nature" (2 Pet. 1:4), overcoming this present corrupt world.

God has graciously given us *"richly all things to enjoy"* (1Timothy 6:17), including our families, marriages, health, *perfect soundness* in mind and body (cf. Acts 3:16), and the rest. The quality and measurement of all things He has given us is described as *richly*. These things are beautiful, handsome and in abundance, just like the life itself that Jesus says He came to give us (John 10:10b). God desires also that *"you may prosper in all things and be in health, just as your soul prospers"* (3 John 1:2); and God gives and consistently supplies you, *"the power to get wealth, that He may establish His covenant which He swore to your fathers, as it is this day"* (Deut. 8:18).

The reason for supplying *the power to make wealth*, according to the passage, is so that He can make all His promises good concerning us. That none of His Word will fail regarding every good thing which the Lord has spoken concerning us (cf Joshua 21:45); and also that we don't boast in our own strength (cf Deut. 8:17). God did all this, that He would ensure as He has promised, *all things are ours*. Things which He deliberately put in place to *serve* us, rather than us being controlled by them. And these things are under our authority, for the purposes of helping us to live as God would love us to, and to enjoy Him and all He has delivered unto us.

> *Therefore let no one boast in men. For all things are yours: whether Paul or Apollos or Cephas, or the world or life or death, or things present or things to come - all are yours. And you are Christ's, and Christ is God's (1 Corinth.3:21-23). Let this mind be in you which was also in Christ Jesus, who, being in the form of God, did not consider it robbery to be equal with God, but made Himself of no reputation, taking the form of a bondservant, and coming in the likeness of men. And being found in appearance as a man, He humbled Himself and became obedient to the point of death, even the death of the cross. Therefore God also has highly exalted Him and given Him the name which is above every name (Philip.2:5-9)*

In the absence of God's glorious *truth* espoused, regarding His revelation, wisdom, *will,* and blessings that I have mentioned, people will still continue to live in panic, anxiousness, worries, in bondage to fear and Satan, and even sickness and the fear of death; the kind of life not intended by God for His people. God's desire for the believer is to have and live a triumphant life, always abounding in His grace and love.

Now, does it concern you that you might be missing God's best, God's purpose for your life, and are now probably living your life below God's expectations and standards? For many, life and living are a mystery; and even God's will is a mystery. But the truth is that God's mysteries for the quality of life He intends here on earth, and life eternal for all His children, are already revealed and are available to those who care to know.

You don't have to live the rest of your life wondering what your life is about. You certainly don't have to allow yourself to become crippled by the fear, anxiety and worries that have unfortunately engulfed so many people, including believers, who are continuously hindered from enjoying all that God Almighty freely and richly offers and imparts to His children. *"And you shall know the truth, and the truth shall make you free* (John 8:32)."

Triumphant Life by Design

Our generation, like most others, is all too familiar with living with fear, worry and anxiety. Frankly, we cannot ignore the fact that an overwhelming number of people, from all walks of life, now consistently suffer from the consequences of having to live with horrible fears, worries and severe anxieties. There are those who hopelessly dread the future, others wonder about the meaning of life, some harbour intense fear of resentment, fear of failure, bareness, accident, death, and so forth. Apart from these, there are now the ever increasing and disturbing fears of aging, getting sick, losing a job, and the fear of living the rest of one's life as a single, divorced or unmarried person, enforced by mounting pressures on families and communities.

Together with other uncertainties which are fast becoming big concerns for modern people, many are seriously seeking ways out of their predicament for a better life of assurance and hope. A life which offers greater prospects of peace, stability and happiness. However, not many know where to turn for such quality of life. Many do not know how to access the grace and power to live free from the consistent torment and domination of fears, worries and anxieties. Yet, God, in His supernatural wisdom and foreknowledge, has already created means by which all who trust in Him can possess and enjoy an enviable life of peace, tranquillity and happiness; more than our own strength or wisdom can provide.

Of course, this kind of life; a life that enjoys consistent peace, might sound awfully strange to a world and a people whose peace is being constantly disrupted by fears. But, measures are available, especially for believers, to amply deal with their fears, to succeed and have a blessed life of peace. One way this is possible, is for believers to apprehend God's desire and purpose for their lives in relation to what has been termed as *the mystery of God's will*. Fortunately, this is available and accessible, and comes to believers as the knowledge of the *truth* that they need to know; or also the *revealed wisdom of God*.

Clearly, the life of the believer is not haphazard, nor is it a product of chance. God has definite thoughts and plans concerning His people, and He desires the best possible outcome for them here and in the afterlife. Except that for some, the wonderful path to attaining such a life, largely still remains shrouded as the mysteries of God or the mystery of His will. Those who find God's plans, purposes and desires to be a mystery sometimes tend to think of them in ways that might be enforced by their readings of certain passages from the

Bible. For example, we read from Isaiah 55:8, 9, in which God declares; *"My thoughts are not your thoughts, nor are your ways My ways."* He says, *"for as the heavens are higher than the earth, so are my ways higher than your ways, and my thoughts than your thoughts."* Understandably, the very assertions of this passage raise two serious issues, or two problematic questions for the reader.

First, one might ask, is it possible to know God's will or purpose and thoughts? The answer is an emphatic, *yes*. Contrary to what people commonly believe about God's will and thoughts being a mystery, it is possible to know His will and His thoughts (see Psalm 25:9,14; Romans 16:25-26). However, His very thoughts are still beyond our thoughts. The reason being that God's thoughts are not human thoughts. When you consider for instance that God thinks 'big' things and man normally thinks on quite a 'smaller' scale, it would be easy to grasp the wisdom behind God's thoughts being higher.

Again, according to the Bible, God's thoughts are always good thoughts (see Jeremiah 29:11), while man's thoughts are generally evil (see Jeremiah17:9). So the problem is never about whether it is possible to know God's will or thoughts, but only that His thoughts and ways are higher than ours, in ways that exceed our judgements and expectations. For examples; *"God is not a man, that He should lie, nor a son of man, that He should repent. Has He said, and will He not do? Or has He spoken, and will He not make it good?"* (Numbers 23:19), and God is *"able to do exceedingly abundantly above all that we ask or think, according to the power that works in us."* (Eph. 3:20)

The other problematic question that the statement we are considering brings about regards just what then are His will and thoughts for us, which are higher than our thoughts? This of course will be the main subject and consideration for this section, with the hope that, by establishing an appreciable understanding into the *knowledge of the truth* regarding God's will and thoughts towards us, we will be better positioned to adequately deal with our fears, worries and anxieties, which normally paralyze, and deny a good number of God's people, from succeeding and having the quality of life God intends for them.

However, this very thing, establishing a good understanding into the *knowledge of the truth* regarding God's will and thoughts towards us for a triumphant life, so to speak, tends not to be the easiest thing to do in life for most believers. The reasons for this may vary immensely but mainly because many have, contrary to God's order, assumed their own style of ascertaining what they believe are the will and thoughts, or purposes, of God.

Many more have ignored the divine provision already supplied by God for establishing His will, thoughts or purposes. So for such people, God's will, thoughts or purposes will always, by their own nature, remain literally the mysteries of God. But, for those following Godly guidelines and seeking the *truth*, the mysteries of God, or *the mystery of God's will*, becomes an '*open secret*', designed on purpose by Almighty God for a triumphant life.

The Mysteries of God Revealed

In order to establish a good understanding about the mystery of God's will for His people, it is helpful to begin with 1 Corinthians 4:1, in which Paul, by the inspiration of the Holy Spirit, declares, *"Let a man so consider us as Servants of Christ and Stewards of the Mysteries of God."* Two important terms and phrases stand out prominently from his assertion and deserve setting aside here. First is the all-important phraseology and description, *Servants of Christ,* which precludes what the believer is not, and functionally defines the most important thing that they, are and could become, in relation to Christ Jesus. The fact is that every true believer in total submission belongs to Christ Jesus and is "the sheep of the Father's pasture" (cf. Ps 74:1; 1 Corinth. 3:23; Col. 1:15-17).

The second description to think about is the term *"stewards"*, which is a designation in the Bible for someone who is entrusted with an important responsibility, for which they are also accountable. A *steward* conducts himself and carries out his duties as one under authority. His rights and authorities, in relation to his functions and responsibilities are always directly linked to the one who assigns him. So, looking at Paul's use of the term *"stewards"*, found in 1Corinthian 4:1, it is clear that servants of Christ who are also stewards, have been entrusted with the mysteries of God. If that is true, as the passage states, then it is reasonable on this basis, and on the strength of other related passages to say that God's will and "mysteries" for His people are revealed and can be known (cf 1 Corinth. 13:2; 14:25, Romans 1:19-21; Acts 17:28-30; Eph. 1-2).

Again, the very fact that the Scriptures claim that servants of Christ are stewards of the mysteries of God, gives credence to the reasoning and conclusion that servants of Christ or believers, can and should know these mysteries. Nobody stewards what has not been first entrusted, given or delivered to their care or stewardship; and you cannot be a steward of something you don't have or know.

The Secrets of the Mysteries of God

By allowing Scripture to interpret Scripture, it is possible to establish what the mysteries of God are, or at least to establish what His mysteries entail and suggest. Paul, in a subtle way, while discussing God's mind and original intent for all His people, gives a very good clue to the mysteries of God. He claims the mysteries have been there right from the foundation of the world. Included in this discussion is God's purpose regarding 'rulers of this age', who were the cohorts of Satan in executing what they thought was their master plan, but indeed was God's subtlety in mystery to bring about their own demise. This is when and where Paul introduces us to, and opens for us a great window into the understanding of the mysteries of God and God's will for believers; *"something eye had not seen, nor ear heard, nor have entered into the heart of man"*, yet have been revealed by God (See 1 Corinth. 2:7–10).

By approaching 1Corinthians 2:6-16, with openness to the Holy Spirit, and biblical 'forensic' carefulness, one is able to literally piece together *"precept upon precept* and *line upon line"*, evidence for the mysteries of God, and also how to discern such mysteries. First, in verse seven, we understand that God's wisdom is housed and encapsulated in mysteries. Hence God's mysteries contain, *incubate*, and convey the wisdom of God. In other words, within the mysteries of God is the wisdom of God, and the mysteries of God are the *containers* of the wisdom of God. So, it is therefore possible to encounter the mysteries of God when you encounter the wisdom of God. Similarly, to recognise God's wisdom as it is, introduces you to God's mysteries. Hence, God's wisdom is God's *revealed* mysteries, or simply God's mysteries revealed.

God's Mysteries as Parables

The mysteries of God work similar to how parables work:

> *But when He was alone, those around Him with the twelve asked Him about the parable. And He said to them, "To you it has been given to know the mystery (secret or hidden truths) of the kingdom of God; but to those who are outside, all things come in parables, so that 'Seeing they may see and not perceive, and hearing they may hear and not understand; lest they should turn, and their sins be forgiven them'" (Mark 4:10-12).*

Within a given parable are the intended moral lessons, yet disguised and unrevealed. Get the intended moral lessons of the parable, and you then understand the parable and its essence. Similarly, get the wisdom of God ("the moral lesson intended") and you get the mysteries ("parables") of God, which house and carry the wisdom of God. Therefore, since a parable is not intrinsically different from its intended moral lesson; in the same way, the mysteries of God are never different from the wisdom of God, which they bear and convey. In relation to God, mysteries are essentially wisdom yet disguised and unrevealed, while wisdom is mystery that has become known and is accessible and applicable for advantage in life.

Samson's *out of the eater came something to eat* enigma in Judges 14:14 left his audience in absolute darkness. The meaning of his riddle and parable remained a complete mystery to them, and frustrated his audience, because they could not unravel its meaning, although they worked feverishly hard at it. It made them vulnerable, but as soon as they were able to impishly gather the meaning of his enigma from Samson's own wife under duress, they were relieved and gained an advantage.

Like Samson's guests, whom he challenged with his riddle, believers too could remain in the 'dark' concerning God's unrevealed mysteries, until He makes it known to them. Unlike Samson, God's mysteries are not intended to remain enigmatic to believers or servants of Christ. He has chosen to make His mysteries known as His thoughts, will, or simply His wisdom to them, so as to help and bless them in diverse ways.

In Deuteronomy 4:6 Moses, God's servant, is able to point to the recorded revelation of God through Scriptures, saying to the children of Israel, *'this is your wisdom and understanding'*, because what was hitherto a mystery has been made concrete and applicable for anyone who cares to know. That is why the Word of God is never a mystery, but always the wisdom of God for believers in things that pertain to life and godliness (See Mark 4:34-35; 4:10-12; Matthew 13:34-37; 15:15&16; cf 2 Peter 1:2-4).

In a sense, this concept of mystery and the wisdom of God, is in effect, similar in principle to the *'Word of God becoming flesh'* for all to behold *its* glory (see John 1:14). Like our Lord Jesus Christ, who became for us wisdom from God, (1 Corinth. 1:30) revealing to us in concrete ways the love of God, which until then was a mystery of endless and fruitless search-in-the-dark through man's personal and vain religion. Now, the Scripture declares, *wisdom is the principal thing, and in all your getting, get understanding (Read Proverbs 4:1-13).*

Satan Does not Know the Word of God

Now, there's a good need for some clarification, especially with me equating the wisdom of God to the Word of God, and saying that the wisdom of God is accessible, available, applicable or even revealed. I chose those words deliberately and I am aware it might sound some alarm bells, or even confuse some people. This will be those who especially believe that *Satan knows the Word of God*, and take their clues from the Lord's temptation passage, which is found in Matthew chapter four.

A good reading of that passage will educate its readers otherwise. The fact that Satan does not know the Word of God, but that he uses it randomly to his advantage, hoping to deceive his unsuspecting victim, whose knowledge of Scripture is scanty and also vague. By the way, this observation explains some of the greatest challenges facing the Body of Christ today. There are believers who continue to pay no or little heed to the Word of God, and as a result lend themselves to Satan's beguiling, to undermine and to create chaos within churches.

We all have a great need to be properly taught the Word of God and to be constantly led by the Holy Spirit into God's truth. By so doing, we can be wise in God and full of the wisdom of God. But, without the help of the Holy Spirit, it is very easy to walk in deception. Even the Pharisees, Sadducees and Scribes always thought they had a proper handle on the Word of God, and prided themselves in great satisfaction to be masters of the Word of God. However, they encountered the Lord Jesus, who clearly shocked them with answers in Godly wisdom, every time they tried to test and entrap Him.

A classic example of such encounters will be, the Sadducees' deceptive and roundabout questioning of the Lord about resurrection, found in Mark 12:18-27 and Matthew 22:23-32. His answer was direct and profound. The wisdom His answer exudes is relevant to the point I am trying to make; that Satan, his cohorts and a good number of people claiming to know the Word of God today, do not in fact know the Word of God. Most of what is claimed to be known today about the Word of God, is simply the letters of the Law of God. Majority might be familiar with the Word of God, but essentially, that is a far cry from knowing the Word of God, or knowing and having the wisdom of God.

Hear what the Lord told the Sadducees in answer to their *tricky* question, carefully designed to entrap the Lord, and in some ways a clever attempt to test Him regarding the Word of God. In response to their question;

> *Jesus answered and said to them, "You are mistaken, not knowing the Scriptures nor the power of God. ³⁰ For in the resurrection they neither marry nor are given in marriage, but are like angels of God in heaven. ³¹ But concerning the resurrection of the dead, have you not read what was spoken to you by God, saying, ³² 'I am the God of Abraham, the God of Isaac, and the God of Jacob'? God is not the God of the dead, but of the living." ³³ And when the multitudes heard this, they were astonished at His teaching (Matthew 22:29-33).*

In Mark's version of the same narrative, he even added further emphasis on the fact that, in Jesus' response to the Sadducees, He insisted that they were actually in error and far from the truth of the wisdom of God. Mark goes on to add that, after Jesus told them that God is not the God of the dead, but the God of the living, He went further to say; *"You are therefore greatly mistaken."* This was a repetition of what Jesus had already said in a previous verse, but this time it carried with it the special emphasis; *greatly*, (Mark 12:27).

Often, most people who are in error, don't even know, and do not recognise that they are also mistaken. It is even an impossible task for them to appreciate that, they are *greatly* mistaken. The Lord Jesus assigned good reasons for why the Sadducees and people like them are *'mistaken'* or *'deceived'*, which is another literal translation for the original term Christ used. The first thing we notice in Christ's answer is His most direct indictment that they did not know the Scriptures, which ties in nicely with the fact that they were *deceived*. Secondly, they did not know the power of God. The third and most subtle, which yet calls to question the integrity of the Sadducees, is the fact that the Lord asked; *"have you not read what was spoken to you by God, saying…?"*

Clearly the passage suggests that God do speak in the Scriptures. If He did speak even in the time of the Sadducees, then the problem might have been that, either the Sadducees read and did not understand or receive what the *Spirit* of the Word was saying, probably because they lacked the capacity to receive and to be taught by the Holy Spirit of the Word (cf 2Tim. 3:7). Or, that they chose to familiarise themselves with the *letter* of the Word, mainly for debates and to ensure their own political ends, as they were accustomed to.

Whatever their motives were, it seems to me that they were responsible for their negligence, which showed in their being *'mistaken'* with the Word of God. The Lord's authoritative and outright dismissal of their claims to Scriptural knowledge, was nonetheless, a direct rebuke of the ignorance of the Sadducees in relation to the Word of God and God's wisdom.

In this context, and given the fact that many restrict themselves to just 'knowing about' the Word of God, as opposed to truly 'knowing' it; then, the relevant question to ask ourselves today, is similar to what the Lord Jesus asked the lawyer who came to test Him: "*What is written in the law? What is your reading of it?*" (Luke 10:26). If similar questions were to be asked today, you might be asked; 'how do you read the Word of God? Like the Sadducees?' There's little wonder why some will only 'know about' the Word of God and not actually 'know' the Word of God, or even receive a revelation of the wisdom of the Word of God. It all boils down to 'how you read the Word'.

Although God might choose other ways of communicating to His children, primarily God has spoken in His Word, and still speaks today in and by His Word. However not many know how to read the Word of God in ways that will enable them to receive all that the Lord says or intends, to say to them. In addition, another problem exists, whereby people who read the Word of God, unfortunately read it purposely for others and seldom think that it refers to them personally. Reading the Word of God in such a detached and impersonal manner will definitely end in *error* or being *mistaken*.

Matthew ended with the commentary on the multitude's reaction to Jesus' response to the Sadducees and observed that; "*they were astonished at His teaching*". Exactly, those who actually are not *mistaken* and know the Word of God, and of course the power of God, because of their right reading of the Word of God, will often leave many people of our world today astonished; because of the power of the revelation and wisdom they exhibit through the Holy Spirit upon Whom they rely.

Furthermore, such people are bound to see and to experience the true power of God, because they are 'fresh' and renewed in their thinking, in their love for God, their love for the things of God and God's people. They do not water down the grace of God by their 'faulty' traditions nor would they attempt to place their traditions or cultures over the Word of God, given that they know the Word of God and of course the power of God also. The Holy Spirit helps them.

Such people will avoid the temptation to be or remain in error like the Sadducees, and will endeavour not to betray and water down the Word of God like the Pharisees and Scribes, whom Jesus also charged with, *"making the word of God of no effect through your tradition…, handed down, and many such things they do"* (Mark 7:13). It is a basic fact that, people who do not know the Word of God and the power of God *"make the Word of God of no effect through their tradition"*, and Satan is no exception.

Satan Knows Some Things about the Law

When it comes to knowing the Word of God, it is correct to say, *Satan knows some things about the law of God.* Hence, it makes it possible for him to prowl successfully as 'the accuser of the brethren', who seeks whom he might devour (Revelations 12:10; 1Peter 5:8). It is even more proper and appropriate to say that Satan is familiar with the letters or texts of the Word of God, and not necessarily the Word of God itself which is the revelation of God. Otherwise, he would know the wisdom of God and also possess Godly wisdom. Also, He would have 'known' Christ, the living Word of God, and would not have attempted to tempt Him with the letters of the Word of God as he did in Luke 4. Had Satan known the Word of God, he would not have attempted to subvert the reign, dominion, power and authority of the Father, who is Himself the very Author of the Word. Secondly, God, through His Word, makes believers wiser than their enemies, including Satan (Ps. 119:98).

There is a clear difference between the *letter* of the Word of God, God's wisdom and the *spirit* of the Word of God. Frankly, the letter of the Word of God on its own is incomplete, and equates to a blunt sword. However, if you know anything about the true Word of God, you will know that it is *"living and <u>powerful</u>, and <u>sharper</u> than any two-edged sword, piercing even to the division of soul and spirit, and of joints and marrow, <u>and is a discerner of the thoughts and intents of the heart</u>"* according to Hebrews 4:12. That, in truth sounds more than the description of mere letters!

First of all no letter is *living* or alive, and no letter is *powerful,* even if we try with all our best human effort to make it look powerful. Secondly, to say that Satan knows the Word of God would equate to him having the ability to discern the actual *"thoughts and intents of the heart,"* which in truth is most impossible for him; especially the *"thoughts and intents of the hearts"* of believers whom, the Bible categorically states, possess the mind of Christ (1 Corinthians 2:16).

We know that only God and His Spirit can discern and reveal the heart with all its thoughts and intents (Jerem.17:9; cf 1Samuel 16:7). Furthermore, not Satan but only the Holy Spirit and God, search the *thoughts and intents* of the hearts of people as well as the deep things of God (1 Corinthians 2:10; Romans 8:26-27). With the believers, Satan's principal means of access to the *thoughts and intents of their hearts* is to gather clues, like a good detective from what they say about their thoughts and intentions and then try to piece together his evidence in order to build a story for his case (cf 2 Corinthians 2:11). Similarly, he uses the same means to influence them, if they are caught off guard. As a result, the believer must always 'be sober, vigilant, and also steadfast in the faith', according to 1Peter 5:8 & 9.

God *"declares the end from the beginning"* (Isaiah 46:10), but Satan only tells and knows what has already taken place. This is the same way that Satan's agents, including sorcerers, diviners, witches, and spiritualists operate, by checking into your history, family backgrounds or 'back-files' in order to accuse you, or to instil fear in you. Unless the information is already available, they have real trouble trying to pre-empt your future or what's on God's mind or your mind. Hence, believers who diligently guard their *hearts* as well as their *mouth* can seriously become problematic for Satan and his agents. For *"you are snared by the words of your mouth"* (Proverbs 4:23) and *"you are taken by the words of your mouth"* (Proverbs 6:2)

Unfortunately, for most of us believers; including church leaders, the mouth or the tongue is often the most untamed and uncontrolled of our 'physical members'. It accounts for most of the personal and family battles we will ever face (James 3:5,6). To illustrate what I am talking about, check with those who sometimes have a good prophecy concerning their lives, but which was delivered carelessly in public. Satan and his agents become immediately interested, and all of a sudden, great spiritual and physical battles ensue, with the sole aim to stop the realization of the words of that particular prophecy.

Most times when the prophecy seems to stall, it isn't that the prophecy was false, but that Satan tries to place an embargo against the fulfilment of the prophecy in this physical realm. Having become aware of the details of the prophecy, he will try every scheme necessary, to interfere with it; sometimes making it twice as difficult for the believer (cf Daniel 10:12-14).

An illustration of this kind of satanic scheme in Scripture, pertains to the wise men's announcement about the birth of Jesus (Matthew 1:1-7). Herod was okay until the birth of the baby Jesus was announced. Then, he ordered the child to be searched for, pretending he also wanted to worship Him. But after the Father hid His Son, Herod ordered that all children two years and below should be killed, hoping that through that process the *child* Jesus would be killed, and His divine purpose on earth permanently aborted (Matthew 2:16).

The good thing is, God knows how to defend and to deliver His people from satanic traps as well as temptation, by making a way of escape for them (cf 1 Corinthians 10:13; Daniel 6:27). May the Lord keep you and cause you to live, in order to see and to enjoy the day of your appointed manifestation and blessings!

The Spirit and Not the Letter

The Apostle Paul speaks concerning the covenant under which believers live and reign saying;

> *Not that we are sufficient of ourselves to think of anything as being from ourselves, but our sufficiency is from God,⁶ who also made us sufficient as ministers of the new covenant, <u>not of the letter but of the Spirit; for the letter kills, but the Spirit gives life</u>. ⁷ But if the ministry of death, written and engraved on stones, was glorious, so that the children of Israel could not look steadily at the face of Moses because of the glory of his countenance, which glory was passing away, ⁸ <u>how will the ministry of the Spirit not be more glorious</u>? (2 Corinthians 3:5-8).*

Obviously, I do not intend to do a whole thesis about the Word of God, but hope to press home an essential point that could be easily overlooked. Paul, and every true New Testament minister or believer serves not the *letter* of the Law or the Word, but the *Spirit*. Simply because, the *letter* dries things off to 'death' and also drives people to 'death', so to speak. Even when it comes to the people we minister to, the effect we have on them goes beyond letters of ink; having the same impact and effect that Paul claims to have had on those he ministered to saying;

> *clearly you are an epistle of Christ, ministered by us, written not with ink but by the Spirit of the living God, not on tablets of stone but on tablets of flesh, that is, of the heart (2 Cor. 3:3).*

Similarly, how the Word of God is delivered or taught has a nature that is far from letters. The delivery is highly spiritual, and is released as the work of the Spirit, so that we concur with Paul when he says,

> *these things we also speak, not in words which man's wisdom teaches but which the Holy Spirit teaches, comparing spiritual things with spiritual (1 Corinthians 2:13).*

In addition, our attention is directed to something that is generally overlooked by many, in Romans 7:14, which gives a brief but powerful description of the Law or the Word of God. It states emphatically that the Law, which in contemporary usage may be referred to as the commandments or in a sense 'the Word of God', *is spiritual.* This obviously agrees with what the Lord Jesus Christ Himself proclaims in John 6:63, that *the words He speaks are spirit, and they are life.* What is even more key, and apparently intended to complement and to complete the earlier description of the Law or the Word as being *spiritual,* comes from verse twenty-two of Romans seven. It quotes Paul saying, that he *"delights in the law of God according to the inward man (my spirit)"*.

Bringing those two thoughts or concepts together, we have a powerful insight as to how the Law of God connects to the person who reads or receives it. At what level or depth of their being it can be received, interpreted, or transmitted. We are also given here an insight into how we should approach the Word of God; that is *according to the inward man*, if we must derive its full benefit in accordance with our desires and God's own will for us.

The logic here is pretty simple and true, spiritually speaking. If the Law or the Word is *spiritual,* then relating to it requires a spiritual approach, for a true lively spiritual encounter. Therefore, anyone wishing to relate to the Word of God must to do so from their own *spirit,* which provides the appropriate spiritual platform for graceful interaction with the Word. So then, to approach the Law or Word of God from a carnal disposition instead of a spiritual viewpoint will be unprofitable.

This is where the Holy Spirit's role and help becomes absolutely critical in the life of the believer. He helps the believer to make the all-crucial connection, enabling his/her spirit, and also providing the enabling environment for their spirit to hear, receive, delight in, and freely appropriate the Word of God according to God's will. The Holy Spirit reveals, positions, and translates God's Law or Word, which is *spiritual*, into spiritually receivable or manageable *nibble* sizes, and grants the human spirit the abilities and capacities to receive, and to comply with what is entrusted to it as wisdom of God, from the Word of God.

In any case, when it comes to the Word of God, the Holy Spirit is the custodian, the communicator, facilitator, dispenser, and the One who works the Word or the letters of the Word, making it living, powerful and effective. In one sentence, the Holy Spirit is the living power behind the letters of the Word, causing the 'letters' to diffuse life to those who read. Without the Holy Spirit, the 'letters' are merely an impossible tasks of vain and fruitless human endeavours.

Now, how can Satan know the Word of God, or even have the wisdom of God if he doesn't have the Spirit of God? How can he have the revelation of God, the *rhema (revelatory)* Word, when the Spirit of God does not live in him or reveal God's truth to him? God teaches the humble His way and makes His secret, or mystery known only to those who fear Him according to Psalms 25 vr 9 and14.

Therefore, given Satan's very adversarial nature and rebellion toward God, which stands in sharp contrast to the spirit of humility, it is impossible for God to teach Satan, and at the same time reveal His Word and truths to him. God, remember, resists the proud. However, under the New Covenant, Satan as a *conman* only has enough sense to sniff on what the Holy Spirit has released to God's children as their *rhema* or revelatory word, and to try through his many schemes, to *steal, kill, or destroy* what God has already released into the life of His people as their assignment or blessings.

There are good reasons why it was impossible for Satan to defeat the Lord Jesus, during the period of His temptation. First of all, the Holy Spirit, the very power behind the Word of God, who brings life to the letter of the Word escorted Christ into the wilderness for His temptation. He remained with Christ and helped Him even before angels came to minister to Him at the end of His temptation.

During His temptation, clearly we see and hear Satan slanderously using the letters of the Law he was familiar with, but what he failed to realise was that the Son of God would act on divine revelation, the wisdom of God and *rhema word*. So while Satan is obviously stuck with his unrenewed stock of old letters of the Law, or even the letters of the Word which he is familiar with, the Lord Jesus consistently, with reliance on the Spirit of God, was downloading fresh revelation as the Wisdom of God in His own defence. Hence, although Satan tried very hard, using various suggestions and tricks, his defeat was imminent and predictable.

You know the end of the story. The Lord Jesus Christ prevailed triumphantly over Satan and went ahead to accomplish the reason why He came, *"to destroy the works of the Satan (*1John 3:8*); to seek and to save that which was lost* (Luke 19:10) and *that they may have life, and that they may have it more abundantly"* (John 10:10). Remember, it was prophesised of the Lord Jesus, that *"the Spirit of the Lord shall rest upon Him, the Spirit of wisdom and understanding, the Spirit of counsel and might, the Spirit of knowledge and of the fear of the Lord"* (Isa. 11:2).

Don't be fooled, the Word of God or the wisdom of God is more than the letters of the Law or the letters of the Word of God. Far from it being the letters or knowledge of the letters of the Word of God; when the mystery of the Word of God is discussed, it is done in the context of the revealed Word and the wisdom of God, which the Spirit of God makes possible, and has nothing to do with the letters of the Word. This is so powerful because only the revealed Word has the ability to truly communicate God's love, power, desire, plans, purpose and His will for His people. Hence, the Word of God is prophetic in nature and character, and is always able to establish the people of God in all things, at all times, especially in obedience and faith towards God.

> *Now to Him who is able to establish you according to my gospel and the preaching of Jesus Christ, according to the revelation of the mystery kept secret since the world began* [26] *but now made manifest, and by the prophetic Scriptures made known to all nations, according to the commandment of the everlasting God, for obedience to the faith (Romans 16:25-26).*

Believers and the Wisdom of God

With regard to the believers, the wisdom of God is now readily available and easy to entreat and to have because the Bible says that, 'wisdom literally calls out in the streets and raises her voice in the open squares, and cries out in the chief concourses, at the openings of the gates in the city and she speaks her words' (Proverb. 1:20, 21; Also James 1:5). What was a mystery from the beginnings has now been revealed; that which was the Lord's secret and treasured possession, been the beginning of His way and His works before there was ever an earth; that which was there when He prepared the heavens and when He drew a circle on the face of the deep; the very wisdom that was beside Him as a master craftsman; and delighted Him and rejoiced before Him and in His inhabited world; this wisdom is now accessible and available for finding life and obtaining favour from the Lord (Proverbs 8:22-36).

This is the very wisdom that sets believers apart, and also assures their continuous victory over Satan, if they know what to do. As it is written; *"You through your commandments have made me wiser than my enemies: for they are ever with me". (Ps. 119:98)*

Wisdom Hidden

We have established that the mysteries of God are the wisdom of God, and at the risk of oversimplification, it is basically *God's thoughts, ways, plans and purposes,* which are now revealed and are accessible to the believers (1 Corinthians 2:7). However, we see in the same verse, 1Corinthians 2:7, descriptions that might seem atypical, being applied to the wisdom of God, when compared to what we have already said about wisdom being available and accessible. The first description or adjective we encounter, which is associated with wisdom in the same verse is the word, *"Hidden"*. Why should something that is available and accessible be *hidden* at the same time? Let's untangle this apparent paradox and oxymoron surrounding this other mystery as well.

Without being tedious, I will throw in Proverb 25:2, which says in fact, *"it is the glory of God to (hide) conceal a matter, but the glory of kings to search out a matter"*. So right away we understand that *God conceals* but *kings* (human beings including believers) *search out* or have the adventurer's task of discovering what is hidden or concealed. Again, just because something is hidden, it doesn't mean it is hidden or concealed from everyone, nor is it undiscoverable by everyone; otherwise every man would marry the right woman!

Now, a keen look at the lines of the passage will soon reveal why the wisdom of God is described as hidden, but fortunately not from everyone. For example we know as the psalmist declares, *"the secret (mystery) of the Lord is with those who fear Him, and He will show them His covenant" (Psalm 25:14)*. Similarly, the 'Lord guides the humble in justice and teaches the humble His way' (Psalms 25:9).

In the verse six of 1st Corinthians 2, the wisdom described as *hidden,* is spoken only among those who are mature (*'the initiated')*. Who are the mature? They are believers whom, by virtue of their dependence on the Holy Spirit, their diligence in study, and in seeking God's will and applying themselves to the Word of God, have trained themselves to the level of godliness with contentment, through the grace of God and by the power of the Holy Spirit. They distinguish themselves in that they know right from wrong, and endeavour to do all things in the love of God. One could go further in trying to define *the mature*.

A mature believer is one who can countenance the wisdom of God without being offended or turning cynical, because they are subject to the Spirit of God and are taught by Him (cf John 8:47). The immature believer does the complete opposite of what the mature believer would do. Hence, the immature believers stand most likely to have the wisdom of God hidden from them. However, while the immature believers are likely to have the wisdom of God hidden or concealed from them (cf Luke 9:44-45; 18:34), they are not the main subject and reason why the wisdom of God could be hidden.

Mainly, the wisdom of God is hidden from the 'rulers of this age', a profound metaphor for the enemies of God and those who oppose His eternal plans and purposes. Such enemies include Satan and his cohorts in the spiritual and earthly realms. So, to a large extent, the wisdom of God is hidden primarily to protect its contents and details from the enemies of God, who intend to use it for their diabolic intentions, intending to hijack, and if possible abort or thwart God's divine plans and purposes prematurely, before they are ever 'born' on earth or realised in the lives of God's people. Satan's agenda has always been the same, *"to steal, kill and to destroy"* (John 10:10).

Well, that must be a good reason for God's wisdom to be hidden, knowing the avalanche of 'spiritual terrorists' and 'wicked' networks out there just waiting to pounce on sensitive information to their advantage. In His awesome and endless wisdom, the Father will do all in His great power to protect His plans and purposes for believers. Even if it means hiding His wisdom just to ensure that none of His good plans for them are interfered with or thwarted through deceptive avenues unleashed against believers by Satan (cf Job 42:2; Daniel 10:12-14).

There is no doubt that God could choose, at anytime, to make His wisdom known to mature believers. However, there's a balance to be struck. Remember, God is sovereign, and in view of His divine sovereignty, His right timing, and of course His activities on earth regarding His ways and purposes, it is possible for God to hide things in mystery from even the most mature believer and to choose instead to reveal the same to *babes*.

> *In that hour Jesus rejoiced in the Spirit and said, "I thank You, Father, Lord of heaven and earth, that You have hidden these things from the wise and prudent and revealed them to babes. Even so, Father, for so it seemed good in Your sight. ^{24} for I tell you that many prophets and kings have desired to see what you see, and have not seen it, and to hear what you hear, and have not heard it."(Luke 10:21,24)*

This outward workings of what I term as 'the grace of God in His sovereignty toward *babes*', to me suggests a striking fact of life in view of who God is, His power, mercies, wisdom, love and compassion. That, there's hope for the willing 'fool' – that even the 'fool' can become wise when the Lord decides, only in view of God's divine sovereignty. (cf. 1 Cor. 1:26-31; 3:18-20; 4:10).

Wisdom Ordained

Another interesting phraseology associated with the wisdom of God is that it was *ordained before the ages for our glory!* What a blessing: that God in His perfect wisdom predetermined, right from the outset, to introduce His wisdom in mystery for our glory – that means our victory in every sense. It was actually for you and every believer, those who are indeed God's children (cf. John 1:12).

God the Father had all of His children in mind, when He put in place a solution for every situation and circumstance they might encounter, including the big one, *SIN*. The battle was already won before it even began, and what we saw on the Cross was indeed the unfolding of God's wisdom for humanity's eternal freedom and glory in Christ Jesus.

However, the good thing is, all this was hidden from Satan and his wicked angels, demons and agents at every level (Ephesians 6:12), but was ordained for our victory. For them it was a mystery not known, but for the believers, it is today the wisdom of God revealed for their glory. Surely, God has you in mind; go ahead and exercise your rights through the wisdom of God for every blessing and praise the Lord!

> *"...'The God of our fathers has chosen you that you should know His will, and see the Just One, and hear the voice of His mouth. For you will be His witness to all men of what you have seen and heard."* (Acts 22:14, 15)

Chapter Two

UNRAVELLING THE MYSTERIES OF GOD: DIVINE WISDOM, SATAN'S LIES AND BELIEVERS' WALK

> *...none of the rulers of this age knew; for had they known, they would not have crucified the Lord of glory (1 Corinthians 2:8). For what man knows the things of a man except the spirit of the man which is in him? Even so no one knows the things of God except the Spirit of God (1 Corinthians 2:11).*

Many tend to give Satan, the devil and his agents more credit than is deserved. By himself, Satan is simply not as powerful as some think (see 2 Corinthians 2:11). Here's a good proof and a reason why. Isaiah 14:16, allows believers into a great secret that has been ignored over the ages. It says about Satan; *"those who see you will gaze at you and consider you, saying: 'is this the man who made the earth tremble, who shook kingdoms?"* Verse seventeen continues; *"who made the world as a wilderness and destroyed its cities, who did not open the house of his prisoners?"*

The rationale behind *'is this the man...'* assumes, and rightly so, that Satan has no real power or authority of his own to truly instigate most of the things believers assign and arrogate to him, except for his cunning tricks under his sleeves. Hence, anyone walking in the wisdom of God is far ahead of Satan and will always outweigh him and frustrate him to utter madness (Proverbs 2).

For example, when David truly walked in the wisdom of God, he became a great source of fear and frustration to King Saul who planed to destroy him. Furthermore, he prevailed always over Saul and his armies, until Saul's final defeat and death at the hands of the Philistines (1 Samuel 18:8-30; 24:1-22; 26:1-25; 31:1-13). We understand that, on every occasion when Saul tried to harm or destroy David by means of some wicked scheme, it was said that *David behaved wisely, very wisely, more wisely,* and of course, *the Lord was with Him* and Saul became all the more afraid of David (1 Samuel 18:9,12,14,15,28-30).

That the Lord was with David is understandable because, to be wise and to behave wisely, God has to be with you and you need to belong to God, being subject to the council of His Spirit of wisdom, who brings us into the unreachable wisdom of God. Like David, believers who have rightly positioned themselves with God, in ways that His wisdom might work for them, have the great privilege of accessing and harnessing the mysteries and wisdom of God for their benefit in both the spiritual and physical realms.

But, the story of David and Saul paints a good picture of both the divine and prophetic advantage that believers who walk in the wisdom of God may have over Satan; his many evil schemes, the wicked works of his spiritual and human agents, including witches, wizards, sorcerers, enchanters and the like. Such believers will outweigh satanic ploys at all levels, if they continue to walk in Godly wisdom at all times. Instead of them being afraid, Satan and his cohorts, like King Saul and his wicked armies, will rather be afraid.

This also is true, and we have records in the New Testament, in which believers acted in boldness and by the wisdom of God, so that those who opposed them rather retreated, having been terrified and afraid. There is the case of Peter and John against the Sanhedrin in Acts 4:1-31, and then in Acts 5:12-42, in which Peter and the other apostles were accosted by the presiding council of religious authority. In both instances, the disciples acted according to the wisdom of God and prevailed. Similarly, believers will always have the upper hand if they trust God, and act in boldness and by the wisdom of God.

Power and Victory through the Wisdom of God

Believers must understand that some things have already been written concerning them. Even before we were conceived in our mother's womb, our lives and situations, including our future were already covered by God Almighty (see Jeremiah 1:5; Psalms 139:13-16; Eccle. 3:11b). However, the specific details of God's plans and purposes for us, which are in a nutshell, the wisdom of God; these are protected as mysteries, so that ideally, Satan and his cohorts cannot grasp them before they take place. At the right time, the wisdom of God is revealed to us as 'the wisdom of God's will' for our lives and for victories in life's affairs (Eccle. 3:10,11). Therefore, just like Moses exhorted the children of Israel in Deuteronomy 4:6, every believer must learn to access, and to walk in the wisdom of God, in order to maximise their purpose and to establish their authority over Satan's cunning schemes and suggestions.

Of course, in practical terms, part of walking in Godly wisdom for a believer, is to be discrete with one's tongue in saying what is in the heart, and keeping quiet about some things regarding their dreams and intentions, until the time is right for their commencement and execution. Many people prematurely shout and tell everyone, including those opposed to them, all their *secrets* before they are ever realised. Obviously, an open *secret* becomes the greatest weapon in the hands of the enemy who has been lurking around to work against his victim. Consequently, many dreams die before they are ever born.

Consider how God go about things in wisdom. He keeps things in mystery and confuses the devil, so He is always miles ahead of Satan.

Don't claim you are speaking in faith when in reality you are being unwise by prematurely and openly spreading your secret dreams and desires, with practically anyone who crosses your path. Even Paul advises to beware, because *"not all have faith" (2 Thessalonians 3:2)*. If God, the Almighty Father Himself, is discrete about what He reveals, how much more His children who are made in His image?

As part of God's divine image in us, we should know better and act discretely in our conduct and approach to life. By the way, His image in us, is His nature in us, so that for example God loves and God thinks in unlimited ways; therefore His children love and think also, but to the extent that has been allowed us, because we are limited.

Our limitation in relation to God's *unlimitedness* of course is no weakness. It's just because we are humans and God is God, and God is Almighty. The truth remains that whatsoever God has given us, regarding His 'image' and *divine nature (2Pet. 1:4)* in us, is good and perfect for all human functionalities, relationships and activities on earth, until sin distorts our ways. But, the good news is, that 'image' is redeemed in the believer who is under full submission to Christ, and who has the Spirit and the mind of Christ (1 Corinthians 2:16 & Galatians 4:6).

Truly, we are 'fearfully and wonderfully made' (Ps. 139:14), and God literally rejoiced over us saying, 'and it was good' after creating us. He blessed us and gave us power in congruity with His 'image' in us to 'be fruitful, multiply, fill and subdue the earth, and to have dominion over other creatures on the earth' (Genesis 1:26-28; cf 2Pet. 1:4). This is why we can be wise, and why it is so important that on the earth, believers are wise and walk in the wisdom of God.

On a practical note, the wisdom that God gives us even applies to how we can shield our marriages from potential threats from without. Take for example, wives or husbands who go about telling all their business to the next door neighbour, who is secretly wishing for their marriage to collapse. By telling all their business, they in effect only hand over to the next door neighbour 'powerful weapon' to speed the process of dissolving their marriage and breaking their home. That's why the wisdom of God would generally advise that we keep very tight lips on some things, especially in the presence of certain people.

The following are some biblical wisdom and Godly counsels, in their perfect form for having power and victory through the wisdom of God:

- *He who guards his mouth preserves his life, but he who opens wide his lips shall have destruction (proverbs 13:3).*
- *A fool's mouth is his destruction, and his lips are the snare of his soul (Proverbs 18:7).*
- *Whoever guards his mouth and tongue keeps his soul from troubles (Proverbs 21:23).*
- *Debate your case with your neighbour, and do not disclose the secret to another (Proverbs 25:9).*
- *A prudent man foresees evil and hides himself, but the simple pass on and are punished (Proverbs 22:3).*
- *Therefore the prudent keep silent at that time, for it is an evil time (Amos 5:13).*
- *A fool's wrath is known at once, But a prudent man covers shame (Proverbs 12:26).*
- *Discretion will preserve you; understanding will keep you, to deliver you from the way of evil… (Proverbs 2:11-12).*
- *You are ensnared by the words of your mouth, you are taken with the words of your mouth. (proverbs 6:2)*

Samson Ignored Wisdom

Lack of discretion and foolishness is not wise, nor can it be a blessing in any form as some falsely suppose. God is wise and expects all His children to walk in wisdom (see Proverbs 2).

In bemoaning the regrettable lack of wisdom among believers, the Lord Jesus Christ announced, *"for the children of this world are in their generation wiser than the children of light"* (Luke 16:18). Likewise, He forewarned His followers explaining to them, *"Behold, I send you out as sheep in the midst of wolves. Therefore be wise as serpents and harmless as doves"* (Matthew 10:16).

The Lord might, in His sovereignty and wisdom, use the 'foolish things' of this world to confound the 'wise of this world' for His glory (1 Corinthians 1:27). But clearly, nowhere does the Lord celebrate 'foolishness' on the part of believers. On the contrary, God Almighty usually searches for, appreciates and promotes only wise and faithful servants: *"Who then is a faithful and wise servant, whom his master made ruler over his household, to give them food in due season? (Matthew 24:45, also see Mtt. 25:1-11; Acts 6:3).*

Samson, the great Judge and leader of his people Israel, was in the physical hugely powerful. But, when it came to walking in Godly wisdom, he lacked discretion in some areas. Ultimately, we understand that he prayed towards the end of his life, from the midst of his humiliation and dreadful sufferings, and God graciously granted him his petition.

However, God's wisdom and discretion would have saved and prevented him from experiencing unnecessary pains, with still greater victory over his enemies, while maintaining profound success in providing leadership for Israel. In the end, Hebrews 11:32 recorded Samson among a company of other great people of God, who accomplished great feats on behalf of their nation and people, Israel.

Yet, this does not exonerate Samson from the fact that the wisdom of God eluded him at some point in his life, causing him to become careless and play into the hands of his enemies.

King David for example, who is mentioned with Samson in the same passage, made a terrible mistake at some point and became directly responsible for murder, in order to cover his sin of adultery and to take his victim's wife. Obviously God was displeased with David, and sent His prophet who helped point out the King's indiscretion.

Afterward we see and hear a very remorseful King in Psalms 51, pleading with God for pardon and forgiveness. This was David, who earlier on in his life, had with every caution acted in wisdom in dealing with King Saul, whose intention was to destroy David's life. He prevailed over Saul by walking in wisdom. This same David, as a young lad acting in wisdom, overpowered and slew the great champion of the Philistines, Goliath, who terrorised all of Israel. He became 'the King after God's own heart' and was anointed greatly by God through His choice prophet, Samuel. But, even David sidestepped God's wisdom at some point causing him great grief.

Looking at the life of David and indeed Samson, there cannot be any more appropriate warning to the believer than what the Apostle Paul wisely sounded in 1 Corinthians 10:12; *"therefore let him who thinks he stands take heed lest he fall."*

So, like David, Samson was not the perfect man as some would like to portray him. He did not always walk in the wisdom of God for his life, although it appears that he, by the grace of God, fulfilled his purpose in defending Israel and leading his people. The most significant instance of carelessness in Samson's life in relation to the wisdom of God, was when he allowed his own lips to divulge his God-given secret about the taboos of His Nazirite birth and anointing for delivering Israel out of the hands of their enemies.

This was a man whose birth was like no other, announced by an angel and anointed and separated as a Nazirite unto God, right from his mother's womb (Judges 13:3-5, cf Numb 6). When Samson grew up, the Lord blessed him and His Spirit began to move upon him (verses 24-25). Afterward we see Samson doing great things, but then in chapter 16 of Judges, things take strange turn. We are told he joined himself with a prostitute in Gaza, among his enemies who planned to kill him by waylaying him.

Samson, however, outsmarted them by rising at midnight and uprooting the city gates with all its posts, while heading for his hometown, carrying the gates and the posts upon his shoulders. He showed great muscular strength, and wonderful battlefield ingenuity, by rising early to leave the city when his enemies had planed to arrest him during the morning hours. But he never learned.

Sometime afterwards, Samson was found with another woman, Delilah, with whom he fell in love. But this time, his enemies got smarter. Now here was a woman he truly loved. They couldn't physically conquer or defeat the man, Samson, but if they could ascertain the secret of his overpowering and unconquerable strength, more than half of the job would have been done. Hence, sooner or later depending on how things turn out, where Samson found his greatest love might also be his weakest point.

The Philistine's lords, exercising great tact with forbearance and eleven hundred pieces of silver, managed to lure and entice Delilah, the love of Samson to reveal the secret of his great strength. She immediately obliged. In fact, she found betraying Samson an exciting challenge and from that moment she began to pester him about the secret behind his mighty strength.

Delilah, on separate occasions, used different forms of blackmailing techniques, spiced up with a few strokes of 'romantic bribery' and incentives. It was her daily persistence, and constant harassing and pestering with words; and not her beauty, love or charm that got to the man of God, Samson. The passage explains that Samson's soul was vexed to death by what he was hearing from Delilah (Judges 16:11), and nothing else; not even all the wars he ever fought vexed his soul to death in that manner. Something was definitely wrong but the man of God did not catch on. His enemies had changed their tactics and grown smarter, but he still remained in the same old place.

So, out of sheer frustration, Samson told 'all his heart', and said to her, *"No razor has ever come upon my head, for I have been a Nazirite to God from my mother's womb. If I am shaven, then my strength will leave me, and I shall become weak, and be like any other man" (Judges 16:17)*. That was it, he was right and she knew this time he had told her *'all his heart'* (verse 18). Samson had disclosed what even God, in His wisdom for Samson, kept as a mystery, and in secret from Samson's enemies. He has acted contrary to Godly wisdom, that,

> *He who guards his mouth preserves his life, but he who opens wide his lips shall have destruction (proverbs 13:3). A prudent man foresees evil and hides himself, but the simple pass on and are punished (Proverbs 22:3). Also see Proverbs 21:23; 18:7; 2:11-12; 6:2*

As long as Samson's secret behind his great strength remained concealed and hidden deep in his own heart, he was unconquerable. Satan and his cohorts stayed and lived perpetually in fear of Samson, not knowing how to deal with him. This was because, Sampson, the man of God and his secret were an unfathomable mystery, and an enigma which his enemies could not resolve except by his own carelessness. God Almighty kept things that way for Samson, and it is the same for believers until we use our mouths to sell ourselves out to Satan and to those who oppose us. Similarly, to Satan, our Lord Jesus and His divine purpose for redeeming us, was a great mystery. That's why 1 Corinthians 2:7-8 says,

> *But we speak the wisdom of God in a mystery, the hidden wisdom which God ordained before the ages for our glory, which none of the rulers of this age knew; for had they known, they would not have crucified the Lord of glory.*

The Father kept His great and illustrious secret from the enemies of Christ as a mystery until He was done, and then, benefiting from hindsight, they realised very slowly that they had been setup, outworked, outmanoeuvred and terribly defeated. If you check the day that Jesus was crucified, they 'feared greatly' and began to say to one another, "*indeed this was the Son of God*" (Matt 27:54). Too late!

In the case of Samson, having disclosed 'all his heart' he became vulnerable instantly, and being lulled into sleep on Delilah's knees, probably in distress, she shaved off his hair. Then she also physically tormented him, herself (verse 19); a sign that he was now weak. The lion killer could now be tormented by anything including the 'feeble' and romantic hands of his 'lover'. There are two very sad but serious commentaries rendered in the passage; one being the natural consequence of the other. They read, '*and his strength left him, …but he did not know that the Lord has departed from him.*' Because of his indiscretion, he put himself in a vulnerable and helpless position where the Lord had no choice but to allow him to see what he had brought upon himself.

The sage cries out aloud, "*Wisdom, is the principal thing; therefore get wisdom, and in all your getting, get understanding*" (Proverbs 4:7). Of course, God abides with those who love wisdom, and walk in His wisdom. The wisdom of God will always save and prevent your 'eyes' from being put out; being bound with fetters, and from becoming a grinder in prison. That is the little wisdom that Samson teaches us from his life. He certainly was forgiven and restored with mighty strength for his final battle, but as they say, *prevention is better than cure*. It is hard work to walk in wisdom continuously, but it's even harder and more deadly to ignore wisdom.

Saul Applied Wisdom

Still talking about the power of hidden wisdom, or the mysteries of God and how it works for the believers, we can certainly learn some valuable lessons from the very early stages of the life of King Saul, immediately before he was crowned king of Israel. We are aware that God, through the incidence surrounding the loss of Saul's father's donkey, caused Saul to meet with the Prophet Samuel who had a special message from God for Saul at Zuph.

They met and their little audience went well. Saul was informed that his father's donkeys had been found, but Samuel also anointed Saul as the 'desire of all of Israel' and the commander over God's inheritance, Israel. When the time came for Saul and his servant to return to his father's house, the prophet gave Saul a series of instructions regarding specific events that would take place before he got home.

Wonderfully, everything happened as the Prophet said. Most importantly, 'God gave Saul another heart', the Spirit of God came upon him and Saul began to prophesy with other groups of prophets, whom he encountered on a hill, as Prophet Samuel had prophesised.

After the great news Saul got from the Prophet Samuel, probably with excitement, about the unequal privilege to experience the prophetic Spirit of God, Saul immediately continued to the 'high place', maybe the place of worship. While he went, or when he got there, Saul's uncle became interested in the outcome of Saul and his servant's rendezvous, and more specifically the minutes of the meeting Saul had with Prophet Samuel. He insisted on knowing all about what had transpired during their meeting with the prophet; and here's how the passage puts it:

> Then Saul's uncle said to him and his servant, "Where did you go?" So he said, "To look for the donkeys. When we saw that

they were nowhere to be found, we went to Samuel." ¹⁵ *And Saul's uncle said, "Tell me, please, what Samuel said to you."*¹⁶ *So Saul said to his uncle, "He told us plainly that the donkeys had been found." But about the matter of the kingdom, he did not tell him what Samuel had said (1Samuel 14-16).*

Notice how Saul answered his uncle. He only told him the obvious things, and the trivial detail regarding the true plans and purposes of God for his life and future. Saul strategically, and in wisdom kept back the most personal details of his conversation with Prophet Samuel, knowing that they were meant for only his own consumption.

Unlike many people today, Saul was very discrete with his word of prophecies, the wisdom of God's will for him. By doing so, Saul followed a pattern akin to the way God protects his plans and purposes for believers from Satan and other wicked people, by shrouding them in mysteries that are otherwise unsearchable. In today's world of computer technology, it will amaze you to know that even within the general World Wide Web, and internet browsing, some things are hidden. There's something called, *the Deep Web*, which is a hidden environment in which high security information travel, and highly sensitive transactions take place, away from the scrutinizing eyes of common web browsers. That's wisdom!

Saul's uncle, because he had been denied the real truth about the prophecy that Saul received, and also refused any significant insight concerning God's purpose for Saul, he could not interfere with the outcome of Saul's prophecy. There was no way he could manipulate Saul or obstruct his destiny in any shape or form, even if he had other ulterior or clandestine motive to sabotage his nephew. Saul's use of discretion in this way establishes the wisdom of keeping tight-lips as we discussed earlier. *He who guards his mouth preserves his life, but he who opens wide his lips shall have destruction (proverbs 13:3).*

Someone may argue, well, Saul's uncle sounded sincere even being really courteous using the word '*please*'; but remember even the Scriptures say, "*... both the inward thought and the heart of man are deep*" *(Psalms 64:6)*. "*... (God) You alone know the hearts of the sons of men*" *(2 Chronicles 6:30)*. Some things, unless very necessary under God's direct instruction, must remain the exclusive purview of the immediate receiver; especially when it comes to God's purpose spoken in secret, until their due time has fully come.

> *The whole vision has become to you like the words of a book that is sealed, which men deliver to one who is literate, saying, "Read this, please." And he says, "I cannot, for it is sealed" (Isaiah 29:11)*
>
> *"But you, Daniel, shut up the words, and seal the book until the time of the end; many shall run to and fro, and knowledge shall increase" (Daniel 12:4).*

In exceptional cases, you may discretely disclose your God given *secret* and purpose, if the *time is at hand* or if it became absolutely necessary. Just bear in mind at all times that protecting your God given purpose or wisdom for your life takes precedence over trying to please others for vain popularity. The goal is always preservation!

> *And he said to me, "Do not seal the words of the prophecy of this book, for the time is at hand (Revelation 22:10).*
>
> *Then the Lord answered me and said: "Write the vision and make it plain on tablets, that he may run who reads it. [3] For the vision is yet for an appointed time; but at the end it will speak, and it will not lie. Though it tarries, wait for it; because it will surely come, it will not tarry. [4] "Behold the proud, His soul is not upright in him; but the just shall live by his faith (Habakkuk 2:2-4).*

Chapter Three

THE HOLY SPIRIT, GRACE, AND THE MYSTERIES OF GOD: BELIEVERS' UNTOLD BLESSINGS AND INHERITANCE

The ninth verse of 1 Corinthians 2 gives us a bird-eye's view into another wonderful truth about the wisdom of God for believers. That, this wisdom contains things, probably many things not yet revealed, and these things have been prepared in advance by God, specifically for those who love God. Secondly, that God has also concealed as a mystery, such wisdom and their contents, away from Satan and his cohorts.

I can't wait to say this. Isn't it incredible, to know for a fact that, buried deep inside of you are a lot more good things concerning you and your future; things more than you know and can see at the moment! Surely, these are glorious things from God waiting to be realized, and that's good news. Central to this good news, is the truth that, the gracious God of heaven, the Father of all creation, loves to do you good, and to cause you to flourish in His blessings.

God desires to shift you from worldly sorrows into His unspeakable joy; to give you His oil of joy for your mourning; His *beauty* for your *ashes*; His gladness and garment of praise for your spirit of heaviness; to make you His own *planting*; to *rebuild, repair* and restore past ruins in your life; to give you *double honour* instead of shame; and instead of confusion, you shall rejoice in every portion the Lord has allotted to you (see Isaiah 61:1-7).

Hidden Treasures in Time Capsules

Let's think about it this way; that the believer's life is like a pregnant woman. This means that every believer carries something of a treasured potential and possession called a *baby*, although not yet seen or heard or comprehended. The conception or the unborn *baby* in the mother's womb is the hidden wisdom of God, 'equivalent' to things already prepared, but again not yet seen or heard or comprehended. Once the *baby* is born, that becomes *things revealed*, 'comparable' to God's wisdom, when it is finally unearthed at the point of delivery. This concept of things is espoused by Romans 1:20 which says, *"for since the creation of the world God's invisible attributes (hidden wisdom) are clearly seen, being understood by the things that are made, even His eternal power and Godhead…"*.

In our 'pregnant woman' analogy, the real mystery falls within the *incubation period* of normally nine months, the time between what God has already prepared for you and the time of the actual birthing or manifestation of that which He prepared for your blessing. But, this mystery, God does not intend that it remains mystery forever to those who love Him, and are believers in Christ Jesus. In short, this period of mystery or the mystery itself is only time bound and also circumstantial as the Scripture alludes; *"to everything, there is a season, a time for every purpose under the earth"* (Eccles. 3:1).

Again, since giving birth prematurely presents its own problems or suggests an abnormality within normal birth circles, God will do everything to disallow *premature birthing* of His mystery, (i.e, things prepared but not yet seen, heard, nor comprehended). This is to avoid your *child* from becoming vulnerable and susceptible to perilous adversities that invariably surround premature birth process.

So, particularly important to this notion of things and the mystery of God is that, by God's own design, He has something good locked *inside* of you and there's something good awaiting you in your future.

The Holy Spirit and the Wisdom of Things Revealed

The succeeding verses, 10 and 11 of 1 Corinthians, claim that this wisdom of things prepared but not yet seen, heard or comprehended, find their expression through the Spirit of God. These things are made visible and certain through the help of the Holy Spirit of God. But just what are these things and what is their importance? Surely they must bear substantial relevance to the believer's life, existence and wellbeing, and their victory on earth. Otherwise, God would not consign the revelation of such things to the Holy Spirit. Likewise, God has also given believers the Holy Spirit who is indeed the Spirit of His Son Jesus Christ (Galatians 4:6; also 1 Corinthians 2:16), to help them to access what He has provided.

The first thing to note about the things God has prepared for believers is that, these things are free of charge. However, believers can only know these things through the Holy Spirit. Secondly, we must admit with humility that to be able to appreciate and to comprehend these things, (i.e their *width, length, depth and height*) Christ must first dwell in our hearts by faith, and we must be rooted and grounded in love (Ephesians 3:17-19).

Furthermore, believers must appreciate that knowing the full extent of these things is only in God's power to reveal, and He is always able to do for us far more, exceedingly, abundantly above human comprehension, and to do more than all that we think, desire or imagine… (cf Eph. 3:20). Hence, believers should not be afraid to expect more, or should not become shocked at the extent of what God would reveal or do through the power of the Holy Spirit. This will cover forgiveness of sins, but also will include creative miracles and healings of diverse kinds, coupled with a variety of cosmic signs and wonders in the earth to the glory of the Father!

The Mysteries of God's Will and the Revelation of the Holy Spirit

In Ephesians 3:1-7, Paul alludes to the mystery of God's will for believers and says *"this mystery has now been made known which was not know before, but now been revealed by the Holy Spirit. And I have written briefly!"* So, what exactly is the content of this mystery or the wisdom of God for His people according to Ephesians chapter one?

A much closer examination of Ephesians chapter one discloses the content of the mystery or wisdom of God for His people, revealed by the Holy Spirit as His 'prophetic Scriptures' or the Word of God (Romans 16:25-26). This revelation comes not only as the wisdom of God for His people, but also the makeup and substance of their blessings and inheritance, through Christ Jesus in a mystery.

Elsewhere in Romans 16:26, we are told why the revelation of the mystery of God became necessary; to inspire *obedience to the faith*, or so that people might believe and obey God. This truth is very critical for the overall understanding of the believer's relation to the mysteries of God. Otherwise, they might get trapped and sidetracked in focusing on the mysteries of God or the wisdom of God as an end in itself; thereby missing out on the true desire of God, which is *obedience to the faith – believing and obeying God.*

It was very crucial to clarify the true purpose of the revelation of the mystery of God, because there's always temptation for human beings to 'abuse' what was intended for good, and to disregard their real function, to their own peril (Deut. 8:12-14, 18,19). Unfortunately, the Children of Israel made a 'Golden Calf' to worship, from the gold God Almighty provided for His own purpose and service (Exd. 32).

Now, drawing mainly from Ephesians chapter one, let's attempt to outline, with some explanations, the actual content and substance of the mysteries of God or the wisdom of God which the Holy Spirit reveals.

(a) *Spiritual Blessings*

We do encounter the first of the mysteries now revealed as the wisdom of God for God's people, in verse three of Ephesians one, although the list continues into verse fourteen of the same chapter. We will simply refer to this first mystery as *Spiritual Blessings*.

Meanwhile, the apostle Paul, is quite keen to describe the nature, extent, capacity or potential and situation of this mystery, now revealed regarding our spiritual blessings. Additionally, he does not leave readers in any doubt that this is already the state of the believers, having already been *blessed* by God the Father with *every blessing*, whose nature is *spiritual* and also situated *in heavenly places* in Christ Jesus.

It's a wonderful thing to know that even the blessings like the One who bestows them, are from above and are seated *"far above all principality or rule, powers, might or authority, and dominion, and every name that is named, not only in this age but also in that which is to come" (Ephesians 1:20-23)*.

Can we find in Scripture what exactly these *Spiritual Blessings* are and their relation to the believers? Certainly.

It has been said, unlike most books of the Bible which specialise in giving details of the handiworks of God, the book of Ephesians exposes the *mind of God* concerning things, as He had designed and purposed right before the foundation of the world. That is why in Ephesians we see the description of the calibre and quality of the blessings with which God, in His wisdom has already blessed His people right from the beginning.

But, to be able to pin down in practical terms the make-up and what these blessings truly entail, we will have to see them at work in demonstrable terms as the handiworks of God for the believers through the life of God's holy Son, Jesus Christ of Nazareth. Helpfully, Colossians 2:11-15 provides us with their very essence and verifiable nature, and also the extent of the works and effects of the believer's *spiritual blessings*.

Bearing in mind that we might not be exhaustive, a good attempt to briefly summarise these *spiritual blessings* from the passage in Colossians looks like this:

1. *Dominion over Sin* (vr. 11) - Speaking of believers' right to forgiveness and reconciliation because of what Jesus has already done.

2. *Dominion over Death* (vr. 12) - Speaking of believers' right to no longer be subject to death, or the bondage of the fear of death, because of what Jesus has already done. *Also see Hebrews 2:14-15; 1 Cor. 15:57.*

3. *Dominion of Life* (vr. 13) - Speaking of believers' right to life and quality of life on earth, while at the same time gaining eternal life because of what Jesus has already done.

4. *Dominion of Victory* (vr. 14) - Speaking of believers' right to triumphant living and life, as opposed to paltry, hopelessness and a lifestyle of defeat, because of what Jesus has already done. *Also see John 10:10; 2 Cor. 8:9; 3John 2.*

5. *Dominion of Authority* (vr. 15) - Speaking of believers' right to freedom, liberty and possibilities because of what Jesus has already done. *Also see John 16:33.*

(b) Chosen in Christ

In Ephesians 1:4, we see another fascinating and significant area within the mysteries of God and 'His wisdom revealed', regarding believers. It is the reality that all believers 'were', and are *chosen in Christ* (see John 1:12,13).

Within the same verse, Paul gives us the timing and the purpose for which believers 'were' and are *chosen in Christ*. They were chosen *"before the foundation of the world, that (they) we should be holy and without blame before Him in love."* A Similar thought is reiterated elsewhere, in which believers are chosen in Christ that they might become the righteousness of God, as it is written, *"for He made Him who knew no sin to be sin for us, that we might become the righteousness of God in Him"* (2 Corinthians 5:21). Also, *for Christ is the end of the law for righteousness to everyone who believes (Romans 10:4).*

Chosen to be *holy* or completely separated to God, to be without *blame* or charge, or defects, and to be complete, lacking nothing was God's original purpose and intent for all who are in Christ Jesus. This in every way conforms to the wisdom of God's will, initially locked up in mystery, for all believers. It ensures that our sins were fully propitiated and fully paid for, including the consequences of our sins. At the same time, our shame, reproach, fear, worry, lack, sickness, and so forth, were catered for. (see 1Peter 2:24)

This means that every time God looks at the believer, He sees him or her through Christ's eyes and righteousness, affirming this great all-time truth that, *"therefore, if anyone is in Christ, he is a new creation;*

old things have passed away; behold, all things have become new... that is, that God was in Christ reconciling the world to Himself, not imputing their trespasses to them, ... For He made Him who knew no sin to be sin for us, that we might become the righteousness of God in Him (2 Corinthians" 5:17,21)*. Peter also affirming that, *"He (Jesus) Himself bore our sins in His own body on the cross, that we might die to sins and live for righteousness; by His stripes you were healed"* (1Pet. 2:24).

This same Jesus helps believers to maintain their *holiness* and to remain *blameless* before the Father. If God chose us in Him to be *holy* and *without blame* from the foundation of the world, then, in the same way that He chose us, God will also have to make provision for us to abide. Hence John concludes, *"My little children, these things I write to you, so that you may not sin. And if anyone sins, we have an Advocate with the Father, Jesus Christ the righteous. And He Himself is the propitiation for our sins, and not for ours only but also for the whole world"* (1 John 2:1-2). The blood of Jesus Christ, that great blood of propitiation, continues to cleanse us from all sins (1John 1:7).

All of this cost the Father dearly, but the good news is that, it clearly delighted Him, and continues to delight Him today, that He fully paid for our 'chosenness', to become *holy,* absolving us of all *blame* and *guilt,* to become children of God in Christ. This is how Paul in his most characteristic way puts it,

> *"For it pleased the Father that in Him all the fullness should dwell, and by Him to reconcile all things to Himself, by Him, whether things on earth or things in heaven, having made peace through the blood of His cross. And you, who once were alienated and enemies in your mind by wicked works, yet now He has reconciled in the body of His flesh through death, to present you holy, and blameless, and above reproach in His sight— if indeed you continue in the faith, grounded and steadfast, and are not moved away from the hope of the gospel which you heard, which was preached to every creature under heaven, of which I, Paul, became a minister" (Col. 1:19-23).*

(c) Predestined by God in Christ Jesus

In verses five and six of Ephesians chapter one, we encounter probably the most controversial subject, when talking about the mystery of God's will or God's wisdom for believers. However, this same subject of predestination also seems, to me, to be the one that holds the most intriguing promise for the believers.

The question of predestination has over the years been a grey area of theological debate, and whenever it has been raised it has, without fail, been a source of unending theorization, confusion, division, upset, and offence, to mention just a few. But we can save ourselves all the unnecessary wrangling and endless debates if we stick to the simplicity of the Scriptures and get on with pursuing God's wisdom and purpose for all His people.

A very helpful place to begin to understand the question of predestination is definitely Romans 8:29, which beautifully unveils the implicit wisdom of God's will for all. This passage with a deep sense of mission and purpose asserts, *"for whom He foreknew, He also predestined to be conformed to the image of His Son, that He might be the firstborn among many brethren."*

In a nutshell, the subject or question of *predestination* according to the wisdom of God's will, is about God's people having all the help required to attain God's standards, and not about simply trying to exclude some or others, as some want us to believe. Whether it is in the book of Ephesians or Romans, as we have already seen, the whole idea of *predestination* powerfully helps to bring to the fore the superiority of the foreknowledge of God, who alone knows the end from the beginning and has no need for anyone or anything else to counsel Him (Isaiah 46:10).

It enforces the very fact that God has no need to now learn His creation anew or the order of things, because He already knows them, being the Omniscient God (see Isaiah 48:8b). That does not mean that God is aloof from His creation, but as a *master of His arts* He has birthed the absolute *best*. This applies especially to His free-moral thinking species called human beings with freewill and the power for making definite choices.

With their freewill, of course, comes the opportunity for making uncorked choices but with attendant responsibilities for the choices they make. Needless to say, most often human beings get things really wrong because they are not omniscient or all-wise, but limited in the wise exercise of their choices and opportunities. Right from the start, human beings, in utter rebellion, got it wrong in choosing to rebel against God's commandments. As a result they became depraved and ruined their God-given opportunities for a profound, heavenly type of relationship even while still on earth.

But God, the loving Creator and Father, took important steps to rectify and reconcile His children back to Himself. And, as part of this process, He sent His only begotten Son, Jesus, the absolute prototype who bears God's ideals and original intentions for His relationship with human kind, but also the One to repair, reconcile and restore the damage done by human being's careless choices, together with their attendant consequences.

Jesus Christ, the holy Son of God, therefore becomes to human beings an archetype that all must aspire to and for. He is the Father's standard (*the first born*) for the rest of humanity, especially for all who might, by the wise use of their personal freewill, recognise and desire the need to please God, their eternal Creator, in ways and manners that create, enable and support a lively, earthly and heavenly relationship.

This certainly is God's ever present desire for humanity; the wise use of our freewill to embrace His already extended, and in the meantime open-ended invitation to all, because "*the Lord is not slack concerning*

His promise, as some count slackness, but is longsuffering toward us, not willing that any should perish but that all should come to repentance" (2 Peter 2:9). All of this captures, reminisces and resonates in a powerful way the Father's heart and delight to restore and affirm His children; the very reason why He has with patience being magnanimously self-giving in Christ Jesus.

In fact, at His own initiative and expense, God *'draws'* people (John 6:44), and *'teaches all'*, that they might hear and learn from Him, the way of salvation, which is Jesus Christ.

> *It is written in the prophets, 'And they shall all be taught by God.' Therefore everyone who has heard and learned from the Father comes to Me (John 6:45).*

Secondly, the Father does His optimum to *'teach'* (lead) those He *'draws'*, through means that are appropriate, according to His own wisdom; whether by general revelation or personal revelation. This is intended to help all to hear and learn, in order to lean into the *call*, albeit, at their own will. (cf. John 6:65-68)

Unfortunately, within the context of freewill, which includes the free moral choice of human beings, there will be those who might *hear* and never *learn*, although they have, like others, been *taught* by God (cf 2Tim. 3:7; Jn. 8:43; 9:27). This has no bearing on God's teaching abilities; but as it is the case, not all who are taught, tend to always hear, or learn. So, they do not respond to God's *'call'*, as they should. In this case, Paul's claim in 2Timothy 3:7 is justified; that indeed, there are many who are taught, and "are always learning and never able to come to the knowledge of the truth". Paul, here, was either admitting to a general human weakness, a lack of will, or a sheer disobedience of individual choice. The latter might be the reality in most cases. Whatever the case might be, we see from the Bible, that God delights greatly in all His people to be saved. For this reason, He has provided amply for our salvation through the Lord, Jesus Christ.

For the believers therefore, their sole concern should be, at all times, *"looking unto Jesus the author and finisher of their faith" (Hebrews 12:2)* and *"keeping themselves in the love of God, looking for the mercy of our Lord Jesus Christ unto eternal life" (Jude 1:21)*. This means that God's true aim for all is for them to be like Jesus, for He is in a sense God's mirror before us to help us dress properly.

Yet, in the process, we are not left alone to struggle things out by ourselves. God's Holy Spirit helps us to make the necessary changes, always helping us to conform to the *image of Christ*. That's the whole aim of our predestination, and we must on our part be willing to take the journey, only trusting God's wisdom, mercies, and grace.

Amazingly, this is not for a chosen few, it is for all who are willing just as the Father Himself is *"not willing that any should perish but that all should come to repentance"* (2 Peter 3:9). Similarly, *"God so loved the world that he gave his one and only Son, that whoever believes in him shall not perish but have eternal life."* (John 3:16) So, His invitation remains in full strength for the entire world, not just a chosen few, as some erroneously think when they speak about *predestination*.

It would be such a contradiction of terms, intents and purposes to say on the one hand, God has in *predestination* already chosen a few people, and then on the other hand to see God throwing out an all-inclusive invitation to the whole world for salvation through Jesus Christ (see *Rom. 10:4,9-13, John 6:45)*. Our God is not hypocritical and never will be – He is faithful, He is all loving and He is just.

The truth is that God has predestined us to conform to the image of Christ Jesus, which gives us something to aspire to, and to look up to (cf Heb. 12:2). It is difficult trying to run a race and to finish, or even trying to excel if there is no set standard or criteria defining and demarcating the level of performance expected. There has got to be a prerequisite and a final qualification point; such is Christ to the believers. We must strive persistently to the finishing line, which entails conforming to the image of Christ Jesus. That of course is the Father's expectation and predetermined goal for all of His children. There is no need to fall short or to deter, *"but we all, with unveiled face, beholding as in a mirror the glory of the Lord, are being transformed into the same image from glory to glory, just as by the Spirit of the Lord"* (2 Cor. 3:18).

Believers, therefore, have a solid and clear roadmap to follow, and are therefore admonished by the writer of Hebrews who says,

> *"... since we are surrounded by so great a cloud of witnesses, let us lay aside every weight, and the sin which so easily ensnares us, and let us run with endurance the race that is set before us, ² looking unto Jesus, the author and finisher of our faith, who for the joy that was set before Him endured the cross, despising the shame, and has sat down at the right hand of the throne of God"* (Heb. 12:1-2).

The Practicalities of our Predestination in Christ

> *Having predestined us to adoption as sons by Jesus Christ to Himself, according to the good pleasure of His will, to the praise of the glory of His grace, by which He made us accepted in the Beloved (Ephesians 1:5,6).*

Taking our lead from Ephesians 1:5 and 6, and of course our discussion so far about predestination, we can easily identify and set aside some great biblical truths for everyday living, concerning our being predestined in Christ.

First, it means that, being predestined in Christ eventually translates into *sonship*. Hence we are children of God, redeemed and blessed by virtue of the finished works of Christ Jesus (see *Acts 17:28*). We are, therefore, a privileged people facing a glorious future; our past having been sufficiently atoned for by Christ, so that now, we can live with a certain, hopeful, fear-free expectation of a glorious future, while living in a victorious here-and-now. Consider what Hebrews says,

> *For you have not come to the mountain that may be touched and that burned with fire, and to blackness and darkness and tempest, and the sound of a trumpet and the voice of words, so that those who heard it begged that the word should not be spoken to them anymore. (For they could not endure what was commanded: "And if so much as a beast touches the mountain, it shall be stoned or shot with an arrow." And so terrifying was the sight that Moses said, "I am exceedingly afraid and trembling." But you have come to Mount Zion and to the city of the living God, the heavenly Jerusalem, to an innumerable company of angels, to the general assembly and church of the firstborn who are registered in heaven, to God the Judge of all, to the spirits of just men made perfect, to Jesus the Mediator of the new covenant, and to the blood of sprinkling that speaks better things than that of Abel (Heb. 12:18-22).*

Second, it is God's will to have us as His children, and in accordance with His purpose, it delights and pleases Him for us to be called His own children, without being in anyway ashamed of us (see John 3:16; 2 Peter 3:9; Psalms 35:27).

Third, God willingly accepted us as Children, not through our good works, but to the sole credit, strength and praise of His grace, He has brought us into His marvellous universal family, being the object of His unconditional love and unlimited blessings (1Pet. 2:9; Eph. 2:8).

Predestination and God's Foreknowledge from Salvation Point of View

> *"For whom He foreknew, He also predestined to be conformed to the image of His Son, that He might be the firstborn among many brethren.* [30] *Moreover whom He predestined, these He also called;*

whom He called, these He also justified; and whom He justified, these He also glorified" (Romans 8:28-30; Also 2Thes. 2:13-14).

"And He Himself is the propitiation for our sins, and not for ours only but also for the whole world" (1 John 2:2). Much more then, having now been justified by His blood, we shall be saved from wrath through Him (Romans 5:9).

I believe that, to make any real sense of the doctrine of *predestination* from a biblical point of view, we need to start and conduct our discussion within the context of salvation from sin, and salvation for sinners, instead of looking at it as a matter of *fate* with regard to good or bad fortune that befalls people in their lifetime (2 Thess. 2:13-14).

Secondly, it is important that our discussion does not hint or present God as intentionally making some people for destruction, or desiring and delighting in the fact that some would be saved while others would be destroyed. In fact, God does not even delight in the destruction of the wicked, let alone the righteous, and this is abundantly clear throughout all Scriptures. He does not even want any to perish (see Ezekiel 18:23; 2Pet. 3:9; John 3:16; 1John 2:2).

"But if a wicked man turns from all his sins which he has committed, keeps all My statutes, and does what is lawful and right, he shall surely live; he shall not die. None of the transgressions which he has committed shall be remembered against him; because of the righteousness which he has done, he shall live. Do I have any pleasure at all that the wicked should die?" says the Lord GOD, "and not that he should turn from his ways and live? (Ezek. 18:21-23)

The Means and the Call

Now, God, who does not desire that any would perish, has freely put in place the *means* by which all people who will choose to be saved can be saved. This voluntary generosity on the part of God in granting unlimited access to all who choose to be saved, could be seen as *predestination* regarding His salvation intended for all (cf 2 Pet. 3:9; 1 John 2:2; John 3:16). This therefore requires, on the part of the one desiring to be saved, a definite choice, preferably in the affirmative, and to unreservedly commit to the *means* which God has put in place for their salvation.

Therefore, to help those who might take advantage of the *means* by which they can be saved, when they desire to be saved, God, who *predestined* all to be saved, throws out a general *call* to all in respect of their *predestination*; allowing them the option to exercise their moral freedom with regards to the *means* of salvation which God has already provided (see 2Thes. 2:13-14; 1:10-12; 2:10, 11).

By so doing, the individual chooses whether to make a personal commitment, to accept or reject their 'inclusion'. And such a choice of course, must be done, taking into consideration the fact that all of humanity by reason of their sins, both *Adamic* and personal, have fallen short of the glory of God, and thus are subject to the just punishment for sins (Rom. 3:23; Rom 6:23).

This general *call* is sounded and heralded, also to all, as a 'free gift of God' (Rom. 6:23) throughout the entire world by means of general and specific revelations to *every creature* (Col. 1:23; Rom. 1:19, 20), God, desiring and encouraging all to receive His free gift of salvation. Those who respond favourably and positively to the general *call* of God, and yield to His will and plan for their salvation, are then *justified* through the blood and finished work of Jesus Christ on the cross (Romans 5:9; Rom. 3:25; 1 John 2:2; Col. 1:19-23). They literally then pass from death to life, having been forgiven all their sins and been freed from the just punishment for sins, and condemnation (Rom. 5:16; Rom. 8:1). The same, that is those who heeded favourably to the general *call* of God, as a free gift from God who loves all people in the world (John 3:16), then get to be *glorified* by God through Christ Jesus (Romans 8:28).

Responses in View of the Call

Under the biblical doctrine of *predestination*, and with regard to the general *call*, there are three different responses to expect, from those who hear the gospel, which is God's clarion *call* to *all nations* and people (Acts 10:34,35; Acts 17:26-28). This pattern of response toward the general *call* or the gospel is observed, literally throughout all the earthly ministries of the Lord Jesus. You can also find similar pattern in most places in the Bible, where the gospel was preached with the intention of bringing God's salvation to the listeners.

But, I have chosen as a reference, Acts 17:22-34; a very typical case, which represents the different kind of response and reaction following the preaching of the gospel, as a general *call* of God to people for their salvation. Without making any fuss about any particular order in which people's reactions or responses might follow, I will present the three different responses, which are always present when a general *call* occurs.

First, you will have the *mockers*. They are those who mock the message and grace of God as foolishness, and therefore reject outright the general *call* of God (cf Psalm 1:1; 1Cor. 1:23). This group of people, by their own choice, exclude themselves from God's salvation plan, and go to the extent of denying and denouncing their place in God's *predestination* package. They will not progress beyond the *call* to become *justified*, let alone *glorified*, unless they personally decide in time to respond favourably to God's general *call*. By their own choice to reject God's *call* for reconciliation (2Cor. 5:18,19; Rom. 5:11), they in effect have chosen to spend their eternity without God, in an awful place normally described as hell, and designated for all who reject God's salvation.

Second, you will have those who *Put-off* for the future. You could refer to this group of people simple as, the *procrastinators*. These, for reasons best known to themselves, hold back, procrastinate and postpone making any true commitment to Christ immediately, in view of the message they heard. Often, they are undecided and choose to simply 'sit on the fence' for one reason or another, and might end up not making a decisive commitment to Christ, who is God's *means* for their salvation. Thus, in the end, they might slip into eternity without God, sharing the same destiny with the *mockers*. If they decide in favour of Christ's invitation for their salvation, before the worst ever happened, they stand to benefit fully from God's salvation plan and to become saved. Otherwise, by their 'lukewarm' attitude, they might hear the Lord telling them, as He did to the church of the Laodiceans:

> *"I know your works, that you are neither cold nor hot. I could wish you were cold or hot.* [16] *So then, because you are lukewarm, and neither cold nor hot I will vomit you out of My mouth (Rev. 3:15,16).*

Third, you have those people who, upon hearing the gospel preached, immediately receive and believe it for their salvation, and right away, go ahead to start a life changing relationship with God through Christ. This latter category of people, who heed and adhere to the general *call* through the hearing of the gospel, forge a lively and rewarding relationship with God, and typify God's desires for people everywhere at all times. They have, through their right response in faith, to God's general *call*, basically fulfilled the requirement of their *predestination* package, so to speak. God has called them to become "partakers of the inheritance of the saints in light", and therefore, present themselves qualified (Colossians 1:20), after their *call* to progress to being *justified* and then *glorified*. They've already passed from 'death to life' (John 5:24), with a good promise to spend eternity with God, and to also enjoy a blissful place called heaven. These are the *Obedient ones*, who become *saints* of God through Christ, for whom the preaching of the cross and 'Christ crucified' is not foolishness. Rather, "Christ is the power of God, and the wisdom of God" (1Corinthians 1:24).

However, God has a further request that this third category of people, the *Obedient ones*, would "*continue in the faith, grounded and steadfast, and not to be moved away from the hope of the gospel which they heard*" (Col. 1:23). That they do not draw back unto perdition, but should continue in their belief to the saving of the soul (Heb. 10:39); that is at the end of their sojourn here on earth, they might be with the Lord Jesus, in glory!

God's Foreknowledge in Predestination

What about the thorny issue of *foreknowledge*? Obviously, we cannot speak about *predestination* without addressing the related issue regarding the *foreknowledge* of God (see Romans 8:29). Often, in relation to God, *foreknowledge* is discussed in the context of the omniscience of God; that God knows all things from the beginning to the end (cf. Acts 2:23; 4:27). Scriptures like these also play a significant role in the discussion of God's foreknowledge:

> *Declaring the end from the beginning, and from ancient times things that are not yet done, saying, 'My counsel shall stand, and I will do all My pleasure (Isa. 46:10).*

> *... for I knew that you would deal very treacherously, and were called a transgressor from the womb (Isa. 48:8).*

> "*Before I formed you in the womb I knew you; before you were born I sanctified you; I ordained you a prophet to the nations*" *(Jer. 1:5).*

However, in regard to predestination, *foreknowledge,* as in those whom God *foreknew* (Romans 8:29) refers to those who might respond to God's general *call* through the preaching or hearing of the gospel, or the revelation of Himself. Therefore, in view of those whom He knows would adhere to the general *call*, God has already pre-populated 'the book of life' with names, which is the general register of all who would decide, by their freewill, not to rebel against God's free gift of salvation (cf Rev. 17:8; 3:5; Exodus 32:32; Phil. 4:3; Rev. 13:8; Rev. 20:12,15; 22:19). Like God's *foreknowledge* of such people, so is God's provision of the *means* for their salvation, which is *"the Lamb that was slain from the foundation of the world"* (*Rev. 13:8, Eph. 1:4, cf. John 17:24,1Pet. 1:20*). In John 6:64, regarding the Lord Jesus and His followers, He knew from the beginning which of them did not believe and who would betray Him.

Secondly, the preceding verse, that is Romans 8:28, throws some interesting light on the next verse 29, which raises the issue of God's *foreknowledge*, declaring that *"for whom He (God) foreknew, He also predestined to be conformed to the image of His Son, that He might be the firstborn among many brethren"*. In verse 28, if we consider the qualifying characteristics of those for whom *"all things work together"*; they are those who *"love God"* and are *"the called"* in relation to God's plan or purpose. Although the same verse does not specifically define the plan or purpose of God, it is easy to know from the pretext, context and post-text, that this plan is the *salvation plan,* or salvation purpose of God (See Romans 8:18-37).

That means that, God's foreknowledge has to do with *"those who love God and are the called";* people we will refer to as God's 'own' because of their love for God, which ultimately translates into adhering to God's *call,* hence are *the called*. These are those who are expected to conform to the *image* of God's Son, Jesus Christ, mainly because they *love God* and will naturally not reject God's *call* or the gospel of Jesus Christ, because of their love for God.

So, God, in His *foreknowledge* knowing all His 'own', born and unborn on earth (cf. Jer. 1:5); He has already *predestined* them to conform to the *image of His Son, Jesus Christ* (Romans 8:29), not by compulsion but through their love for God, leading them to adhere to the *call* or voice of God as their own free moral choice in their life time. Depending on their individual response to the general *call* through their love for God, they are then *justified* through Christ, and then subsequently *glorified* (Romans 8:30; 2Thes. 2:13-14), willingly satisfying and concurring to their being *predestined*.

(d) Redeemed in Christ Jesus

Part of the mystery of God's will for believers, now revealed and captured by the book of Ephesians, is the fact that they are redeemed in Christ, and their redemption was only made possible through His blood, according to the riches of His grace (see Eph. 1:7). The fact of the believer's redemption presupposes a previous state or condition of bondage, servitude or slavery to another; precisely Satan, sin, curses, and vile nature, against which they initially stood helplessly.

But, in and through Christ Jesus, the believer is redeemed, made free and restored by the blood of Christ. The blood of Christ was the worthy price for the redemption of believers, because nothing else would have sufficed. The Bible is replete with such great testimonies:

> *... for it is the blood that makes atonement for the soul (Leviticus 17:11).*
>
> *And according to the law almost all things are purified with blood, and without shedding of blood there is no remission (Hebrews 9:22).*
>
> *For it pleased the Father that in Him all the fullness should dwell,* [20] *and by Him to reconcile all things to Himself, by Him, whether things on earth or things in heaven, having made peace through the blood of His cross.*
>
> *And you, who once were alienated and enemies in your mind by wicked works, yet now He has reconciled* [22] *in the body of His*

> *flesh through death, to present you holy, and blameless, and above reproach in His sight (Colossians 1:20-22).*

Equally, our redemption in Christ bears endless spiritual, physical, visible, invisible and psychosomatic implications and provisions. Among other things, Christ took away all our curse, disease, sickness, shame, reproach, condemnation and fear of death, to bring us into His glorious blessings. These truths about our victory and blessings are found throughout the Bible, and here are a few:

> *Christ has redeemed us from the curse of the law, having become a curse for us (for it is written, "Cursed is everyone who hangs on a tree"* [14] *that the blessing of Abraham might come upon the Gentiles in Christ Jesus, that we might receive the promise of the Spirit through faith (Galatians 3:13 -14).*

> *Who Himself bore our sins in His own body on the tree, that we, having died to sins, might live for righteousness—by whose stripes you were healed (1 Peter 2:24).*

> *Having wiped out the handwriting of requirements that was against us, which was contrary to us. And He has taken it out of the way, having nailed it to the cross.* [15] *Having disarmed principalities and powers, He made a public spectacle of them, triumphing over them in it (Colossians 2:14-15).*

(e) Forgiven in Christ Jesus

Believers are forgiven in Christ Jesus, as part of the mystery of God now revealed as God's wisdom for His people. This truth connects directly with the other truth of their redemption as seen in Ephesians 1:7, which proclaims, *"in Him we have redemption through His blood, the forgiveness of sins, according to the riches of His grace"*. Having been redeemed, believers are also forgiven of all their sins under the grace of redemption. According to Daniel 9:9, 'mercy and forgiveness belongs to the Lord our God', although we have rebelled against Him. Likewise, the Psalmist rejoices that, *"as far as the east is from the west, so far has He removed our transgressions from us"* (Psalm 103:12). John, writing to fellow believers says, *"I write to you, little children, because your sins are forgiven you for His name's sake"* (1 John 2:12).

In Christ Jesus, *"we have redemption through His blood, the forgiveness of sins"* (Colossians 1:14); *"and you, being dead in your trespasses and the uncircumcision of your flesh, He has made alive together with Him, having forgiven you all trespasses"* (Colossians 2:13). But unfortunately, some believers, because of their lack of knowledge of this blessed truth, still walk with a 'sin and guilt consciousness', so much so that they are unnecessarily, heavily burdened by a deep sense of shame, reproach and defeat, even after they've repented of their sins.

They allow Satan to accuse them and to rob them of their joy and victory already purchased by Christ Jesus through His own blood. With their overwhelmed sense of guilt and feeling of shame, such believers inadvertently ruin their lives and the lives of others around them, by being awkward in many ways. God has forgiven them and even others have forgiven them, yet they find it impossible to forgive themselves and to let go of their past. Remember;

> *For by grace you have been saved through faith, and that not of yourselves; it is the gift of God (Ephesians 2:8).(God) who has saved us and called us with a holy calling, not according to our works, but according to His own purpose and grace which was given to us in Christ Jesus before time began (2 Timothy 1:9).*

(f) Access to God's Rich Grace for Wisdom and Understanding

> *Through wisdom a house is built and by understanding it is established (Proverbs 24:3).*

A good examination of Ephesians chapter one verses eight through ten lends itself to the following conclusion. First, the mystery of God's will, or 'His wisdom revealed' for believers can be summarised as God's rich grace in Christ Jesus, transmitted to them as God's forethought, wisdom and understanding. As a result, the true essence of the believers' freedom and forgiveness totally rely on, and are entirely credited to, what Christ Jesus has done. It is through the power of His blood that our sins are forgiven. However, we have been set free because God's grace is so rich. This grace He poured out on us by giving us great wisdom and understanding in keeping with what He wanted to do, and by showing us the mystery of his plan that was purposed in Christ.

Second, in time to come, the full extent of the mystery of God's will shall be fully manifest, the culmination of it being God bringing together all things in heaven and on earth, under the Lord Christ Jesus as the head and ruler. But in the meantime, and in keeping with God's plans and purposes for us, we were also saved and chosen to belong to Christ. He works out everything for us to fit His plans and purposes for us, in accordance with His grace and love that we might be to the praise of His glory.

(g) *Obtained Inheritance of all Things Good and Richly to Enjoy*

According to Ephesians 1:11-14, we who belong to Christ have an inheritance, and the Scripture refers to this as been already *obtained*, appointed and predetermined by God, who works out all things to fit His plans and purposes for us. This inheritance is first and foremost Godly and kept aside for those who put their trust in Christ, having heard and responded appropriately to the message of truth, which is the good news of their salvation.

On the whole, this inheritance in reality is also the good news of salvation and the things that accompany our salvation, which Hebrews 6:9 also calls *better things*. They are *better things* because they contain God's best aspirations, promises, provisions and expectations for all His children. They are the blessings of the Lord, bestowed by His rich grace towards us, in this present time and for the future.

Our inheritance encompasses *all things good and richly to enjoy*, not of uncertain riches that fade and rot away, but of the glory of the living God in things that pertain to life and godliness; supplied by His divine power through the knowledge of Him who called us by glory, virtue and goodness *(1 Timothy 6:17; 2 Peter 1:3 cf Romans 2:4)*.

Peter claims that, by this very act of God's magnanimity, we have been given *"exceedingly great and precious promises, that through these we may be partakers of the divine nature, having escaped the corruption that is in the world through lust"* (2 Peter 1:4). *'Partaking of His divine nature'*, that's part of our inheritance, having been *'bought with a price'*, to become children and heirs of God, and joint heirs with Christ (1 Corinthians 6:20; Romans 8:17). Joined to our Lord Jesus Christ, we are now one spirit with Him and *"we have the mind of Christ"* (1 Corinthians 6:17; 2:16).

In conformity with the terms of our inheritance, when we believed, God marked us with a seal indicating that we are His own people (cf 1 Corinthians 6:19). This seal is the Holy Spirit that He promised, *"the guarantee of our inheritance until the redemption of the purchased possession"*, to bring praise to His glory. By the seal of the Holy Spirit whose *temple* we are (1 Corinthians 6:19), we have a surety and can now be sure that someday, we will receive all that God has promised.

Indeed, possessing all the promises of God, in their entirety, will happen after God sets all of His people completely free. But meanwhile, our inheritance has been bought and fully paid for in Christ; guaranteed perpetually by the Holy Spirit (Ephesians 1:14). With time, and according to God's plan and purposes, we can have all that the Lord has bought and promised, including *"all that eyes have not seen, ears heard, and mind comprehended"*.

However, while we wait, we have been given a *down-payment*, a good measure of our inheritance, which the Holy Spirit supplies, obviously sufficient for all that we need right now to richly enjoy, until the fulfilment of all things, when the proper time, according to God's timing and purposes arrives. God actually can not wait for His children to claim their inheritance in full to the praise of His glory! Those He has already given, and which His children are presently able to receive, form part of the mystery and wisdom of His will for us. This is so that, we can live victoriously, and fully fulfil our God given purpose on earth, without shame or regrets, in the fulfilment of the Lord's offer of abundant life to all His children in John 10:10.

Overall, when it comes to the wisdom of God's will for you and the covenant of your inheritance in Christ, He has already released and given to all, through Christ Jesus, everything we need for *life and godliness* (2 Peter 1:3). Your health has been paid for. Your marriage supplied, and the job you need is available. You can give birth to children as far as God is concerned, and you can walk again from your paralysis. You can live a debt free life, and live holy and in righteousness. Your children can be redeemed and you can experience household salvation. Your protection has been given, and you can have peace and be happy by virtue of your inheritance in Christ Jesus.

And, when it comes to you having peace, with dominion over the struggles of life, Paul cries out in prayer for you today as he did before; *"now the Lord of peace himself give you peace always by all means. The Lord be with you all"* (2 Thess. 3:16 KJV). *"And the God of peace will crush Satan under your feet shortly. The grace of our Lord Jesus Christ be with you. Amen* (Rom. 16:20). *"But the Lord is faithful, who shall establish you, and keep you from evil."* (2 Thess. 3:3 KJV)

Chapter Four

BELIEVERS' SECRET WEAPON: THE GOLDEN TRUTH ABOUT GLOSSOLALIA IN THE MYSTERIES OF GOD

> *For he who speaks in a tongue does not speak to men but to God, for no one understands him; however, in the spirit he speaks mysteries. ...For if I pray in a tongue, my spirit prays, but my understanding is unfruitful. (1Corinthians 14:2, 14)*

One of the greatest spiritual blessings, as well as spiritual weapons, that God has given His people against the wiles of the devil is, 'speaking with or praying in tongues'. Sometimes, it is referred to as 'praying with the Spirit'. In theological circles, this wonderful phenomenon is more typically referred to as *glossolalia* (see Ephesians 6:18; Mark 16:17).

Without a doubt, the battles that believers often face are mainly spiritual rather than physical. Even Paul admits, *"for we wrestle not against flesh and blood, but against principalities, against powers, against the rulers of the darkness of this world, against spiritual wickedness in high places"* (Ephesians 6:12). These are potent forces with regard to their various schemes and the effectiveness of their cruel manoeuvres. However, believers have the greatest power on their side, not just to outmanoeuvre their enemies, but, to also be able to dislodge and to destroy every wicked scheme of their enemies, through the power of Christ Jesus.

Since our focus here concerns the mysteries of God vis-à-vis the wisdom of God, and their purpose in relation to God's people and the works of Satan; we will therefore endeavour to discuss the significance of tongues to the believers, within the same context. Whether we speak with tongues, pray in tongues or even pray with the Spirit, the advantage for believers is still the same, especially when it concerns the activities of Satan and why the wisdom of God is spoken in mystery.

We have earlier established that the primary reason for the wisdom of God being hidden or spoken in mystery, was for protection *(security)*, preservation, or prevention (also see Mark 4:10-12). God Almighty, through this process is able to keep the details of His wisdom, plans and purposes from His enemies, whose main aim is to discern what God has by His hidden wisdom kept from them. The enemies' true aim of course for attempting to discern God's hidden wisdom is for their own diabolic intentions; hoping to usurp and possibly abort at their embryonic stages, God's divine plans and purposes for His people and the earth. This ties in well into Satan's sole agenda; *"to steal, kill and to destroy"* (John 10:10).

Now, if God speaks His wisdom or plans and purposes in ways that they rather become protected and hidden from Satan and his cohorts, then God must also have ways by which His people can also securely speak to Him while communicating their desires or responding to His plans and purposes. This kind of protection is unavoidably essential, because believers must respond to the Father and if they should, then there must be a safer way to do that.

As a result, God, in His unique wisdom, has given His people the blessing of tongues, an encoded means of communication, a spiritual prayer language that is decoded only by the Spirit of God, but also a complete mystery to Satan and his cohorts. This, in some ways works on similar principles akin to the use of parables in communicating, allowing those *inside* and not *outside* to gain understanding into what is being communicated. (see *Mark 4:10-12*)

Keeping to the principles of parables, let's say that those *inside* ('the initiated'), are the children of the Kingdom of God to whom He has given the grace to understand the mystery, secret or hidden truths of the kingdom. As a result, such hidden truths are no longer a mystery to the children of the Kingdom, but they become the wisdom of God's will to and for them. Those that are *outside* include Satan and his cohorts, who have placed themselves in opposition to God and His agenda for His Kingdom. They are the adversaries of God and God's people, from whom the wisdom of God or even the truths of His Kingdom are kept hidden in secret and in a mystery.

For those *inside*, God has made available the gift and blessing of tongues to communicate with Him directly and securely. In *1 Corinthians 14:5*, Paul's wish is that all *(believers)* spoke with tongues, but more so, he desired that those who spoke with tongues prophesy. By this, Paul does not diminish the desire for speaking with tongues or the use of tongues by any means, but he makes this comparison and preference based on the expediency of the common benefit for all in prophesying, especially when believers gather in one place (see 1Corinth. 14:3, 9-11).

However, in 1Corinthians 14:5, Paul strikes the balance between the wisdom of speaking with tongues, and prophesying using intelligible language, especially for the common good of all within a church context. He further argues that speaking with tongues, which involves speaking in an unintelligible language; if it is accompanied by interpretation could equate to prophesying in view of their desirable function and benefit to a church.

So, although prophecy in a sense could be substituted by tongues with interpretation, we cannot argue the same for prophecy in the place of tongues. Here again, the indispensable and irreplaceable significance of the blessing of tongues to believers' spiritual walk, faith, and life, is established. True, God can speak to us and we can also speak to Him by other means, but for having the purest, more intimate, more secure, and more protected conversation with the Father, He has given to believers the gift and blessing of tongues.

I understand that these are controversial areas among theologians and believers alike, especially when the question arises; should everyone speak with tongues? And even more problematic, is this lingering question that many people tend to ask; is the gift of tongues still available and relevant today? My aim is not to add to the debate, but to present the facts as they are (cf 1Timothy 1:3-6). The gift of tongues and speaking in tongues is a Godly thing. It is good, and believers should desire to speak with tongues. Speaking with tongues is God's own provision for His children, and part of their privileged endowment, to help them to enjoy a richer, purer and a more secured prayer life and worship experience, among other things.

Now, since the purpose of speaking tongues, to the life of God's children has not changed, and equally so, God has not yet found a need to replace or exchange the gift for another, it is inconceivable to think that the gift of tongues is no longer relevant, or that it has ceased. Also, the Holy Spirit who is ever present, and who blesses people with this marvellous gift, has never said that the gift of tongues has ceased. On the contrary, the Holy Spirit continues to pour His gifts upon those who truly desire them.

The following passages ascertain the notion that when we speak with tongues, our prayers or worshipful singing in the spirit is highly, spiritually sophisticated, and exclusively private; with only the Holy Spirit having the means to decode what is being said or sung. Most of what we know about this truth, comes from Apostle Paul, who says,

For he who speaks in a tongue does not speak to men but to God, for no one understands him; however, in the spirit he speaks mysteries (1 Corinthians 14:2)

For if I pray in a tongue, my spirit prays, but my understanding is unfruitful. ¹⁵ *What is the conclusion then? I will pray with the spirit, and I will also pray with the understanding. I will sing with the spirit, and I will also sing with the understanding (1Cor. 14:14-15).* Verse fifteen encourages the combination of praying with the spirit and also with the understanding, which ensures that we can derive the full benefit of prayer, whether in private or congregational.

Now, brethren, if I come unto you speaking with tongues, what shall I profit you, except I shall speak to you either by revelation, or by knowledge, or by prophesying, or by doctrine? (1Cor. 14:6). This passage assumes that when we speak with or pray in tongues, others cannot benefit because we do not make sense to them, because we release mysteries. However, God, who knows and understands all mysteries, knows what we say.

Wherefore tongues are for a sign, not to them that believe, but to them that believe not: but prophesying serves not for them that believe not, but for them which believe. If therefore the whole church be come together into one place, and all speak with tongues, and there come in those that are unlearned (immature), or unbelievers, will they not say that ye are mad? (1Cor. 14:22-23).

"Deep Calls Unto Deep"

At the spirit level, something wonderful takes place when a believer speaks with tongues. There is a certain amount of vital supernatural transaction occurring between God and the 'born-again' spirit of the believer, who is speaking with or praying in tongues. He or she ascends from the human mind or soul's level, and allows the Spirit of God to help his spirit to pray appropriately; praying and interceding for *true* needs, which the Holy Spirit quickens. Obviously, He knows more than the believer's mind or intellect can presently conceive. That's why this kind of prayer, intercession, or conversation with God, has been described as the purest form possible to human experience, where prayers and spiritual singing are concerned. The reason is, although in the physical, we see the person, praying or singing with the spirit; spiritually, all that he or she is offering up in prayer or worship, is apart from their own selfish ambitions, plans, and purposes, and is rather sourced from the Spirit and resourced by the same Spirit, who gives the believer the utterance.

As believers make their requests known to God, they tap into the heart of God by the power of the Holy Spirit. Having known God's heart through the mediation of the Holy Spirit, they then can literally pray in accordance with God's heart or will, concerning areas of their own life, their deep concerns in life, including families and friends, and of course issues within the body of Christ, and the world in general. This level and intensity of prayer, and engagement with the Spirit of God, can be appropriately described in the same way the great psalmist saw his encounter, as, *'deep calls unto deep'* (Psalms 42:7). In this case, the *deep* in the believer's spirit vehemently cries out to, and concords with, the *deep* in the Spirit of God; receiving wave after each wave, an awesome flow of the grace, mercy, love, wisdom, and revelation of God.

> *Likewise the Spirit also helps in our weaknesses. For we do not know what we should pray for as we ought, but the Spirit Himself makes intercession for us with groanings which cannot be uttered.* ²⁷ *Now* <u>*He who searches the hearts knows what the mind of the Spirit is, because He makes intercession for the saints according to the will of God*</u> *(Romans 8:26-27).*

> *But God has revealed them to us through His Spirit. For the Spirit searches all things, yes, the deep things of God. ^{11} For what man knows the things of a man except the spirit of the man which is in him? Even so no one knows the things of God except the Spirit of God. ^{12} Now we have received, not the spirit of the world, but the Spirit who is from God, that we might know the things that have been freely given to us by God. ^{13} These things we also speak, not in words which man's wisdom teaches but which the Holy Spirit teaches, comparing spiritual things with spiritual. ^{14} But the natural man does not receive the things of the Spirit of God, for they are foolishness to him; nor can he know them, because they are spiritually discerned (1 Corinthians 2:10-14).*

Psalms, Hymns and Spiritual Songs

Whereas God has given us tongues for us to communicate with Him directly in a protected and secured way, when it comes to the fellowship of the believers, or believers speaking with one another in an intelligible way, God has provided us these great vehicles; *psalms and hymns, and spiritual songs*. Of course, the contents of the psalms and hymns, and spiritual songs are by nature a high concentration of the Word of God. Hence the need for the Word of God to dwell in us richly at all times. So, Apostle Paul admonishes all;

> *Let the word of Christ dwell in you richly in all wisdom, teaching and admonishing one another in psalms and hymns and spiritual songs, singing with grace in your hearts to the Lord (Col. 3:16).*

> *And do not be drunk with wine, in which is dissipation; but be filled with the Spirit, ^{19} speaking to one another in psalms and hymns and spiritual songs, singing and making melody in your heart to the Lord, ^{20} giving thanks always for all things to God the Father in the name of our Lord Jesus Christ, ^{21} submitting to one another in the fear of God (Ephesians 5:18-21).*

Embrace and Celebrate It

Like everything else, the blessing or gift of tongues, possibly has a down side, which is not innate with the gift itself, but with those who exercise it. Due to misunderstanding of the gift of tongues, their functions, and place within the body of Christ, some have caused unnecessary grief for the Church, similar to what happened in the churches of Corinth. None of that is the intension of our discussion, but rather to help believers to know the grace accorded to them by God to fully assert their authority over Satan's wicked works and schemes. We can only claim our victory over Satan and his cohorts by not being ignorant of his devices (2 Corinthians 2:11), and through the wisdom of God already available to believers, including the appropriate use of the gift and blessing of tongues.

One of Satan's devices concerning the wisdom of God, in reference to praying in or speaking with tongues, is to keep us in darkness. His agenda is to lead believers into denying the gift of tongues, the fact that it is available to all believers; and its huge power and potential. In most places, the gift of speaking with tongues, has eluded believers because, they have been more concerned with *dissecting* and scrutinizing the gift, more than celebrating it. Such attempts profit nothing as far as the gifts are concerned. There is no place for doubt, unbelief or cynicism, if you want to walk in the power of God. It is high time for believers, who appreciate God's wisdom in the earth, and His divine provision, through the supernatural gifts of tongues for their victory, to begin to embrace and to celebrate it.

Your Defence but Satan's Nightmare

I believe, and I say this cautiously by inspiration and not for doctrine, that apparently, Satan was able to eavesdrop on God's instruction to Adam, about not eating from the *"tree of the knowledge of good and evil"*. Somehow, it seems, that the detail of this special and specific instruction leaked unprotected to Satan (Genesis 2:17). If that was the case, then, it probably happened around the time when Adam was recounting to his wife, Eve, what God had instructed him about the *forbidden tree*. It is possible that, Satan, cunningly and subsequently took advantage of Adam and Eve's lack of discretion and wisdom, about the serious nature, ramification, and devastating effect of their choice, across the earth.

Apart from what the Bible says, no one can say with certainty how Satan got to know about the instruction God gave to Adam. But, reading the passage of the temptation of Eve and Adam, we know that Satan was aware of the content of the initial commandment of God to Adam regarding the *forbidden tree*; so, he was able to deceive Eve and then Adam.

Now, when it comes to the believer, God has a special way of communicating His wisdom to us, by using means that are safe and secure from Satan. What He tells us in wisdom becomes mystery to Satan and his cohorts. Knowing Satan's intention to derail God's purposes for our redemption, and knowing our human frailties in resisting Satan's devices, God, on purpose, spoke the wisdom of our salvation in mystery (1 Cor. 2:6-8; Ephesians 1:7-12). Even today, He continues to do the same, in relation to His special instruction regarding our lives, so as to secure and protect His plans and purposes from Satan, who doesn't know the heart of the Spirit of God. For, *"... Even so no one knows the things of God except the Spirit of God"* (1 Corinthians 2:11).

Likewise, God has provided us with His wonderful gift of tongues; an important part of its benefits being, the ability to securely speak directly from our spirit to God in a mystery; by which means, we circumvent possible intervention from Satan and our own human weaknesses. The reality of this simple truth come to us in Scriptures like, 1 Corinthians 2:11, which says, *"for what man knows the things of a man except the spirit of the man which is in him?..."*. Also,

1 Corinthians 14:2; "for he who speaks in a tongue does not speak to men but to God, for no one understands him; however, in the spirit he speaks mysteries." We cannot afford not to walk in God's wisdom provided for our benefit, and advantage over adversaries in this world. To wage and to certainly win our wars or challenges, intended by Satan and his cohorts to distract and disrupt our lives, and the purposes of God for us, the wisdom of God is paramount.

Even David, as we saw earlier in a previous chapter, prevailed against his enemies through wisdom. Our Lord Jesus, while on earth walked in wisdom and prevailed in wisdom always, and for that reason right from His childhood, He *"grew and became strong in spirit, filled with wisdom; and the grace of God was upon Him"* (Luke 2:40). Every serious minded believer intending to do well, and to enjoy God's continuous blessing in their life, would start and win by wisdom. As it is written; *"for by wise counsel (wisdom) you will wage your own war, and in a multitude of counselors there is safety"* (Proverbs 24:6).

Chapter Five

WALKING IN THE LIGHT OF HIS MYSTERIES: "THE CLOUD OF WITNESSES"

Therefore we also, since we are surrounded by so great a cloud of witnesses, let us lay aside every weight, and the sin which so easily ensnares us, and let us run with endurance the race that is set before us, ² looking unto Jesus, the author and finisher of our faith, who for the joy that was set before Him endured the cross, despising the shame, and has sat down at the right hand of the throne of God (Hebrews 12:1,2).

Let me quickly remind you, that many things about your life, that seem like huge disappointment today, are quite purposeful in the wisdom of God's will for you. Note, this has nothing to do with what other people believe and teach called, *fate*; that works on the principle of chance. With *fate*, misfortune is idolised, and life and destinies are set in a concrete, usually toward a predetermined end, and there's nothing anybody can do about it. Our Bible does not teach that!

What I am talking about is far-far from that, and has everything to do with looking at things from the perspectives of God, who is all loving and ever gracious and just. To appreciate this concept and truth, one needs to wear and begin to view things through the right pair of lenses, which will help us to see our lives and challenges, or seeming setbacks, from God's standpoint.

With regards to God's plans and purposes, some things might look like disappointments, only because they are still God's wisdom in a mystery, which are yet to become God's wisdom that is revealed. For *"eye had not seen, nor ear heard, nor have entered into the heart of man the things which God has prepared for those who love Him"*. Take for example men and women in Scriptures, whom we now read about with glee and excitement.

While the wisdom of God was literally being spoken in a mystery concerning their lives, at times, they also felt nothing was working for them, and doubted if there was a promise of a good future. But a time came, when the wisdom which was spoken hitherto as a mystery of God, became God's revealed wisdom, and with great satisfaction their eyes began to see, their ears heard, and it entered their minds what the Lord has prepared. They lived their dreams, so to speak.

Borrowing from a courtroom scenario, let's allow in a moment, to serve as 'witnesses', some of the men and women who have both experienced, 'God's wisdom in a mystery', and 'God's wisdom that is revealed'. They will each take the stand and briefly state their case, with the hope that you can identify with some of them. I intend to offer their stories as their testimonies, from their own point of view from the 'witness box'. Let's call it an *illustrated sermon*, but an abridged and a paraphrased version, to help us to appreciate the dynamics between the hidden and revealed wisdom of God for us.

Case #1: Stand, Moses:

"I was born a great prophet and deliverer *(initially a mystery to me)*, but missed my way. I became confounded to exile for many years, and also abandoned to the backside of the desert as a wanted criminal and murderer. I returned after what seemed like a fruitless and endless years of waiting; and after God had cleared my criminal record. He then called and anointed me to lead His great nation out of their bondage and captivity in Egypt. I'm now so glad that I lived out my purpose fully, as a deliverer and a renowned prophet of God, with whom God spoke 'face to face'". *(Case Ref: Exodus 2- Deut. 34)*

Case #2: Stand, Joseph:

"I was a Prime Minister and a saviour to many people *(initially a mystery to me)*, but was hated by my own brothers without a cause. I was subsequently dumped into a scary pit, separated from the beauty of family relationship, robbed of the assurance and comfort of fatherly love; declared dead, sold into slavery, and then accused of betraying my master's trust. I ended in prison wrongfully charged as a rapist, leaving me hopeless. I was forgotten in prison even by those I helped. At times, it seemed to me like my prayers were being ignored.

Often, I became shattered in a deep sense of loss and frustration about why my own brothers hurt me so badly, and caused me to lose my opportunity, to see and play with my little brother, Benjamin. I terribly missed everyone including my aging Father, my little brother and the ever-present memories of my late mother, Rachel.

Many times I got frustrated with everything, but in the end God let me know why. Thank God, I lived to accomplish all of God's plans and purposes for my life by saving many lives including my own brothers and Father, and many more in Egypt and the surrounding nations". Thank you, Joseph. *(Case Ref: Genesis 37-50)*

Case #3: Stand, David:

"I was a mighty king and God called me a man after His own heart *(initially a mystery to me)*; but despised and forgotten by my own father, and consigned to the wilderness to look after my family's few sheep. There, I fought with lions and bears, to keep me and the flock safe. My youth was stolen from me because of our family's hardship. I had to grow up and mature quickly in order to cater for myself.

In my zeal, at a very young age, I did something that surprised me. Seeing a great giant defying God's army and reproaching the Name of God, I had to stand up for my people and the Name of God, on behalf of my country. In sheer disbelief, but by the grace of God, I suddenly killed the great giant with a sling and a stone. So, all of Israel including the King was free, although I later got into trouble with the King because I suddenly became popular as the *giant-killer*.

Now, I am so glad God allowed me to be kept in the wilderness with the sheep, the bears and lions. While in the wilderness I discovered my gifts and talents, and had all the time necessary to perfect them. It was there that I learned how to use the sling skilfully, and also learned to make my own instruments and to sing without people being over critical about my voice, or even my efforts on the instruments as I developed them. In the end, unlike many young men, I had the great privilege of staying in the King's palace to help heal him by playing my instruments and singing for him. That was my very first experience of the palace, but little did I know that in the end, I myself would rise to the throne as the King of Israel.

I became the King, and the Lord blessed me richly with all things. But, again I made some foolish decisions and became responsible for the murder of a man after I took his only wife. Certainly, I deserved to die then, but God was gracious to me because He made me realise my outrageous sins against Him and I quickly repented.

The Lord blessed me so much, I had enough that I conceived a vision to build God a temple for His worship, but I wasn't the most qualified to carryout that vision to completion. So, I raised all the monies, prepared the materials and the people, to help with the work of building. In the end, God was even much more gracious by choosing my son, Solomon, to reign as king after me and to construct His temple. All of this, and much more God did for me including His covenant to always bless my lineage. I am so very grateful, in the end." *(Case Ref:1 Samuel 16-2 Samuel 23)*

Case #4: Stand, Gideon:

"I was a mighty man of valour, a powerful warrior elected by God to lead and to save my people from their toughest enemies, and God was with me *(initially a mystery to me)*. But, I was caught hidden and frozen with great fear, in the wrong place, because of threats from our enemies.

I questioned God's love and faithfulness, and even thought He had forgotten me and my people, Israel. All through our struggles, He seemed to have allowed our enemies from foreign nations to dominate us, without doing anything about it. Later, I had pretty interesting times, but I will never forget how I had to ensure that God was really going to do what He had promised. I had to put fleeces before Him, and asked for tangible signs. Otherwise, I was not in the position to believe that God was going to do what He said He would do.

Well, God was quite patient with me, and honoured all my requests. Amazingly, in the end, He gave me unqualified victory over our enemies. One all-time unforgettable victory, which was really a miracle, was the day God caused me to defeat an entire nation of great armies with only three hundred men, having no special weapons but only trumpets, and torches inside empty pitchers. That was truly a miracle, and thank God that life actually turned out in the end to be far better than I expected. We became a free people again, triumphing over our enemies!" *(Case Ref: Judges 6-8)*

Case #5: Stand, Naomi:

"I was a woman of great promise, instrumental in all that led to the birth of God's greatest King in Israel, and also 'furtively' regarded in the lineage of the Lord Jesus Christ *(initially a mystery to me)*. But, I was so deeply devastated by the loss of my own husband and two sons, that I became embittered by life. I bemoaned my widowhood and state of poverty terribly, to the point of despairing of life itself. There was nothing more I could wish to live for and all that was left of me were shattered dreams, and perplexing emotions. I couldn't reconcile with myself what I actually did wrong to deserve all the trouble that suddenly came upon me.

But then with time, as God could have it, I regained my life and honour among women and my own people, Israel. People began to count me blessed and highly favoured of God. It took lovely Ruth, a God sent woman, standing with me through all my trials. Of course, Boaz (bless him!), stepped into both Ruth and my own life to help, just when I was at the breaking point.

Ruth stuck with me, although she too had her own challenge as a very young widow, who was in fact one of my deceased son's wife. Surely, now I know that God brought Ruth into my life for a good reason, and with everything that happened, I can now see how God redeemed the situation and caused me to be remembered throughout the history of Israel. Ruth and Boaz gave birth to a handsome boy, Obed, who was also called my son, who became the grandfather of David the King. I never thought in a million years things would work out so well for me in the end; thank God!" *(Case Ref: Ruth 1- 4)*

Case #6: Stand, Jephtath:

"I was a great champion and a judge for my people in crucial times in my nation's history *(initially a mystery to me)*. But, I started out as a gangster; previously disowned by my own kinsfolk and banished into exile in a foreign country, because I was born to a prostitute. I had no good sense of identity, was a terrible emotional wreck, because of how my own family treated me and right from the outset denied me of any rights to family inheritance.

But, in their distress they remembered me, which was not so fair to me, when I remembered that they were the same people who didn't want to have anything to do with me because of my background. Anyway, I conceded in the end to help them, knowing that life can be unjust sometimes. I took upon myself to put in my best on behalf of my people, and I prayed to the Lord God making vows to Him at the risk of anything, including my own daughter, if He gave me victory over the enemies of my people.

We defeated our enemies in the end, but I lost my only child, my young beautiful daughter. That was excruciatingly painful to bear, however she remains an honourable lady whose memory is cherished and commemorated by the daughters of Israel today. I too have learned, in the wake of all my experience, what true sacrifice for one's nation and people entails, and my life is changed for good.

One thing, among others, that I appreciate through all this is the fact that, it really doesn't matter one's deformed background or personal difficulties; anyone has a great potential to rise to the top if they don't give up and let others decide their destiny through abuse or social rejection. Now, I can truly say with Apostle Paul, *'that all things work together for good to those who love God, to those who are the called according to His purpose!'* Thank you, Jephtath, well said! You've definitely given us something to think about. *(Case Ref: Judges 11-12)*

Case #7: Stand, Paul:

"I too was a great apostle of God, Bible writer, prolific church planter, and an ardent defender of the truths of Jesus Christ *(initially a mystery to me)*. But, I became a great religious 'terrorist' who terrorized and threatened the church even to breaking point. I chased and pursued believers even into foreign countries. The day that God's great martyr, Steven, was stoned to death, I was there in person; consenting to his death. I even volunteered to keep an eye on the clothes of those who were stoning Steven, because of my hatred for everyone who followed Christ and called themselves Christians, or people of the Way.

I was so zealous for my forefather's tradition and the Jewish religion, that I worked harder, surpassing all of my colleagues in the effort to preserve our Jewish religious laws and tradition. But, I will never forget what happened on one of those occasions, when I had a go-ahead from the High Priest to get down quickly to Damascus, to arrest more Christians and to violently disrupt their activities.

Just about entering the city of Damascus, a voice and a great light shinning from Heaven arrested me, and knocked me down to the ground. The light and the voice were that of the Lord Jesus Christ Himself, asking me 'why I was persecuting Him?'

Well, truth be told, I never thought about it that way; that when I troubled Christians, I was persecuting Christ Himself. In fact, I didn't even think He was alive until I heard His voice and later saw Him, when I was caught into the third heavens. His power was so awesome and overwhelming, but His unconditional love that I felt that day on the Damascus road, is indescribable.

Although I knew all the arguments against Christians, and was well schooled in all the Jewish laws and the Old Testament, and had great zeal; yet when I encountered the Lord Jesus, my words were so few. I only asked, "Lord what will You have me do?" Obviously, that has changed my life forever!

Here I was, I had just encountered and literally seen the Truth. What did I do? I went on straight ahead, after a few days of recovering from my encounter, to preach that Christians were right after all, and that Jesus Christ was, is and will continue to be Lord, forever. That brought me some troubles, but it was worth it. I vowed to stand up for the truth no matter the cause. I regretted and repented of all my unguided actions in the past, against Christians and the Lord Jesus Christ.

Now, I am just so glad that He forgave me and restored me to my original purpose. God is so merciful and gracious. Today, some consider me, if not the greatest apostle of Christ, then maybe one of the greatest of all times. I appreciate that God is the great restorer as well. I never thought things will turn out this way, so pleasantly amazed at the wisdom and works of God"! *(Case Ref: Acts 7–28)*

The Verdict

You've heard the testimonies of the great "Clouds of Witnesses", as they stepped forward, one after the other, giving you their personal, unbiased evidence of how they came to realise and to appreciate the wisdom of God through their circumstances, and of course their lives. What do you think? Is there hope for you also? Do you see God at work in your life and circumstances?

Certainly, our 'witnesses' offer everyone more hope than was initially thought. In fact, they validate the claim of God's hidden wisdom for His children; that, concerning the mysteries of God's will for those who know Him and trust in Him, they are never 'finished' just because they failed somewhere along the line, or because times are tough.

On the contrary, God, no matter the difficulties of life, has good plans for those who trust in Him, to deliver them and to bring them into a good future. He says to all, *"I know the thoughts that I think toward you, says the Lord, thoughts of peace and not of evil, to give you a future and a hope"* (Jerem. 29:11). That means, even if Satan should do his worst, God Almighty, your Father and mine, will do His best to ensure all is always well with you.

The great *Jury* of heaven above, God the Father, Son and Holy Spirit, the eternal One, has a verdict for all of His children, including you, that in the light of His mysteries, you're already blessed and highly favoured – that as part of your heritage as a servant and child of God whose righteousness is from Him, *"no weapon formed against you shall prosper, and every tongue which rises against you in judgment you shall condemn"* (Isa. 54:17).

Concerning your future, He has also reached a verdict; that because you love the Lord, *"eye has not seen, nor ear heard, nor have entered into the heart of man the things which God has prepared for you"* (cf 1 Corinth. 2:9). How can this be? Well, God Himself shall execute it, *"for with God nothing shall be impossible"* (Luke 1:37). Only believe (Mark 9:23), and *"blessed is she (he) who believed, for there will be a fulfillment of those things which were told her (him) from the Lord"* (Luke 1:45). May the Lord fulfil and perfect all that concerns you, according to Psalms 138:8. As He has already said, "He will never leave you nor forsake you".

# LIVING THE REALITIES
OF THE MYSTERIES OF GOD
[*The Possibilities and The Price*]

Chapter Six

MORE THAN CONQUERORS: YOU MUST PREVAIL

> *These things I have spoken to you, that in Me you may have peace. In the world you will have tribulation; but be of good cheer, I have overcome the world." (John 16:33)*

"In the world you will have tribulations". What a promise! Sounds like a very unusual kind of farewell from the Lord to people who depended on Him for everything. But, those were the last few words to those He was leaving behind as He prepared to depart. Aware that He was about to leave His disciples, who had gotten used to Him being always physically present, the Lord Jesus had to prepare them for the unexpected.

Obviously, the disciples had grown very accustomed to the comfort, security, and authority and power that they had and exude, because of Jesus been physically there with them. Now, all of a sudden, He brings them 'bad' news. They are shocked, and the Lord can sense the terrible fear in their eyes. He feels their sense of loss, hopelessness and discouragement, as their faces dropped and their hearts began to race. Then, Jesus, softly but sternly, says to all, *"be of good cheer!"* (My rendering: *'guys, rejoice, and put on a winning spirit'*!)

Suddenly, the 'world' of the disciples fell apart; it turned rough, and their faith was almost gone. Having been told, that *"In the world you will have tribulation"*, it is not difficult to guess what was penetrating their minds. Earlier on, in John 16:16-19, when Jesus, told His disciples, *"a little while, and you will not see Me; and again a little while, and you will see Me, because I go to the Father"*; they could not handle it. Then, how else could they bear with the notion of having tribulations in this world, after Jesus' departure? One can only imagine them helplessly swinging their heads from side to side, in total disbelief and bewilderment, saying, "Lord not again. We've already had enough troubles and have suffered sufficient set-backs and disappointments, anyway. Please save us this one, Lord Jesus. We trusted you. We literally entrusted our destinies to you and you just can't quit on us like that. We can't handle this." But, the Lord Jesus still insisted, 'guys, you must *"be of good cheer"*, and put on a winning spirit, because I have overcome the world'!

Have you ever had the Lord insist on what His will, plan or purpose is, in spite of your personal fear and trepidations? Sometimes, when life hits really hard against us, it feels so wrong and it feels like God doesn't know or understand our challenges or battles. But, remember that His ways and thoughts are higher than ours. Think about Moses and the children of Israel, who were caught in between the Red Sea and Pharaoh with his armies, the fiercest enemies of Israel. They were absolutely bent on destroying Israel. Yet, it didn't matter how loud or hard the children of Israel cried out, whinging to God about what seemed certain to be their impending doom; God still commanded them to go forward (Exodus 14:10-15).

Did He not care that they were about to perish? Of course, He cared more than they thought. However, God was not ready to respond to their fear and 'protest'; but His favourable plans He had already put in place, for their total deliverance and salvation, as He always does.

Similarly, He cares about you too, my friend and God is watching over His good Word for your life to bring it to pass (see Jer 1:12). He might not react or respond to your 'protest', but at the right time, He will perform His good plans and cause to come to pass the *end* that He intends for you. God is awesome at what He does, and,

> *"Indeed we count them blessed who endure. You have heard of the perseverance of Job and seen the end intended by the Lord—that the Lord is very compassionate and merciful" (James 5:11).*

Scattered not Shattered

> *We are hard-pressed on every side, yet not crushed; we are perplexed, but not in despair; ⁹ persecuted, but not forsaken; struck down, but not destroyed— ¹⁰ always carrying about in the body the dying of the Lord Jesus, that the life of Jesus also may be manifested in our body (2 Corinthians 4:8-10).*

The closing words of the *'be of good cheer'* exhortation from the Lord Jesus to His disciples, holds a little secret about the true nature of their problems. They were afraid of this *world,* and the very thought of them been left on their own in the *world* was terrifyingly frightening. Why? From their experience, the *world* had already been hostile to them in many ways, and the *world* as they knew it, didn't hold much promise for them. Now, with Jesus telling them in fact 'you will have trouble', it did not help matters, no not in the least.

He prophesied that His disciples would be persecuted and they 'will be scattered' (John 16:32). However, Jesus also promised that the disciples would have peace in Him, (vr. 33) notwithstanding the trials and tribulations that might come their way in this *world.* The reason why the disciples would have peace in Him was, because as their Master promised, He has essentially done something about the bitter, stinging powers of the *world* by overcoming the *world* (vr. 33).

How would you react if someone, who definitely knows your future, emphatically tells you that, without doubt, you will suffer persecution and be 'scattered'! – Shock? Disbelief? Relief? Disappointment? Or, just happily, *thanks for telling me, I will look forward to it*! Using a bit of sarcasm, we would say that, the latter reaction would only come from someone with 'a lot of faith', or else a known psychotic. Because it is not natural, to gleefully welcome a promise of troubling pain.

But for many 'normal' people, especially a zealous 'Christian', the initial reaction to a promise of persecution will be to 'refuse it', 'reject it', 'bind it', and '*bin* it', in the name of Jesus! This is what many are used to as the desired spiritual response there is, to '*bind it* and *bin* it... in the Jesus of Name!' Those who respond this way believe, far from being *spooky* they are just being spiritual.

On the other hand, others will respond with rage and anger, and storm away sometimes in denial. If they were 'church members' who were used to only having things their way, they would simply leave the fellowship and head for the next available church, where they hope to hear something more of their fancy.

Whatever and however one chooses to respond in view of potential sufferings in relation to our faith, or God's purpose for our lives, it still does not change the fact about the harsh realities of pains and sufferings. Often, we can only bear, cope or even endure under such circumstance for a little while, especially if they are connected with our purpose, faith and eternal destiny, and if there's an escape determined, as Jesus promised His disciples.

Unfortunately, we might sometimes get hit too hard, through the heavy hands of horrible circumstances and tribulations of this *world*, sometimes leaving us emotionally and physically 'scattered' and drained. However, the idea is, never let up, let down, or get 'shattered', because Christ has promised us a lasting peace in Himself, leaving us a great example of how to overcome the *world*. When things really get tough, there's a great place for solace and a wonderful world in Christ to '*be of good cheer*'. As the Scriptures says,

> *No temptation has overtaken you except such as is common to man; but God is faithful, who will not allow you to be tempted beyond what you are able, but with the temptation will also make the way of escape, that you may be able to bear it (1 Cor. 10:13).*

And again,

> *(God) You will keep him in perfect peace, whose mind is stayed on You, because he trusts in You. Trust in the Lord forever, for in Yah, the Lord is everlasting strength. (Isaiah 26:3-4)*

Living the Disciples Experience – My Story

I remember at age eleven, when we lost our father, I and my brother, without any prior knowledge of what had happened, went as normal to make a telephone call. We needed to know how he was coping in the hospital. Sadly, we were told he did not make it.

Returning from the telephone booth, which was about three miles from where we lived, my brother warned me not to break the sad news to anyone. We had to wait for the arrival of other family members, who were returning from the capital city, where our late father was kept in a hospital. About an hour or two later, they all arrived on a minibus, totally devastated.

But, between hearing the news of our father's death and when the others arrived, I still believed our father was alive. I went through a few different emotions and finally got to the place where I didn't know what to do – cry or not to cry, to believe that he was dead or not to believe that he was dead. I really thought that he would awaken from what seems more like a deep sleep than death. I even had myself thinking he was yet to return from America, where he had just recently visited before he succumbed to the sickness that took him. With mixed emotions and frustration, in the end, I couldn't believe that he could leave us, without me having the opportunity to say my final goodbye. I was seriously 'scattered'!

This was not the last time the Lord's word about *tribulation in this world* would be so real in my young life and experience. Just days after my father's untimely death, a relative, who had promised to give me a new start by taking me abroad to the United States to study and live, was brutally murdered in one of our country's brief but fierce military uprisings.

Four years after my fathers' death, and at age fifteen, I was completely 'scattered' again; this time like many others, forced to leave my country in an unprecedented manner. This was huge, because it was not like anything I have known before. Our entire family displayed and 'scattered' all across different places in various nations. The effect of our civil war was extensive, and was literally felt throughout most places in the West African region.

It was towards the end of ninth grade, and I was playing basketball, looking forward to my senior high school years. University was just about three years away, and getting a university degree for me was a top priority. Part of the reason I aimed so high for tertiary education was because, my late father would have been highly impressed. He worked so hard while he was alive just to ensure that his children had decent education. So, it was a matter of family honour in our little city for children to go to university and turn out to become medical doctors and engineers. I wanted to do that for my father even though he was now dead. I vowed to live 'his dreams and expectations' in some ways. I was always so proud when people, who really knew my father, saw me and remarked that I looked just like my father. In fact, my entire name is really not my own, I was named after my father.

We did most things together even as a little boy. He took me most places he went, and sometimes he told me never to tell anyone where we had been. I kept his secret even as a boy. I loved to wear the same colour of clothes on the same day he wore his. He loved to wear shorts and boot-like shoes, so I wore shorts also. In fact, he would ask his tailors to cut his dress trousers into short-trousers, and then make mine from his trimmed pieces. So we wore the same material as well. He loved Toyota Hilux pick-ups, and I loved Toyota Hilux pick-ups.

He loved hunter's guns (*single barrel slim-22*), and talked about hunting, but I remember only one real successful *game* hunt. I was really impressed, and apparently, it was intended to show me just how good he was. I could not imagine that it was possible that he could aim from that kind of distance. Although I saw nothing on the very tall log tree, just across a two-way gravelled motor lane; he kept aiming at his target. We were then standing near the entry to our farm's junction; with our backs to the junction, but facing the tree on which the *game* sat, across the gravelled motor road.

In some ways, I believe he wanted to give me something to talk about when I was with my friends and the rest of our family. So, not only was he so glad I would hear the gun fire; possibly, I would help to recover whatever it was that he was intending to take down. No sooner had the gun sounded and I was across the road, among the dense bushes of tall straw and grass with my father, looking for what I was convinced, had fallen from the height it initially was.

I was very excited, but anxious at the same time, and following dad, while watching as well with x-ray eyes for poisonous snakes beneath the bushes. I would be lying if I told you that I found anything. I desperately wanted to know what we had, but I was not sure I was brave enough to face it. But, dad finally found it. It was a very large fluffy *game;* it was already dead. But he had to slash the neck, which I believe was a cultural thing. My Lebanese friends, who were Muslim, did the same whenever we went hunting, but maybe my father was just following the Leviticus code concerning life-blood.

My dad was my friend, and I assisted him with his work in his drug store (pharmacy). He built it after serving his time with the local Methodist Hospital as a laboratory technician, where he gained the reputation of 'having eyes as good as the microscope' he operated. I read with great pride, an article on the internet not so long ago, that my father had the ability to tell the type of worm or infection, simply by looking at a specimen from a patient with his naked eyes.

So, you can see that I owed quite a bit to the man who was my earthly father and that's why it was reasonable to try to live his dreams as well as mine. I wanted to show him that I appreciated him. But all this was massively threatened. It took a civil war, something that began initially as a military up-raising, a foiled coup d'état and then full scale war, purportedly backed by western forces, to run us out of our country. The war itself took a nasty turn, degenerating into tribal conflict. More than two hundred thousand precious lives of a total population of only 2.5 million people, were destroyed.

I myself was arrested on three different occasions to be killed during the heat of the crisis. Still, in the midst of all this, and in the absence of any fully functional hospital, I became sick with crippling appendicitis, that the doctor said would require surgery. Lack of basic amenities, food and safe drinking water was about the commonest occurrence. In the end, left with no school to attend, and no future to look forward to in my country, a friend and I escaped to Ivory Coast, a former French colony as refugees. Again I became very 'scattered.'

But in all of my trials and difficulties, God was ever faithful. I miraculously escaped death on all of those occasions, when it was certain that I was going to be killed or could possibly die for lack of basic necessities. In fact, the best one was what I could only term as seeing a *vision* of Psalms 23, which later led to my immediate release, just before the time appointed for me to be killed. As soon as I finished reading (*audibly or not –I don't really know*) what appeared like a scroll version of Psalm 23, immediately I became aware of my surroundings and the danger I was faced with.

After that, the first human voice I heard was a stern command from one of the rebel soldiers saying, that I was free and should run on.

And indeed, I ran from their custody a free person! What became of the troubling appendicitis condition? I didn't have to go through any human surgical procedures. God in His mercies, divinely healed me, and I must admit it was not because I had a lot of faith. I know God, out of His sheer mercy, grace and love, decided to take my infirmity away, and to give me a future.

Even as a refugee, God was with me. By the grace of God, I did not have to stay on designated refugee camps, which was a huge privilege. The Lord provided for me and my friend, and we had our own rented room. It was a single room, but it felt like having a mansion in our condition. Hence, though I suffered 'scattered' experiences, yet I was never 'shattered'!

Because of my background, as you have already read, I have learned, and continue to learn, that God is ever gracious and merciful, and what he has done for me, He will do much, much more for you. If you won't quit, but keep looking up to God, He will come through for you, and as He taught me before, God is never late – *He is the on-time God*. Although you suffer trials and tribulations, He is with you, and the good thing is, even as Christians or followers of Christ, sometimes,

> *We are hard-pressed on every side, yet not crushed; we are perplexed, but not in despair; persecuted, but not forsaken; struck down, but not destroyed— always carrying about in the body the dying of the Lord Jesus, that the life of Jesus also may be manifested in our body (2 Corinthians 4:8-10).*

In all our difficulties and hard circumstance, we too can say with Paul,

> *Who shall separate us from the love of Christ? Shall tribulation, or distress, or persecution, or famine, or nakedness, or peril, or sword? Yet in all these things we are more than conquerors through Him who loved us. For I am persuaded that neither*

> *death nor life, nor angels nor principalities nor powers, nor things present nor things to come, nor height nor depth, nor any other created thing, shall be able to separate us from the love of God which is in Christ Jesus our Lord. (Romans 8:37).*

It's Common to All

> *No temptation has overtaken you except such as is common to man; but God is faithful, who will not allow you to be tempted beyond what you are able, but with the temptation will also make the way of escape, that you may be able to bear it (1 Corinthians 10:13).*

Sometimes in life, like the disciples of Christ, we might suffer setbacks or similar situations that leave us 'scattered'. Some of those might relate to our own fears, disappointments, sudden change in some aspects of life, traumatic experiences including loss of love ones, shattered dreams, financial difficulties and so forth.

Within such context, often, we might be presented with the option to choose how to respond and what to make of our experiences. At this point, the wisdom of Christ comes in handy. He, throughout the Scriptures, encourages those who know and follow Him not to deny the fact that things might go wrong sometimes. But, they must put their total trust in Him to find the needed *peace*, which everyone requires, when they go through unexpected and unpleasant situations that might leave them 'scattered'. This is His *peace* that surpasses all understanding and that guards, and 'governs' the hearts of believers through Christ Jesus, while trusting Him for their help which comes from the Lord (Philippians 4:7; Psalms 121:1,2).

Notice, He does not ask us to fight our own way from the situation or through it, relying on ourselves and relying on the ways of this *world*. He says, only in Him shall we have *peace*, but turning to this *world* for any other answer will only lead to more complications and further difficulties, because the *world* has no true and permanent answer or solution to offer. In essence, the *world* can not solve the mess and problem it has created, because the *world* itself is the problem. *"In the world you will have tribulation"*, but Jesus has overcome the *world*. He definitely has the answer and the solution to the world's problems as well as the problems believers face while living in the *world*. As the Scriptures say;

> *(God) You will keep him in perfect peace whose mind is stayed on You because he trusts in You (Isaiah 26:3).*

> *If they obey and serve Him, they shall spend their days in prosperity, and their years in pleasures (Job 36:11).*

Chapter Seven

THE OVERCOMER: YOU CAN GET UP, TAKE UP YOUR BED AND WALK

> *Then behold, they brought to Him a paralytic lying on a bed. When Jesus saw their faith, He said to the paralytic, "Son, be of good cheer; your sins are forgiven you"* (Matthew 9:2; see Mark 2:1-12 for full story)

Here comes the paralytic man and his good friends. It has been a long haul of great effort, just to get to the venue of Jesus' *'gospel* & healing crusade' in Capernaum. Historians and archaeologists now believe that the venue was no other than, the 'home of Simon (Peter) and Andrew'[1] (Mark 1:29), where some of Jesus' greatest teachings and miracles took place in Capernaum. Although, the building was later modified in a small way to accommodate crucial events; we are told that during the *'healing of the paralytic'*, it was packed to capacity, with no room to receive anyone, not even near the door (Mk 2:1-2).

Jesus had already begun to teach, and everyone was listening keenly. Since He was always on the go, as an itinerary evangelist, this crusade probably was his last day of revival meeting in Capernaum, before he would return later. All of a sudden, there was a big banging sound. A *paralytic* man, carried on his own bed by his four friends, found himself right before Jesus, as He preached. What happened? Because of the multitude, the men could find no other way of getting inside, but to tear part of the roof of the building. They would do anything to get their friend inside, to be prayed for. *I'm so glad that the rains were not on. Imagine the 'out-pouring', or should I say the 'down-pour'.*

One could not help but notice how the *paralytic* man got in. When Jesus and the multitude looked up to see what was happening, then they saw four men quickly descending from the roof, while using the middle beams. Having descended from the top, and standing in the midst of everyone present, they put themselves together; rushed over to help their *paralytic* friend, who was still tied to his bed. He's quickly untied and properly centred on his bed. Then, with all eyes fixed on Jesus, He moved forward, just enough to appreciate the paralytic man's condition. The four men including the paralytic did not have to explain themselves; their effort paid off, causing Jesus to literally 'see their faith'. (*I have narrated the story using my own style*)

Unlike others, who conceal their faith so well, some people's faith becomes immediately apparent, and you have no need to ask them further questions. For such people, you just have to get down to business with them, because they are ready to receive their miracle. There is no need for any 'form filling exercises', so as to ascertain the background to the cases of people whose faith can be seen.

Therefore, Jesus, obviously taking compassion on the *paralytic* man, looked intently in his eyes, and called out to him, '*son, be of good cheer*'. Then He leaned over slightly towards the *paralytic*, as if meaning to touch him, and also said to him '*...your sins are forgiven you*'. No doubt, Jesus knew what He said would arouse the critics' interest; but He was not so concerned about being criticised. He was more impressed with the faith of the *paralytic* man and his colleagues, and their need for a healing touch from God Almighty.

After all, it was the *paralytic* who was suffering, not the critics. It was the *paralytic* whom the *world* and Satan had been nasty to. So, in Jesus' mind, those deserving of His priority were the *paralytic* and his good friends, who in fact saw his pain and the need for him to be healed. They have managed to 'disrupt' His sermon, and claimed His complete attention. So also, they must get what they came for.

Now, why was Jesus saying to the *paralytic* 'rejoice' or *wear a winning spirit* although he was paralysed? Couldn't He see that the man was a cripple and an acute paralytic? Was there any thing to 'be of good cheer' about in his personal world full of trouble? Was Jesus asking the *paralytic* to deny the reality of his situation? Certainly not. Maybe Jesus was saying, 'once again the facts are there and so obvious, but the choice lies in your power to be 'cheerful' not for the wrong reasons but *wear a winning spirit* despite what you are going through.'

In essence, you can be happy, you can *wear a winning spirit* when you decide, not when other people allow you or your situation permits. Your ability to overcome, win and be happy need not be physically dependent on your culpable senses, nor should it be circumstantial, but should be drawn from the deep recesses of the Spirit within you, who helps you with your battles and who helps you to overcome. And it works pretty well especially at Jesus' command! (Rom. 8:26)

Overcoming and Winning

Two important, but modest scriptural instructions that capture what is needed for overcoming life's challenges, as well as maintaining the victory, are found in John 2:5, and Mark 9:7. They involve a simple word of command, that says; "*Listen to Him, and whatsoever He (Jesus) says unto you, do it!*" That way, you are guaranteed God's help for deliverance, victory and true happiness. If you felt sickly and Jesus came along and said, 'hey, you are well'; simply listen to Him, do and be what He says concerning you.

Speaking of listening to Jesus and doing what He commands, Jairus' daughter in Mark 5:35-43, readily comes to mind. She is pronounced dead after a brief illness. Her father who had initially gone to seek the help of Jesus, to heal his daughter, got a bad report from some people who had news that his daughter was already dead. They told him, "do not trouble the 'Master' any longer, because your daughter is dead". In other words, Jairus had to accept that, all hope was gone, and the only reasonable thing to do was to return home, to bury his daughter.

But, Jesus saw things differently. Instead of agreeing with the bad report and the 'naysayers', He spoke the opposite concerning the girl's situation. 'She is not dead but sleeping', He said. Then, Jesus also cautioned, Jairus, to stand his ground and to listen to Him. Well, that's my way of putting it plainly. However, if you want Jesus' own words, here they are: *"He said to the ruler of the synagogue, do not be afraid, only believe"*.

Evidently the text did not say that Jairus believed, but the fact that he still took Jesus to his house to see the dead girl, indicates something more than just believing. A faithless and doubtful person would have bowed in shame, and advised Jesus; 'let's stop here and not make matters even worse by making fools of ourselves before the group of mourners that have already gathered. They will certainly count us for fools and being beside ourselves, because we have travelled much distance only to pray for a girl who is already dead.' This sort of response of doubt and unbelief was fortunately, not how Jairus saw things. He rather persisted with the 'Master', who coming into Jairus' house, prayed for the dead girl and brought her back to life.

Do you know why Jairus received his dead girl back to life, 'turning his mourning into dancing'; his sadness into happiness? He listened to the 'Master', and did what he was told. It is good to believe, but you have got to take it to the next level, by obediently doing what Jesus says. That, I tell you, is the greatest secret to an overcoming life and maintaining the victory as a believer – always do what Jesus says!

Let me remind you of the twelve disciples who, although were afraid of facing their *world* without Jesus, received a strange command, to 'be of good cheer'. Jesus promised them divine peace in Himself, and the fact that He has already overcome the *world*. You also saw how a man, bound and made crippled probably due to his *sins* is told to 'rejoice'. I said probably due to his *sins*, because the first thing Jesus addresses apart from the man's condition is his *sins*.

Now, was Jesus telling those He spoke with to be a bunch of naïve clowns? Certainly not. He was simply saying, there is always a way out, and never let things get to you so much, that you cannot see hope beyond them. For *"with God all things are possible, and to those who believe, all things shall be possible"*. Hence, there's always a reason to be happy in spite of our challenges, and should endeavour to see beyond the present limits that are imposed on us by our challenges. Be like the psalmist; believe and say with him:

> *I lift up my eyes to the hills— where does my help come from?* [2] *My help comes from the Lord, the Maker of heaven and earth.* [3] *He will not let your foot slip— he who watches over you will not slumber;* [4] *indeed, he who watches over Israel will neither slumber nor sleep.* [5] *The Lord watches over you— the Lord is your shade at your right hand;* [6] *the sun will not harm you by day, nor the moon by night.* [7] *The Lord will keep you from all harm— he will watch over your life;* [8] *the Lord will watch over your coming and going both now and forevermore (Psalms 121).*

Few wisdom keys for Winning and Overcoming:

(1) Your *paralysis* does not cancel your "son-ship" or "daughterhood". God's kingdom never discriminates against paralysis. Furthermore, your paralysis should not take you away from God. On the contrary, challenge all *paralyses* by bringing them to God, for a glorious opportunity to experience the kind of love, compassion, forgiveness and healing, which could set you apart from a vast majority of people. Our Lord Jesus did not hesitate to call the paralytic 'Son'.

> *Then Peter opened his mouth and said: "In truth I perceive that God shows no partiality. But in every nation whoever fears Him and works righteousness is accepted by Him (Acts 10:34-35).*
>
> *So ought not this woman, being a daughter of Abraham, whom Satan has bound—think of it—for eighteen years, be loosed from this bond on the Sabbath?" (Luke 13:16).*

(2) Your *paralysis* provides an uncommon platform for you to receive more than is due and allows you to offer more than is common. Let's call it the *law and work of uncommon grace*! (see Luke 1:58)

> *Therefore I say to you, her sins, which are many, are forgiven, for she loved much. But to whom little is forgiven, the same loves little." (Luke 7:47)*
>
> *… For everyone to whom much is given, from him much will be required; and to whom much has been committed, of him they will ask the more (Luke 12:48).*

The law and work of uncommon grace always sets one apart from another. Most certainly, not many will be able to speak and work like Paul, for Christ, and who counted his own life nothing for the sake of Christ and His gospel. He deemed himself privileged to serve Christ.

Surely, not very many will love like Mary of Bethany, who broke and poured on the Lord's feet a costly bottle of perfumed oil, to the dismay of Judas, the *treasurer* (John 12:3-7). Mary Magdalene even loved Him more. She provided for Christ out of her own substance (Luke 8:3); was present at His crucifixion (Matt. 27:55, 56); sat to watch over Jesus' tomb while others went away (Matthew 27:60, 61). She still called Him her *Lord*, even in His death and while still in the grave (John 20:13); wept and stayed alone and longer at the empty tomb of Jesus on the third day, to find Him after the rest of the disciples, including Peter, had deserted (John 20:1-11); and she was the first to see and to announce the risen Lord (John 12-18).

Scarcely, will we have another Magnificat, or a soul rousing song of glorification to God, as did Mary, the mother of our Lord in Luke chapter two. Equally, the Elizabeths of this world are very rare on earth for their unique experiences, which forge deeper relationships out of their depth of appreciation for the Lord, who favours them when they least expected it. Elizabeth, the wife of Zacharias and the mother of John, was already discounted as barren, and in her very old age, God gave her a promised son (Luke 1:23-25).

There will always be very few Davids, who literally were hand picked by God having been denied, deprived, and kept in isolation, but who rose to heights of unprecedented glory and beauty. David did not only become the King of Israel, he was the *man next to God's own heart (1 Samuel 13:14).*

(3) Your *paralyses,* no matter how crippling they are, have a great potential to prepare and propel you into greatness. A lot of this truth only comes by wisdom of hindsight, but they are a reality of life.

Barak Obama became the president of America, but we know that his challenging background did a lot to prepare and propel him into that great office. He mentioned difficult circumstances regarding the absence of a biological father, his mother's second complicated marriage relationship; the subsequent loss of his mother, and the unfortunate racial tension existing during his formative years. What could have been major *paralyses* to hinder Obama, rather worked together to drive him to make something of his life. Mainly, he found grace in another faithful Father, God who made it possible for Obama to study at Harvard, leading to the Senate and then the presidency.

The Spirit for Winning and Overcoming: My Own Background

Had it not been for war in the country of my birth, and the death of my father at an early age, life might have been far from what it is today. I would probably, be pushing papers and doing a regular forty-hours-a-week job, for a monthly salary, which is a very honourable thing to do. But, I could have continued far from my true purpose.

I had other issues as a boy – my tongue was tied so much that I became shy, self-conscious and nervous even to speak. My friends openly teased and jeered at me, and made me feel insignificant. Due to my slurred speech condition, I had to repeat myself again and again, as a result of people saying to me; *'pardon me – come again'*. Nothing was more frustrating to me, and sometimes, my father, who even tried without success to find what exactly was responsible for my then slurred speech condition. I still remember, as a boy, being with him on our farm, and asking me to open my mouth wide and to raise my tongue, for him to check if the 'roots' of my tongue were okay.

Also worryingly to me, a number of my close childhood friends did not find me satisfactorily skilful at key sports, which every boy of our age then, grew to love and use for forming their social identity. So, when it came time to play football, I mostly became what was then sarcastically known as a "bench warmer". It was the description of a substitute, who only matters if the team were short of a more skilful player, or if they were late, injured or absent. Even then, during a game, I was conscious that most teammates reluctantly gave me a pass only if they were out of options.

Most times, I went out of my way to be unusually kind, buying the balls for the games, hoping that my friends would in return select me, to play on their teams, instead of snubbing me. I was nicknamed, and some of those horrible names I still remember today, even though they mean nothing to me now. If anything, they helped me to grow up quickly. In the process, I also develop early in my life, some essential survival skills for living in an intimidating environment. I learned to be myself, and to major on my strength, and to appreciate my difference from others.

Through my challenges, I grew to consider my choices in life, and ultimately I was driven to God, when the right time came. When God found me, no friend could lure me away from Him or convince me otherwise. Because of my background, I had learned that friends will not always be there for me, but God will. Because, I became familiar with teasing, taunting and selfishness to some extent, nothing of such sort really surprised me any longer, so I bought my freedom from people's unfair opinion.

But God definitely healed me. My *heavy* or tied tongue condition, which was largely responsible for my poor accent and slurred speech, improved and then vanished miraculously. I don't remember making any real conscious effort or specifically praying about it. Somehow, I might have grown up believing that I must learn to live with having slurred speech. Later, by the grace of God, I became the 'intelligent' and well spoken person, whom even foreigners easily understood, compared to some of my friends with backgrounds similar to mind. That became the start of my 'internationalization'.

Like Joseph, my own people will give me away but the world will embrace me, simply because God was up to something different and bigger even with all my "paralyses" of my growing-up experience. I was and am still God's boy today. I love to see myself as His son because God's Word says so. My relationship with the Father has been incremental since then, and I now love Him more than I did in the past, as I reckon where He has brought me from, and where He is taking me to. He brought me from afar, and my being in Britain is clearly symbolic of my journey with God. In other words, my geographical transition, in a way parallels my spiritual transformation; something I entirely credit to the grace of God.

Some have heard me make jokes about the remoteness of my birthplace, as I try to demonstrate the goodness of God. I tell people, just imagine, "I am the only British citizen from Ganta – an unknown village-city not in the United Kingdom, but somewhere in Liberia". Ganta, given the global scheme of things, is so out of the way that a United Kingdom border agent, who was once inspecting my passport, could not hold back his inner urge to make an inquiry about my place of birth.

I patiently endured his 'interview' because, ironically, I hold a British passport which names Ganta as my place of birth; something which probably raised a red flag for the border agent, who was attending to me. So, he asked, "where is Ganta, I have never come across that in my entire career?" Well, he was right! When God decides to lift His own, He brings them from strange and unknown places, just to thrust them into the lime light of the great and honourable. Thank God for His goodness!

This certainly could be your story, my friend. God is able to take you from the back of nowhere and to place you right in front of somewhere. From nobody to somebody; from unknown to known, and from obscurity into His limelight! The psalmist says, *"when your father and mother shall forsake you, then the Lord will take care of you"* (Psalms 27:10).

Never allow your *paralysis* to stop you, anyway. Don't even empower your *paralysis* by giving it more than the attention it is due. Let your *paralysis* work for you. The good news is, just like the paralytic at the beginning of this chapter, your own *paralysis,* if properly positioned, could bring you before the King of Kings. Instead of being alienated, you are already loved as a *child* of the King. You are the child of God and He loves you more than you now know. *Be of good cheer*, your 'sins' are forgiven; get up take up your bed and walk! You're a winner and an over-comer

Chapter Eight

THE COMEBACK: YOUR FAITH MAKES YOU WHOLE

> *But Jesus turned around, and when He saw her He said, "Be of good cheer, daughter; your faith has made you well." And the woman was made well from that hour (Matthew 9:22; Mark 5:25-34).*

Everyone knows her. She has been ostracised because of her 'awful' issue that has persisted year after year. She is embarrassed to show up in public, because her private condition has become a public concern.

Of course, she will not let her condition to isolate her forever, and she is determined to find a cure, against the advice of her customs and religious belief. In their eyes, she was no good, but in herself, she knew she had to fight back to regain her life, dignity and purpose. This drove her into taking some unusual steps toward a solution, including sneaking under the cover of the dark, hiding and mixing quickly into a crowd.

As a regular woman, her daily life was difficult, because every time she ventured out, her issue would make her terribly self-conscious and afraid; knowing that she was an easy target for possible public ridicule and execution, by stoning. While she busily sought a way out, her issue did not get better, but rather grew painfully worse, intending to cut her life short, in spite of all of best effort and dream.

A Rare Woman

The woman I have just described is the same person the Bible officially calls, 'the woman with the issue of blood'. Unfortunately, she was tagged by her condition, and that name remains today. She visited some of the best doctors and physicians of her time, but her case only got worse and was declared incurable. And, as the Bible says, *'she had suffered many things (a great deal) at the hands of many physicians.'* Yes, 'many things'. This shows that she was a rare woman. She was determined and ever persistent, that's why she is a rare woman with an extraordinary integrity. For many other women or men, they hardly could bear to suffer a 'few things', let alone 'many things' at no other hands, but *physicians,* the type of her era. In some cases, she might have been their 'guinea pig' for experimentation; and that's how hard it was for the woman.

Let me take my liberty and define *Physicians,* as I know it and in relation to the woman's situation. In this case it means, *those who examine you, other times 'cut' and 'poke' you here and there, when they need to, hoping to make you well.* They are people before whom you lose your 'dignity', so to speak. The physicians see and know things that you have kept and covered as your major secrets, which are also personal to you; matters and issues you would otherwise never willingly reveal to an outsider. To put it plainly, for our context, the physician is the only one person you must readily allow and pay to invade your privacy.

I know what it means to sit, lie or stand before physicians. Even my wife cannot bear the thought of visiting physicians for any reason. If she did at all, it is always with great reluctance and some coaxing that she agrees to attend, even a standard check-up, which is a prescribed, preventative requirement for all women of certain age range, in the United Kingdom. Although the procedure is normally carried out by female nurses sometimes once every three to four years, my wife finds it terribly invasive and hugely embarrassing. Think about what the woman with the issue of blood would have had to endure with the physicians of her time. I don't think she looked forward to seeing any of them, but she had to see as many, who seemed to offer some form of relief for her condition. So, the woman was not only denied her personal dignity; she also lost her life's savings in the process of trying to gain healing, and trying to regain her dignity, *womanhood* and life. Yet, the Bible says 'she was no better but rather grew worse'.

At least, after all this while and after all the pains, one would hope to get better, having spent one's savings and oneself. But, she only grew worse, the text says. Surely, there can be nothing more frustratingly painful than doing all the right things you know to do, but getting no where as far as your condition is concerned.

Although this woman lived in the days of Jesus, there might still be a good number of people today, who identify with her pains, sufferings and frustrations. Especially, when it comes to doing all you know to do, but still with no improvements; whether it regards a need for healing, a child birth, or some pertinent issues that must be resolved. Whatever your personal circumstance might be, there is still a good reason not to give up now. There are many good physicians out there who are trained to help in every way they can, and thank God for them. However, the ultimate physician and our great High Priest who is always "touched by the feelings of our infirmities" is the Lord Jesus Christ. You can always approach His "throne of grace to obtain mercy, and find grace to help in time of need". (Hebrews 4:15-16)

The Rare Woman, Jairus' Daughter and the Mystery of God's Will

It was known that Jesus was in the city of the woman, and a great multitude followed and thronged Him. And then, a man, Jairus by name, who was a ruler of a local synagogue, came to Jesus, earnestly begging Him to come and heal his daughter. He quickly hurried Jesus to go to his house, because the daughter was at a point of death.

Jesus, wasted no time, and straight away, He went with Jairus to pray for his daughter.

Interestingly, Jesus did not ask any qualifying questions, not of the background of the ruler or his daughter. He simply allowed His compassionate nature to overrule His theological stance. He did not resort to settling old theological scores; neither did He raise any theological issues with this Jewish leader about Sabbath, washing of hands and the rest. As the Son of God, sent to help those in need, Jesus will always respond to any person in need, who will also seek and trust Him for a way out. (see John 6:37; Heb. 11:6)

Like Jairus, if anyone is willing to swallow their pride and disregard their self-imposed theological and traditional barriers, Jesus will travel the road with them wherever they need Him to go. This Jesus even sat and ate with sinners and talked to some of the most despised people of His day, when He knew, without doubt, that He would be harshly criticised for doing so.

As a matter of curiosity, I find it very amazing that the same people who criticise, reject and despise you in public, suddenly come running after you, when they are in real deep water, despite their bias and criticism. Probably, this is the one positive thing which comes of needs, trials, sufferings and desperate circumstances; they drive the doubtful, the proud, and self-righteous to God in time of their needs.

Some needs have the ability to pull temporary barriers down very quickly. My firsthand experience of this was in Liberia, where the civil crises of fourteen years, somehow taught many Liberians to pull together in unusual ways, to help one another the best they could. We saw a similar situation in Haiti during their ill-fated 2010 earth quake that sadly destroyed precious lives, and devastated the country. That disaster brought more people together, both from with-in and with-out, to help, than they have ever seen in recent history. The same was true in Great Britain during one of our worst winter seasons in many decades. From December 2009 to February 2010, we saw a semblance of real neighbourliness, compassion and communal spirit being reborn, which was an exception to the deplorable state of ungodliness in the country; mainly encouraged by a ruthless secularization of the culture and society.

With similar patterns even becoming more prevalent elsewhere in the world, it is almost tempting to say that the easiest way to turn your 'enemy' to a friend again, will be to hope that your 'enemy' will have an issue only you can resolve. Then, hopefully, they might just come rushing to you because of their need, or you might end up going to them out of compassion – no more enemies!

Let's see how the rest of the story unfolds involving Jesus, the Man of compassion, the 'rare' woman with a grisly stubborn and culturally disgraceful condition, and Jairus, the devout religious Jew who is a ruler of the synagogue, but who also finds himself critically in need, because of his young daughter. There is a good irony to all this, especially having a ruler of the synagogue, a very religious Jew of his day, publicly meeting with Jesus, and then, also having in his company a religiously 'unclean' woman, with a blood flow condition.

A Timely Move

While Jairus is himself amazed, intrigued, and probably rejoicing within himself, because of Jesus' swift and unconditional willingness to go to heal his daughter; suddenly, Jesus is intercepted by a rare woman. She quietly, but quickly picked her chance at the very least opportunity. As if divinely orchestrated, she eagled directly upon her target, as she had set in her heart to do, and eluded the crowd. Amid the multitude of eager people pressing in around Jesus, she went straight for the hem of His garment. Immediately, she was healed of her perineum blood flow condition. And the way she got her healing, is a great teacher in itself.

Here is a profound wisdom key for a faith that gets results, which this woman's reaction to her issue and Christ, teaches us. She teaches that anyone who aims unwaveringly at their target will get their target. Also, those who set honest goals will achieve them, even amid crowds of distractions that surround their goals.

The passage says, that, *'and she felt in her body that she was freed from her suffering (limitation)'*. The word *'freed'*, as used in this passage brings us to a truth about this woman's condition that has been overlooked, or hardly visited. It unveils and uncovers something beyond what is openly happening in this passage[2]. It relates to regaining her total body-soul functionality with social ramifications. The truth is, her *flow of blood* condition went beyond and required more than just physical, biological healings; her soul and mind, her heart and thoughts needed to be healed as well. After her body was healed, her mind had to be renewed, (Rom.12:2, 2) for her whole self to experience total transformation and holistic soundness.

Well, the Bible says that her condition had persisted for twelve very difficult years. That was enough, not only to start to mourn about, but also to cause her to give up on life itself. I believe the reasons why some of these terrible conditions persist for a long time, is because Satan strategically preys on the situation to his advantage. Through what seems like a delay, Satan intends to use it to break any resolve to fight and break his controls from over his victims' lives. These conditions are formed to stretch his victims to the breaking point, so that their only option remaining might be to throw up both hands into the air, in despair saying, 'enough is enough; it's not worth continuing anymore. It's not worth the fight.'

But, I tell you, *'those who wait on the Lord shall renew their strength, they shall mount up with wings like eagle...though they run they shall not grow weary, walk and shall not faint'(Isaiah 40:31)*. Is this not what this rare woman teaches us, who are going through any trouble or situation that has outlasted their normal course? She teaches us something that only life can teach; to *stand,* because *'tough times don't last but only tough people do'* (Dr. R. Schuler). "For the Lord God will help Me, therefore I will not be disgraced. Therefore I have set My face like a flint, and I know that I will not be ashamed" (Isaiah 50:7).

Healed and Delivered

Jesus' answer to all that is happening around Him is so typical. A woman had just picked her opportunity to touch Him. Obviously, He senses a stream of power leaving Him. Who knows, probably immediately the woman touched Christ, she withdrew to check herself quickly. At the same time, Christ was asking about the one who touched Him. Being as wise as she was, she was not going to reveal herself unless she was convinced that it has really happened as she set in her heart.

After all, many other physicians before then had given her false hope, only to realise in the end that they had even left her worse than she was originally. After she became sure that she was completely healed, she appeared from nowhere in the crowd and threw herself right at the feet of the Lord, Jesus Christ.

Meanwhile, she was terribly afraid with trembling, not knowing the consequence of her action, with her touching Jesus, while was deemed unclean. Been healed was a legitimate reason for her to be unrestrainedly excited. Yet, she suddenly became all too aware of the traditions and stringent laws, including their horrible consequences that cruelly barred her from mixing with 'good' and 'clean' crowds. Let alone, to touch the *Rabbi,* Jesus Christ; she might have put herself into real danger with the surrounding crowd, she thought.

In the heart of the avid traditionalists, people who were well steeped into the details of their religious and cultural laws, she would have been guilty of defiling their *Rabi,* and even those she had touched along the way. Remember, how Jesus' visit with Matthew, the tax collector presented real trouble for Him, and in the minds of some traditional Jews, placed a *dent* on His claim as the Son of God? How much more to be touched by a woman with a *flow of blood*? It could have given a reason to the religious loyalists to consider extreme measures, including a justification for the woman to be stoned.

It is amazing to know that our Lord Jesus never subjects himself to manmade bottlenecks and stringent laws. He does not allow Himself to be affected by mundane methods, like they do with human priests, before and after Him? Actually, whatever touches Him and whoever comes to Him becomes cleansed, washed and holy, without any repercussions for His own holiness and cleanliness. The logic is simple, Jesus, who makes clean, cannot Himself become unclean. Our Lord abides clean eternally to be able to pull sinners from their uncleanliness. Hence, He pleads with all persons to come unto Him saying, "*all that the Father gives Me will come to Me, and the one who comes to Me I will by no means cast out*" (John 6:37). Furthermore, Jesus beckons all to Himself, "saying *come to Me, all you who labour and are heavy laden, and I will give you rest*". (Matthew 11:28)

The Final Confession and Healing the Unseen Wounds

This rare woman is going to do another rare thing; hold her hand up and admit her 'offence'. She owns up to her responsibility in public, no matter the consequence. At least she has done something that others would never dare do; to take practical steps in the direction of what they believe to be true in their heart; putting faith in action. She resolved in herself, just like before, if I must die for daring to come to Christ for my infirmity and healing, which was the right thing to do, then so be it. I believe, as she whispered that in her own heart, she suddenly remembered what she might have heard before; this saying of Jesus, '*that He had promised that He will in no way cast away anyone who came to Him*' – that He is compassionate and has done "*all things well*". (Mark 7:37)

Anyway, she made up her mind not to be deterred by anything and decided to tell *'the whole truth'*. Twelve years of truth about life's constant battles would seem eternal to tell. Remember it's the 'whole' not 'partial' truth. This, to me is the main thrust of the entire story; rehearsing and re-living unpleasant memories about horrible times in public. I call it, *the final confession*; denouncing the past and breaking free from satanic totalitarian controls and their strangle holds.

She poured it all out to Jesus. For a moment, just imagine someone holding a microphone and giving their true testimonies before a cross section of crowd, who are listening attentively in a capacity packed stadium, where an open-air healing and miracle campaign is being held. While she is trying to get through telling the *whole truth (her fears, trepidations, anxious moments, pains...)*, of course, the self-righteous critics, who had no iota of patience or compassion for her, are already insinuating and making their judgements. The disciples, like in the case of blind Bartholomew, are maybe urging Jesus to hurry and follow course to Jairus' daughter who is dying at home.

Remember anxious Jairus is a ruler, a man with authority, and in our world men with authority must not be taken lightly. This might have even spurred her critics more in their accusations. They may have thought of her as an opportunist and a lair, who is only seeking occasion to show off. At this point, I am reminded of the situation involving the woman who was unjustly criticised and ridiculed in the house of Simon, the Pharisee, as she sobbed at the feet of Jesus, pouring on His feet her tears mixed with expensive fragrant oil.

This rare woman had a story to tell and she was telling it with all her ohms, guts, emotions and strength. In her case, it was all about the unfairness and unkindness of life and people, and the battle she had with her culturally disgraceful sickness that striped her of every bit of self-worth, personal pride and dignity, and her inability to live a normal life. Her troubling condition had also negatively scripted her mind and personality, and she could not help herself.

But, her real moment came for her true healing. The *blood flow* was a daunting challenge, but her emotional disabilities, mainly due to ill treatment meted out to her by all kinds of people, who probably misunderstood her or who just blatantly took advantage of her. This indeed was the worst *disease* of her life.

Unfortunately, it all took place in her 'little world' like some people do experience today. Many are having similar kinds of *diseases*, not bodily pains but real deep psychological wounds. They are not physical infirmities, but are the real sicknesses in the invisible places of their lives. Many can cope with back ache but the same people will collapse under the sheer weight of depression due to neglect, abuse, marital failure, family dysfunctionality and rejection. Many can cope with headaches but not the mental illnesses arising from accumulated trauma of non physical abuse including verbal tortures.

The Lord, together with His disciples and the crowd, has listened to all her moving testimonies, and then He says something that changes this rare woman's life for good. The woman had initially touched the hem of His garment for her physical healing, and now Jesus speaks only a few words back to her, one of which connects with her other struggles, and which was necessary for her complete deliverance and restoration. The Lord Jesus, in speaking with this woman, refers to her as *'Daughter'*, and then continues, "…*'be of good cheer, your faith has made you well. Go in Peace."* Again, He adds a key and significant adjunct, "…*and be freed of your suffering (affliction)."*

Just in case someone was thinking well, it was a cultural practice for an elderly person to refer to a much younger person as son or daughter, let's visit the facts. Bear in mind that this woman had had twelve years of *'blood flow'* or menstrual problem, so it is very unlikely that she was younger than Jesus. Calling the woman, *daughter* was far from adhering to cultural nuances, but was deliberately done by the Lord as part of the woman's healing process in a supernatural way.

For example, Jesus' use of *daughter*, in referring to the woman who was bound for eighteen years due to physical infirmities in Luke 13:16, was not cultural. He calls her *daughter of Abraham*, whom Satan has bound …, and then in a clear defiance of what most held as law and culture regarding the Sabbath, Jesus healed this woman. His reason for healing her, apart from it been a good thing to do was mainly because she was a *'daughter'* of Abraham; a reference which evokes a covenantal relationship with certain rights and privileges including healings.

To not be a *daughter of Abraham*, or a *daughter* of Christ, or just simply a *daughter*, or generically *son*, with regards to the Faith and Christianity negates *relationship* and all its attendant rights and privileges, without which one was easily deemed as illegitimate or an *outcast*. (see John 1:12; Gal. 3:26; Romans 8:15-17; Hebrews 12:5-9) An *outcast* was simply an outsider and the term itself excluded people for various reasons, ranging from biological to sociological; thereby, creating and ingraining identity problems. Somehow, in legal terms, it suddenly barred and put you outside of covenantal rights and privileges if you were not a *daughter* or *son*.

Remember the text says when the woman with the *blood flow* problem touched Jesus, the fountain (continuous flow) of her blood immediately dried up (Mark 5: 29), and *"she felt in her body that she was healed of the affliction (suffering)"*. Obviously, she came not for anything else but to attend to her *blood flow*, which was causing her much suffering, which was healed in the first instance, after she had touched Jesus' clothes.

But, now after explaining and telling the *whole truth*, she is told by Jesus, 'be freed of your suffering' and He begins addressing her with a reference to her as *'Daughter'*. In this reference a deep seated and a subtle but truly significant need of this woman was brought to the fore, touched and healed.

Invariably, given some of the reckless cultural and religious practices of her time, she perhaps might have been presumed to have brought shame and disgrace to her biological family, and also her matrimonial family, if she ever were married. Her condition could have perhaps led to her husband divorcing her because of her *blood flow (cf* Matthew 19:3). Her earthly mother and father, because of cultural laws deeply steeped in religious high grounds, might have had nothing to do with her; and maybe that's why the passage is so silent about any contribution they made to help to find cure for her illness. She may have been told she was under a curse of a sort for some sins, that's why the physician could not even heal her.

However the passage mentions her personal efforts and that of the physicians from whom she sought help. Like all of us, it's quite often easy to bear our difficult tests, trials and tribulations with the support of families. But, where such supports are clearly absent, it is easy for one to give up in despair. The situation was not the same for this rare woman; absolutely, nothing would discourage her quest for the right and a lasting solution to her struggles, until she found it.

Even when all else fails, and everyone else turns their backs on you, don't ever quit searching and looking until you find the Lord, with whom all things are possible! The Psalmist is right in saying, "*when my father and my mother forsake me, then the Lord will take care of me*" (Psalm 27:10)

Restored

Remember, we said in previous chapters, *your 'paralysis' or situations do not negate your opportunity for relationship.* This woman, despite her woes in life, she still was in fact a *daughter*, and Christ was her Father. Biologically, Christ might have not been older than she was to be able to father her physically, but this was beyond biological parenthood. It was spiritual and it was supernatural. It is true that,

> *For as many as are led by the Spirit of God, these are sons of God. ¹⁵ For you did not receive the spirit of bondage again to fear, but you received the Spirit of adoption by whom we cry out, "Abba, Father." ¹⁶ The Spirit Himself bears witness with our spirit that we are children of God, ¹⁷ and if children, then heirs—heirs of God and joint heirs with Christ, if indeed we suffer with Him, that we may also be glorified together (Romans 8:14-17).*

> *Christ has redeemed us from the curse of the law, having become a curse for us (for it is written, "Cursed is everyone who hangs on a tree"), ¹⁴ that the blessing of Abraham might come upon the Gentiles in Christ Jesus, that we might receive the promise of the Spirit through faith (Galatians 3:13-14).*

> *Inasmuch then as the children have partaken of flesh and blood, He Himself likewise shared in the same, that through death He might destroy him who had the power of death, that is, the devil, ¹⁵ and release those who through fear of death were all their lifetime subject to bondage. ¹⁶ For indeed He does not give aid to angels, but He does give aid to the seed of Abraham. ¹⁷ Therefore, in all things He had to be made like His brethren, that He might be a merciful and faithful High Priest in things pertaining to God, to make propitiation for the sins of the people (Hebrews 2:14-17).*

Hear what the Lord Jesus says about how old He was. He told His listeners, *"Most assuredly, I say to you, before Abraham was, I AM"* (John 8:58). In other words, He has been there right from the beginning, and He is 'old' enough to father all and to become the Father of every person who will gladly receive His forgiveness.

No wonder the Spirit of God in us attests to our adoption as children of God. The Holy Spirit who also has been there from the beginning, and who is the eternal Spirit of God, confirms to us that as part of His fatherly privileges and love towards His children, the Lord Jesus 'never leaves us nor forsakes us' (Hebrews 13:5). It is understandable that 'the Father to the fatherless' (Psalm 68:5), Jesus our Lord and saviour would reach across to this rare woman, who obviously was in dire need of being restored. He wanted to give her back what society and her unfortunate illness had stolen from her; her dignity, humanity, love and identity. So, He called her *'daughter'*.

Telling the *'whole truth'* indeed was a formidable part of her journey to total soundness, but hearing Jesus call her *'daughter'*, I believe, felt like a calm relief balm, purposely applied to bring about stillness right through her scared and scarred heart and emotions. That did it finally, taking the stings off prolonged abuse and dejection, and replacing it with an overwhelming love and sense of personal worth, value and appreciation.

By calling her *'daughter'*, Jesus healed areas of her life that her personal effort at reaching out for Jesus' garment did not touch. She was definitely set free and perfectly made *whole*, receiving faultless soundness with instant positive psychosomatic effect. The poison of bitter stings of hatred, anger, grief, confusion, despondency, loneliness, and frustration; the injury that cut right deep into her heart due to a long circle of inner emotional tortures, the bruise and anguish of violence probably received through verbal torments, abuse and trauma - all of those dried out in a moment.[3] The anger, grief, and troubling emotions of similar nature that pertain to long term suffering which Satan had intended to use to enslave this woman perpetually, all of these were broken and the woman was restored beautifully by Christ.

In the same way that her *flow of blood* ceased immediately after she touched Christ, this last miracle of restoring her to perfect soundness came also with instant result when Christ 'touched' her.

Can you be of good cheer in a spiteful *world* and through your challenges? Yes, it's possible, and yes you can. Jesus says, 'be of good cheer'! You don't need the *world* to cheer you up, you need just one person to make the difference, and Jesus does. As in the case of this rare woman, Jesus is your only bridge to true recovery; restoring to you your real humanity with perfect wholeness.

You have probably tried other solutions in vain, and you certainly can go so far to touch Jesus' garment with dramatic and instant physical healings. But, let Him free you also in those invisible areas from the nasty stings, poisons and striking scars left by your physical concerns and disabilities, so that you can be healed and be fully restored. Allow Him to 'touch' you as His *child* with His healings, whoever you are and whatever your case may be.

When It Doesn't Hurt Anymore

Years ago, I heard a famous preacher narrate a story on one of his preaching tours in Ghana, West Africa. He spoke about how his little son, out of true compassion toward a man, who had had his leg surgically removed, asked if his father, the preacher, could pray for him. This little boy, in all innocence, approached the man saying, "*look, my father is a preacher and he will pray for your leg and heal your leg.*"

Obviously, this child might have seen the man's scar, or the stump of his leg and, moved with compassion, thought about what he could do to help. But, the preacher said, the man looked into the curious eyes of the young child and with a broad confident smile responded in love – "*son, it's okay.*" And obviously appreciating the young child's offer, the man continued, "*I am already healed and it doesn't hurt anymore.*"

Wow – what a response! "*I am healed, it doesn't hurt anymore*", he said. Friend, one of the ways to test your healing is to see if it doesn't hurt anymore. Anyone can claim to be healed but if it still hurts, emotionally or physically, then there's a need to be healed of that which still hurts. In such situations, there is a need for a second healing – a second freedom (Gk, *Hygies*) that Jesus offered the woman with the issue of blood. If it hurts, it is not healed, and if it is healed, it will not hurt. The Lord Jesus wants to offer that full, total and complete healing to you today.

Prayer for Your Healing

Lord Jesus, I have read and now know that You are the only Physician, who gives total healings, and makes completely whole. You did it for the woman with the issue of blood, and also for the blind man by applying ordinary mud on his eyes. Now Lord, You are no respecter of persons, you did it for others, I believe You can do the same for me also. I know you love me. I now ask You to please make me completely whole. Heal my body and heal my emotions. Heal my mind and take every hurt from me. Heal my past and give me your perfect peace and soundness. I thank you Lord Jesus and thank you Holy Spirit for helping and healing me. I receive my complete healing and I am free right now, in the Name of Jesus Christ, AMEN.

Chapter Nine

THE FAITH-*ER*: ... DO NOT BE AFRAID

> *For they all saw Him and were troubled. But immediately He talked with them and said to them, "Be of good cheer! It is I; do not be afraid" (Mark 6:50; Matthew 14:27)*

Are you afraid? Well, here we see the disciples of Jesus startled, perplexed, frightened and amazed with their eyeballs literally roving and almost popping out of their sockets. Beneath them a tumbling and an unsettled boat, losing stability and welling up with rushing water, emanating from powerful waves of sea water. The sea beneath them is bouncing furiously. Their nerves are calling for help as the restless and unfriendly sea fast becomes a matter of grave concern. The serious risk posed by the continuous rage of the sea means that sooner than later, if care is not taken and their prayers are not heeded, the vexed sea will abruptly end their lives.

They are too far away from shore, thereby endangering their safety, and leaving them most vulnerable in a place where there is nothing solid in sight to cling onto. So, in their desperation their minds had begun to overwork, entertaining ideas about possible ways of escape. Not able to find any quick-fix solution, and with a rising, simmering tension now reaching its maximum, one thing was certain; they could rapidly lose their minds if things had continued the way they were.

A fast scan of the disciples' secret thought processes could have probably revealed something like this: "Are we going to die this way, fed to the fish? What if we jump out of the boat; could I swim to shore safely? Should we have set course at sea and got the boat rolling in the first place? If the Master really loves us and thought well of us, then why did He allow us to leave without Him? He being God's Son, why didn't He perceive that there was going to be trouble at sea and never send us this way?" (Remember, the passage says, "*immediately <u>He made His disciples</u> get into the boat and go before Him to the other side, to Bethsaida, while He sent the multitude away*".)

"How long before the storm calms down, and what if it doesn't calm in time?" It's unimaginable, the flood of thoughts that would have filled and cluttered the highways of the minds of the disciples. To even consider that all of that was happening in just a few moments, was also incredible. Some were probably screaming one thing, while others were totally overwhelmed by their collective plights, and then idly looked on.

After a good while, Jesus came, leisurely gliding on the waves of the stormy and turbulent sea. He had just finished praying, and then descended from the mountain. Why is He walking on the sea and not waiting for the next available boat? Did He see a vision of His disciples tumbling and toiling upon the stormy sea, making Him to want to hurry and not wait for a paddling boat? Or were His 'men', the disciples calling out to Him in prayer from the midst of their troubled tour upon the sea? This most probably was the case, that He heard their 'prayers', because the Bible says, '*call upon me in the day of trouble, and I will deliver you and you shall glorify Me (Psalm50:15)*'.

Truly, the disciples were in trouble and, in answer to their fervent prayers, the Master, Jesus, came swiftly and quickly with the precision of a five-star rapid response team in times of emergencies. Like Jonah who called out from the belly of a big fish to his God; Jesus has just heard His disciples cry out loud to Him from the 'belly' of their desperation. It is an awesome thought to know that Jesus is just a sincere prayer distance away from our most horrendous experience.

The passage specifically defines the problem the disciples had; 'the wind was against them'. Sounds to me like 'the *world* was against them'. Just one of those spiteful *world* experiences when things or people vehemently oppose you from reaching out for your goals, or from being what God truly wants you to be and become. So, the wind was against them.

But, there was an interesting twist right from the beginning of their journey. Immediately after Jesus made them set sail at sea, He went up to the mountain to pray, and the text says; *'then He saw them straining at rowing....'* In other words, He became aware, even while at the top of the mountain, in prayer, that His disciples at sea were paddling and rowing their boat with serious and grave difficulties.

The word *'straining'* suggests that they were pulling hard on their paddles, strenuously twisting from side to side, and painfully hurting with groaning and suffering as the wind opposed them. All this was occurring in the *evening*, while Jesus Himself was still on the shores upon the mountain. When He saw them *'straining at rowing'*, He decided to make a move only at the *fourth watch* of the night.

Finally, when He decided to walk on the same sea toward His disciples, we understand from the passage that He went walking on the water as if He would pass the disciples. How long was the evening to the *fourth watch* of the night? It was nine solid and long hours, the time the disciples had to strain at rowing on the sea on their own.

The *fourth watch* was about dawn or the break of day.[4] For practical purposes, let's say the disciples started toiling from 9pm to 6am, and Jesus saw them, but was in prayer on the mountain. Did Jesus realize they will die, sooner rather than later, if nothing was done about their plight at sea? Remember, *the test or leading of God will never lead you to where His grace can not reach, to take care of you.* First Corinthians says, *"with every test or trial the Lord makes a way of escape, that you may be able to bear it" (10:15).* Deuteronomy says, *"God's tests are to humble us and to prove what's in our hearts" (8:2).*

So, Jesus is on the sea heading right in the trajectory of the boat that was carrying His disciples. By now, they certainly are on the last string of their strength, battling the bulging tempest and boisterous seawater. It has been a long haul of a fight trying to save themselves from the restless swelling sea waves.

Does any of this sound familiar? When you have to deal with issues of your life that are constantly nagging you, constantly driving you crazy, so persistent that it never seems to abate? Well, I have had real tooth ache before, and I know exactly how it feels. You sometimes literally don't mind having to take off your whole head just to get rid of the persistent and nagging pain of it all! Yes, some of life's challenges are just like 'tooth ache', so stubborn that you wish to remove the entire jaw that bears the bad tooth.

Probably, this whole fight against the waves and tide of the sea was the strongest, inorganic opposition that the disciples had to face so far. They have had head-on confrontation with demonic forces, but through spiritual battles in which they easily had the upper hand under the authority Jesus. But, at sea they were facing the elements, a physically tough and demanding challenge, which required all the strength they could possibly marshal individually and collectively. If they had never stood together and fought together before, now was the time.

What a blessing it will be, the day that every church congregation realises that, when there is a battle against the body of Christ, it is a battle against the individual Christian as well as the entire body of Christ. That, the way to sustain is to stand side-by-side and to 'fight' with all our might in order to save our own lives, as well as the life of the body of Christ. This is so important because we are all on the same boat; when it goes down we all go down with it.

Unfortunately, this fact is often overlooked and as a result we find in the body of Christ some who believe they are *lone rangers* on their own. So then we see in the body of Christ an unfortunate problem, of men and women who stand aloof when part of the body of Christ is being 'lynched', as if it doesn't concern all of us. Part of the revealed mystery of the will of God for all His people, as Jesus taught His disciples, was that; the body of Christ will love one another and be one, and in unity serving one another (John 13:15, 34-35;17:23). This fact agrees with words of wisdom left to us by the sages, which says, *"united we stand, and divided we fall"*; and *"though one may be overpowered by another, two can withstand him. And a threefold cord is not quickly broken"* (Ecclesiastes 4:12).

Clearly, the wisdom of standing side-by-side in the face of great challenges will always defeat the option of selfishly standing alone. Agreement, usually in prayer for one another, which is the number one symbolism of our unity and willingness to stand side-by-side, makes a strong and victorious church and an undefeated family in every situation. 'If we will brave it together, we will win it together', could be the underlying message the disciples of Christ leaves with us, as they brave the storm of the sea together.

The Power of Prayer and Faith - Practical Lessons

Jesus, the Lord, has just descended from the mountain after a long period of prayer in *charging up* and *sharpening* His anointing, so to speak, as He wisely sought His Father's will (cf. Act 22:14,17,18). By the way, I think everyone should pray before venturing at 'sea'! Have you got any real life decision to make right now? Are you considering marriage, having children, setting up new business or ministry? Please pray beforehand. You do not want to have to suddenly succumb to the overwhelming and overpowering waves and weights of your choices, decisions, or activities, due to your inability to pray first.

Be like Jesus, be wise, and don't be like the disciples. They rushed to sea and didn't pray (at least the passage does not say they did). When you pray, you have an advantage of pressing on and pressing through to victory, commanding the 'tides' and 'waves' of your challenges to work for you rather than work against you.

After prayer, Jesus immediately stepped upon the water, striding and gliding effortlessly. The wind and rage of the sea could not stop Him. In fact, He allowed the wave to quicken His pace and to shorten His distance to get on the other side. This was indeed the same wave and crest which opposed His disciples, causing them to cocoon in fear, not far from where Jesus was.

Isn't it interesting, that some would gladly surf and ride on the same kind of challenge that scares and drowns others? Well, that's exactly what Jesus is helping His disciples to understand; that challenges, no matter how immense and threatening, could become stepping stones and bridges to our next possible destination.

The passage says, 'the disciples saw Him walking on the sea.' Being a master teacher, it seems Christ was using this entire episode as an occasion for practical teaching experience, in relation to His disciples; endeavouring to show them plainly the power of faith and prayer. On other occasions, He had done similar things subtly, but in practical ways, using His spiritual authority to demonstrate the power of faith and prayer. For example, in the hearing of His disciples, He openly cursed a fig tree to die from its roots, and did it while they looked on. When they returned later from Jerusalem, they found the same tree dead. By this act, Jesus simply schooled His disciples in the lesson of faith and prayer, and how to get things done by vocalizing one's faith in prayer, no matter how small their faith may be (Mark 11:14,20-24).

Remember also, when He said He was the *'Bread of Life'*, He caused bread to rain from heaven for a whole crowd of five thousand people. When He confessed to be the *'light of the World'*, He got a blind man and gave him his sight back in the most unusual manner. Similarly, I believe He was showing His disciples, whom the Bible suggested were at times stubborn and hard of hearing, (Mk. 6:52) that even the sea and waves obey Him, for He made them. Jesus could have been saying by what He did, that if the disciples including ourselves would dare exercise our faith correctly, we too could attain the same result, or even greater than He did, in terms of signs and wonders (John 14:12).

Easy Error, Know the Difference

The disciples had still not figured out things, and were having a really rough time at sea. On their faces were unmistakable signs of serious fear as they hollered at the top of their voice, with one of them pointing the others to an unusual spectacle far away in a distance. It was something totally alien to their collective experience. The description best to their mind was the name, *'ghost'*. Sounds odd, but very often scared and overwhelmed people will either misdescribe, or at best over embellish their actual experience so as to captivate, mesmerize or create a real sense of urgency about their plight.

That's just the way it is; people usually try to make their own experience seem impossible and incomprehensible compared to similar experiences others might have had. Sometimes, especially in the case of Christians faced with dire situations, they tend to speak in ways and terms that betray their professed faith. They say things like, *'I'm dead!'* Think about that, how can a dead person speak? It's amazing how many 'dead people' speak in the 'world' of the fearful, frightful and over apprehensive! Apparently, it's just part of the drama of curious human existence, be it Christians or non-Christians.

Jesus really did not want His disciples to think that He was a *ghost*. He was so aware of how easily people could be deceived. Already, He had had some call Him all sorts, including Beelzebub (Mark 3:2; Matt. 12:24). Remember in Caesarea Philippi, Jesus questioned His own disciples about whom the crowd says and thinks He was (Matt 16:13-14). He saw the need to set the record straight, especially for the sake of His followers. Jesus did not want to leave them confused about His identity, nor His works, purpose and assignment as the Son of God.

It was as if He was making a statement saying, 'let the crowd misjudge the Lord. Let the crowd misunderstand His purpose, His love and power, and let the crowd be confused about His saving grace, the power of His stripes (1 Pet 2:24) and blood; His death, burial and resurrection and the fact that He is alive today, seated at the right hand of the Father interceding for us. Let the crowd mistake the fact that He became poor that we, through His poverty, might become rich (2 Cor. 8:9). But, for those of us who have come to know Him and follow Him, we need to ensure that we are not caught into the toxic deception of what has now come to be called *crowd mentality* or *crowd psychology*, in which everyone somehow loses their true sense of judgement of what is right, in favour of what is appeasing.

We are called to know and abide in the truth always; especially truths regarding the Lord Jesus and our salvation. We are never called to follow 'the crowd' but 'the cloud'. That was how a pastor friend of mind, in his own style tried to reiterate God's instruction to Moses about when it was appropriate for Israel to break out from their existing camp toward the next. The *'cloud'* represented the tangible glory and presence of God among Israel in the wilderness. When the *'cloud'* which was hovering over the tabernacle was taken up, immediately, they knew it was time to go (see Exodus 40:37).

The truth about our Lord Jesus Christ, which has been amply described by Apostle Paul as the gospel of Jesus Christ, (1 Cor. 15:1-

8) in fact continues to be the 'Power of God unto salvation' (Roman 1:16). We who believe and have come to Christ are 'the fragrance of Christ among those who are being saved and among those who are perishing' (2 Cor. 2:14-16). This truth, the gospel of our Lord Jesus Christ, contends that, *"But even if our gospel is veiled, it is veiled to those who are perishing, whose minds the god of this age has blinded, who do not believe, lest the light of the gospel of the glory of Christ, who is the image of God, should shine on them"* (2 Cor. 4:3-5).

Obviously, with 'veiled' understanding and 'blinded mind', which normally seems to be the disposition of the crowd when it comes to how they see Christ, the message of the Cross, or the gospel which truly introduces and speaks about Christ, will always be foolishness to them until their 'veil' and 'blindness' are taken away. *'... But for us who are being saved it is the power of God' (1 Cor. 1:18).*

According to Matthew 16:13-14, Jesus did not give credence to the crowd's conjecture or speculation about who they claim He was. What the crowd says He was, was in fact far from the truth. In truth, only Peter is noted for getting it right; something the Lord accredited as a revelation from the Father who is in Heaven (Matt. 16:17). Does it surprise you that many times most people might attribute and accredit an authentic work and power of God to Satan? Of course, evidence has shown that it is a prevalent thing today, even among Christians, to confuse what is genuinely the work of God with the charming counterfeits of Satan, and vice versa. *'And no wonder, for Satan himself masquerades as an angel of light'* (2 Cor. 11:14).

Many believers who have failed to read their Bible and to rely on the Holy Spirit of God cannot even tell the difference between a real man of God and a fraudster. Although, the difference should be very clear and unmistakable, if we allow *'the eyes of our understanding to be enlightened'* (Eph. 1:17-21), still many need true discernment to tell the difference between 'Jesus walking on *water*', and a 'ghost' appearing over the same *water* or platform. Many can not even differentiate between the *'Hand of God'* at work and the *scheme* of Satan at work; "for you shall know them by their fruits" (Matt 7:16).

On these issues, the real battle that genuine believers unfortunately have to deal with is along the line of Christians gripped by nagging fear and deception, something which is responsible for some of the acute spiritual 'blindness' and 'deafness' we see today. Because of fear, they open themselves in desperation to anything that offers an immediate remedy, and thus become even more vulnerable. Sadly, many seeking such quick fixes cannot tell who and what is right, which *church* is real or which is a *ghost*. As a result some have tried casting out and 'binding the work of God', but 'loosing the work of Satan.' Just like the Pharisees of Jesus' day, who accused Jesus of casting out Satan and his demons by Beelzebub (Matt 12:27), some believers also find it difficult to distinguish the work of the Holy Spirit from the work of spurious eerie *ghosts*.

There are probably many desperate Christians nowadays queuing ignorantly at spiritualist centres to hear their 'fortunes' being told by demon possessed persons, who contact weird ghosts or spirits of suspicious origins, including *familiar spirits*, which the Bible utterly condemns. These desperate ones are those that continuously make the works of true pastors burdensome (Lev. 19:31; 20:6; Deut. 18:10,11). Every time they visit these strange places, they bring along to church terrible baggage that needs to be dealt with, sometimes over a long period, because they have 'sold' their souls to a rather stubborn and evil demon that demands a payback. So, instead of focusing on building faith, the pastors have to again and again, deal with unnecessary 'baggage' which victims of demons persistently trail.

No wonder Jesus was very intentional about getting it into His disciples' heads that He was not a *ghost*. He insisted, because he knew how, like bush fire, bad rumours spread often too quickly. He knew that *nipping errors and lies in the bud* was the best cure! The great revivalist and evangelist, Moody, once said that 'lies, falsehood and rumour will make a trip around the world while truth is still putting on its shoes'; and that's true.

So, first thing, Jesus quickly drew near the disciple's boat and shouted out loud to them *'It is I, be of good cheer, do not be afraid!'* Yes, He had to scream to be heard. Most certainly, His disciples, who were thinking nothing but that a *ghost* was encroaching, needed to be assured it wasn't what they feared it was. Jesus, knowing their unpredictable nature, and the easy human tendencies to often believe their fear induced 'imaginations', thought His disciples could probably concede the worst and leap out of the boat to their own peril if He had not assured them.

By saying *'it is I'*, the Lord was not just saving their lives and settling their abject confusion, He was also throwing a challenge to them; *that walking over water* was possible. 'You can literally walk over your troubles, seeing that I have done it', He seemed to have been implying, but in a demonstrable manner.

Maybe, that is why Peter responded to the challenge by *answering* "Lord, if it is You, command me to come to You on the water" (Matt 14:28). Of course, for those who are steeped in doubt, and who *walk by sight and not faith*, it takes something that extreme to make one's point. For the disciples, who always requested and relied on *signs* to believe, now they had a big sign right before them that spelled, "It is Possible – you can literally surf on the crest of your trouble without a surfing board!"

The Approach of Christ

There's something about how Jesus, our Lord, deals with and handles His people who are in trouble, and require His quick assistance. I call His approach, *the indirectedness of Jesus*. Whether it was feeding the crowd of five thousand, the healing of blind Bartimaeus, or even the healing and raising of Lazarus from the dead, His custom was the same; not to come straight at the issue. He always set Himself to what seems to be a conscious, prolonged delay or a deliberate questioning as if He were oblivious to the obvious need right before Him.

For example, in John 6:5-6, seeing the great multitude of people who were now famished because they had been at His 'gospel' crusade all day without eating, the passage says that, He had compassion on them, because they were 'like sheep without shepherd and were hungry' (cf Mark 6:30-44). The disciples' solution, even without consulting with Jesus, was simple; 'the day is far spent... the hour is late,...*send them away* that they may go into surrounding country and villages and buy themselves bread for they have nothing to eat' (Mk 6:35-36).

But, Jesus remained calm as usual, and then John (6:5) says, Jesus said to Philip, "where shall we buy bread that these may eat?" In verse seven of the same chapter, Philip answered; "two hundred danarii (about $4000) worth of bread is not sufficient for them, that every one of them may have little". Andrew, the other disciple who heard Jesus asking Philip also responded, "there is a lad here who has five barley loaves and two small fish, but what are they among so many?"

Does that surprise you that Andrew picked on the lad's bread and fish? Well, I know what's happening, from my civil war experience, in which we suffered great lack of daily necessities and food; I can say that in times of famine or hunger, the easiest thing to spot, see and sense is food (edibles), not danger! Present and impending physical dangers are nothing to a hungry man, who wants food anyhow, and that is why people go out to loot stores in search of food under torrential bullets during anarchy and wars.

But, here is wisdom for the wise, "*... man shall not live by bread alone; but man lives by every word that proceeds from the mouth of the Lord*" *(Deut. 8:3)*. His unchanging Word, the impeccable Word, and the

Word of His power (Heb. 1:3), is bound to make all the difference in every situation. So, trust Jesus and His Word.

God is not a Man

A few things to note about Jesus' interaction with His disciples about feeding the crowd: First, John 6:6 exposes Jesus' hidden motive behind His question to Philip. It says about Jesus' question that, "But this He said to test him, for He knew what He would do." Isn't that an interesting tilt to things from the Lord? He knew exactly what He wanted, and was going to do for the famished crowd, which He had already shown compassion by healing their sick folks, before the feeding episode.

Obviously, Philip and Andrew were not aware of the Lord's motive and intension then. We are now benefiting from the wisdom of hindsight. But, something about this whole event, right from the outset, should have prompted Andrew to be just a little more careful about how he picked on the Lord's question. Jesus, although He walked with them, was never in their 'category'. He is a miracle worker, performing signs and wonders at will. He had, only moments ago, healed the many sick among the multitude that came to Him.

I am pointing out this fact because we, men and women alike, are often caught in the clever trick of the devil to make our personal limitations the Lord's limitations. We have this false assumption in place, to think that just because something did not work for us, it invariably would not work for others. Or, if we were denied, others will also suffer the same plight. It takes conscious effort to free ourselves and others from thinking in such a way that limits our faith, and what God would possibly do, if we ask. I believe, for the same reason, many finally give up on their prayers and persistency in trusting God for a desired result.

Somehow, we tend to give into the temptation to allow our personal limitations to impose on us a world-view, through which we *see* God, and also determine the future of our own circumstances. Instead of seeing the 'bigness' and supernaturalness of God before the 'bigness and tallness' of our crises, we have the whole thing in reverse; where we empower our crises and circumstances through a lack of clear vision of the power and provision of Almighty God. This often is the case because we simply set before our eyes the 'bigness and tallness' of our crises. That is why we tend to become easily bedazzled and paralyzed in the face of our crises.

Question: how big is your God compared to what you are going through right now? How large is your God compared to your challenge for increase in finances and what not? Remember, *'but with God, truly nothing shall be impossible, and He is more than able to do far more exceedingly above all that we ask or think'* (Luke 1:37; Ephesians 3:20).

The way the Holy Spirit helped me to begin to think more about the greatness of God, rather than the size of my challenge or problem, was through a simple statement. One morning, while I was feeling discouraged and overwhelmed, about what we regarded as a 'huge' challenge that we had, relative to our own strength and what we could afford at the time, the Lord spoke to me. The statement was so liberating and empowering, and I thank the Holy Spirit for speaking to me that morning in no place but on a treadmill in our little backroom; like Gideon, my own 'winepress' at that time.

Here's what He said, *"if you will believe me to heal cancer and to heal the sick, then you've got to believe Me to be able to buy you a building!"* As I began to think about what the Lord said, I was directed to spend some more time with Him. In my brief stay in His presence, He illustrated exactly what He meant, and how it works, by pointing me to the passage in which Jesus literally spoke to the tree to wither and to die from its roots. Later, in teaching His disciples, who were astonished that the tree had actually withered, Jesus promised them that they too could do the same. Even to the extent of speaking to a mountain to be removed into the sea, and it would obey, if they had faith that was no bigger than the size of a mustard seed.

What was the underlying message? Here it is; the bottom-line is *faith*. *The same faith for healing cancer is the same faith for buying a building*, and God is the One who performs all. So, nothing is ever too big or too small for God Almighty to do. To God, whether it involves raising a valley or lowering a mountain for His children who cry out to Him in prayer, they are all the same and do not require any more or less power from Him. Whether He blows against your obstacles or touches them, it is the same, and nothing is too hard for Him to do, hence our God is above all and over all. Amen!

> *God is not a man, that He should lie, nor a son of man, that He should repent. Has He said, and will He not do? Or has He spoken, and will He not make it good (Numb. 23:19)?*

> *And you shall remember the Lord your God, for it is He who gives you power to get wealth, that He may establish His covenant which He swore to your fathers, as it is this day (Deut. 8:18).*

> *He who calls you is faithful, who also will do it (1 Thess. 5:24).*

Qualifying the Called

Now, according to the *feeding of the multitude* passage, Jesus had on his mind a plan 'to test' Philip, and maybe all His disciples, because we also have Andrew answering to the Lord's question. In this case, let's take Andrew and Philip to be the type of believers who have known and walked with the Lord for a good while; people who have seen the Lord consistently working and displaying supernatural signs and wonders. This very fact allows me to know that the Lord will not 'test' anyone considered to be a novice. He will put you through a 'test' only after He has given you enough time to gain knowledge and experience in the area of your 'test'. Remember, our Lord is just. But, with every 'test', I believe His intentions are clearly to qualify us for the next level, with respect to our faith, obedience, and confidence in Him, or our maturity regarding stewardship, before He can commit more to us.

In the Old Testament, God used a similar pattern, the use of 'tests' as His way of qualifying Israel for the promised land, for increase, and of course perpetual confidence in God's ability to protect and to provide for them at all times. A good example of this is found in Moses' farewell address to the children of Israel, saying;

> *And you shall remember that the Lord your God led you all the way these forty years in the wilderness, to humble you and test you, to know what was in your heart, whether you would keep His commandments or not. ³ So He humbled you, allowed you to hunger, and fed you with manna which you did not know nor did your fathers know, that He might make you know that man shall not live by bread alone; but man lives by every word that proceeds from the mouth of the Lord. ⁴ Your garments did not wear out on you, nor did your foot swell these forty years. ⁵ You should know in your heart that as a man chastens his son, so the Lord your God chastens you. ⁶ "Therefore you shall keep the commandments of the Lord your God, to walk in His ways and to fear Him. ⁷ For the Lord your God is bringing you into a good land, a land of brooks of water, of fountains and springs, that flow out of valleys and hills; ⁸ a land of wheat and barley, of vines and fig trees and pomegranates, a land of olive oil and honey; ⁹ a land in which you will eat bread without scarcity, in which*

you will lack nothing; a land whose stones are iron and out of whose hills you can dig copper. ¹⁰ When you have eaten and are full, then you shall bless the Lord your God for the good land which He has given you. ¹⁶ who fed you in the wilderness with manna, which your fathers did not know, that He might humble you and that He might test you, to do you good in the end (Deut. 8: 2-10, 16).

Question or Answer

This leads me to my second point; that whenever the Lord asks a question or gives an instruction, as seen in the case of Philip and Andrew, it is never a sign of weakness or lack of proactiveness. It is simply, as the passage says, 'to test'. Whenever He asks or gives an instruction, He always has something in mind. He is literally saying, 'something is about to happen, or change'. Christ, in essence, is usually suggesting by His 'tests', that 'I have an idea but first what do you think, or are you ready for this?'

Remember the story of young David, at the battle field where the armies of Israel and Philistine were locked up in a stalemate, resulting in mere battle of words, before the real clash between David and Goliath? At the battlefront, Israel was literally paralysed in fear of the formidable giant, Goliath, whom no one dared to challenge, because he was thought to be unbeatable. In his innocence and also curiosity, while visiting his brothers at the battle front, David asked a few simple questions. And, the way he asked his questions was similar to the style of Jesus, seeing that Israel had caved away from Goliath.

In 2 Samuel 17:26, David asked "What shall be done for the man who kills this Philistine?" In verse 28, his oldest brother, Eliab, heard him speaking to the other men and 'his anger roused against David ...' and he said, *"Why did you come down here? And with whom have you left those few sheep in the wilderness? I know your pride and the insolence of your heart, for you have come down to see the battle."* To Eliab, Goliath was, by all standards, an insurmountable challenge. He and the rest of Israel's army were already hiding from Goliath. So, in Eliab's reckoning, David also had to behave like everyone else and hide from Goliath.

Similarly, verse 33 reveals Saul imposing his inability on David, in the same way that Philip and Andrew tried to impose their limitations on Jesus regarding His 'test' and suggestion about feeding the multitude. Saul does something very much akin to what many of us do. Just because Saul could not face Goliath himself, even with his army, he concluded that Goliath was impossible to defeat.

In verse 34, David retorts, *'hey, I am a man with much experience, my background naturally qualifies me for the task at hand.'* So, David, like Jesus, asked a question but was really indicating the answer he was about to provide; a great deliverance for all of Israel, who were on the run from their fiercest enemy, the great Goliath of Gath.

Ultimately, as the passage unfolds, we see David prevailing over Goliath, the Philistine giant, 'with a sling and a stone', using two very ordinary and unsophisticated weapons of war (vr 50). And so Israel was given the victory. David fought as their champion, but Israel had the victory! As our Almighty Champion, this is exactly what the Lord Jesus does for His people, for "*A mighty fortress is our God, a bulwark never failing*"!

Andrew Failed but Ezekiel Passed

When the Lord asks a question, He always has something on His mind. Andrew failed to recognize this but Ezekiel, even in the Old Testament, knew that there's something more to the questions from the mouth of God. The book of Ezekiel chapter thirty-seven narrates the prophet's encounter with the Lord in his great vision of 'Dry

Bones'. In this vision, Ezekiel had one of those subtle questions thrown to him by the Lord Himself. He takes Ezekiel right into the bottom of a vast valley full of very dry bones, and He says to him, 'well you've seen these very dry bones, and no doubt they are dried to the core.' Now, 'Son of man (that's Ezekiel), can these bones live?' (vr 3). There it is; Ezekiel, who was a great prophet to the nations with marvellous precision in the gift of prophecy, now was confronted with a very pointed question from the Lord. Let's see what he makes of this 'test' and if he responded appropriately.

Ezekiel seems quite adept and, relying on his years of experience with God would without doubt help him to come away clear and clean from his 'test' question. 'Son of man (that's Ezekiel), can these bones live again?' And right in the same breath and in the same verse, Ezekiel answered, 'O Lord God, You know'.

He got it spot-on! That's how to respond to the Lord's 'test' questions. Ezekiel replies with a wisdom of the Spirit to the Lord's subtle question. Like the question to which Ezekiel responded, His answer was just as coded. The Lord asked a 'coded' question and Ezekiel replied with a 'coded' answer. Remember, whenever the God stands within the midst of your trial and ask a question that indirectly suggests the answer, no matter how impossible the trial might seem, God has a ready answer and the solution that you need.

For example, when the Lord Jesus visited a pool at Bethesda in John 5, where a great number of sick people lay, He simply asked a man with an infirmity of thirty-eight years, "do you want to be made well?" The man answered, "Sir, I have no man to put me into the pool when the water is stirred up; but while I am coming, another steps down before me." Anyone who knew the Lord, and His style in questioning what He already knows and desires to do, would have answered differently from the way the infirmed man answered.

Certainly, the Lord, as the passage explains, *'when He saw him lying there, Jesus knew that he already had been in that condition a long time'* (John 5:2-9). If someone knew about your condition that much, without ever meeting you or being told about you, and approached you with a question like Jesus did to the infirm man, that person is not a fool. He or she knows something more than you know, and instead of complaining like the infirm man did, you rather must be asking for them to do the good thing they intend to do quickly, or simply ask them to quickly give you what they brought with them. It's no time for complaining; your time has come for your miracle.

God's Expressed Interest as His Readiness

Let me further illustrate the point I am making about the kind of questions, or even the kind of statements, God would make most often amid our situations and moments of trials. In short, what I intend to drive home to you is that *God's peculiar questions and statements are not simply innocent, disinterested questions or statements.*

For example, I have a pastor friend, who has a wonderful grace from God to prophesy and to bring God's divine healing miracles to people. Often, before he prays for a person, he says that the Lord might point out to him, or he might hear the Spirit of the Lord saying to him, *such and such* a person has a certain disease.

Other times, it might even be in a question form; something like, *'have you realised that person is unwell?'* Now, my friend says in such circumstances, he never waits for the Lord to say what He intends to do about the situation. My friend immediately goes ahead and commits the Lord by making a general announcement of God's readiness to heal. And when it regards specific persons, he promises them God's ready solution and miracle, and goes ahead to pray for them. As he prays, God definitely shows up and heals His people.

But, here is the point; my friend takes *God's expressed interest as His expressed wish and already finished work*! He told me that there are times when he commits the Lord to healing someone and then the Lord will reply to him and say, *"son, I did not say I will heal. I only pointed that out to you, and I have only asked a question."* But, you see, my friend has so developed his relationship with God in this context that he knows God and how He does what He does. In my friend's church services, God would still heal even when He had only asked a 'question', instead of making a direct promise or statement about healing. My friend simply goes ahead and interpret God's 'question' as a statement of fact about possible healing, and also position God's questions as Divine answers. Sounds risky, but he knows his God!

Now, it is understandable that the book of Ezekiel does not do any interpretation or give us the motive of God behind the question that Ezekiel was asked, concerning the dry bones. There was absolutely no need, because prophet Ezekiel's answer does not contradict his faith and confidence in God's abilities to perform the impossible. Surely, he knows God can do anything, if and when He chooses (cf Job 42:2). Surely, he understands there's no limit to what God can do, including giving life to 'dry bones', no matter how dry they might seem physically.

I believe that getting God's 'test' questions right has a lot to do with our overall knowledge and understanding of the nature and power of God – that *"God is not a man, that He should lie, nor a son of man, that He should repent. Has He said, and will He not do? Or has He spoken, and will He not make it good (Num. 23:19)?"* I like the way Job sees God, *"I know that You can do everything, and that no purpose of Yours can be withheld from You (Job 42:2).*

If believers would see God in the light of His divine nature, power and of course His sovereignty, we would have no need to transfer our inabilities and limitations to Him. We often do this, either through fear, intimidation or our lack of faith, and lack of Godly wisdom and understanding in the face of adversities and challenges that come against us. Remember, our God is the *'can do God'* according to Job, and He is able *'to do exceedingly abundantly above all that we ask or think, according to the power that works in us'* (Job 42:2; Eph. 3:20).

Accessing and Enjoying God's Opportunities

As a sign of God's approval for Ezekiel, He issued a command for Ezekiel to carry out a spectacular miracle involving the *dry bones* of Israel, by simply speaking *the Word of the Lord* (37:4). Interestingly, we have a similar occurrence in the New Testament, in which Peter walked over the water by the command (word) of the Lord. Surely, when God approves and sanctions you because of your faith in Him, He allows you to share in His miracle working prowess. You also have His assurance as a vessel worthy of honor and prepared for His use (2 Tim. 2).

See the difference; God stepped aside, and then asked Ezekiel to personally prophesy to the dry bones. But, with Philip and Andrew, Jesus Himself is the One who blesses and multiplies the bread to feed the multitude. What made all the difference, one passed the 'test', and the others did not. Ezekiel had the uncommon privilege of participating in God's miraculous power. The result is what we have in Ezekiel 37:7, in which he admits, *"so I prophesied as I was commanded; and as I prophesied, there was a noise, and suddenly a rattling; and the bones came together, bone to bone."* In other words, it happened just as Ezekiel prophesied.

First, I will reiterate for the sake of emphasis that the 'questions' that God often poses to us are not as innocent as they sound or appear. They usually represent a 'test' with realistic consequences for our faith and confidence, and broadly determine the way He responds to us in our challenges.

Second, you may respond to God's 'questions' in faith and see, and be a part of a miracle, or respond wrongly, either in doubt or fear and forfeit an uncommon experience of participating in the workings of miracles. In any case, God would choose whether to do His miracle but with you as a spectator instead of being an active participant or catalyst. This is like Jesus telling Mary and Mary Madalenge, the sisters of Lazarus, that "if you believe *you* will see the power of God".

Third, Andrew and Philip showed themselves up as serious doubters, reflecting a good picture of believers today, who easily conjure up excellent and convincing reasons why things cannot be done. Some people habitually specialize in looking at numbers, amounts and what they do not have, and how limited their gifts and resources are. Just imagine them explaining to Jesus why things cannot be done. The man with thirty-eight years of infirmity at Bethesda did the same. Have you caught yourself trying to explain to Jesus why you think your particular challenge can not be helped, or why you cannot succeed, and so forth?

It is so natural for people to see things as impossible, because the world and all its negative situations have made us to see things that way. They tell us, 'be reasonable', 'check your facts' and so forth. But you see, Jesus already knows the fact of your limitations and weaknesses, and He sympathises with our weakness (Hebrews 4:15). In fact, sometimes He brings you to that level so that you can begin to look beyond yourself, to the One with whom there is no limit.

Why do you think that such a great crowd, like the one Jesus was preaching to, would forget to bring their own packed lunches, when they have always been with Jesus and knew just how long His 'gospel' crusades lasted? Why was there only the little boy's five loafs and two fish; just the exact quantity the Lord needed for His miracle of multiplying bread and fish? Don't you just think that there was something divine about the little boy alone having a few leftovers?

Why hadn't he finished his lunch beforehand, considering how wild and insatiable lad's appetite can be for food?

It is truly amazing the wisdom of God. No wonder Paul celebrates God's wisdom and knowledge in such a style confessing, *"Oh, the depth of the riches both of the wisdom and knowledge of God! How unsearchable are His judgments and His ways past finding out"* (Rom. 11:33). All this affirms that, in the most unusual way, God uses what we term and class as few, weak, little, or even foolish, to bring great glory to Himself in unimaginable circumstances. This is attested by I Corinthians 1:26-28:

> *For you see your calling, brethren, that not many wise according to the flesh, not many mighty, not many noble, are called.* [27] *But God has chosen the foolish things of the world to put to shame the wise, and God has chosen the weak things of the world to put to shame the things which are mighty;* [28] *and the base things of the world and the things which are despised God has chosen, and the things which are not, to bring to nothing the things that are,* [29] *that no flesh should glory in His presence.*

Think about Gideon, that fearful and terrified young man, who was hiding in the wine press from the Midianites. In the eyes of God he was a man of great might and strength, and yet in himself he felt like a nobody. Here is part of his story showing him very despondent;

> *Now the Angel of the Lord came and sat under the terebinth tree which was in Ophrah, which belonged to Joash the Abiezrite, while his son Gideon threshed wheat in the winepress, in order to hide it from the Midianites.* [12] *And the Angel of the Lord appeared to him, and said to him, "The Lord is with you, you mighty man of valor!"* [13] *Gideon said to Him, "O my lord, if the Lord is with us, why then has all this happened to us? And where are all His miracles which our fathers told us about, saying, 'Did not the Lord bring us up from Egypt?' But now the*

> Lord has forsaken us and delivered us into the hands of the Midianites." ¹⁴ Then the Lord turned to him and said, "Go in this might of yours, and you shall save Israel from the hand of the Midianites. Have I not sent you?" ¹⁵ So he said to Him, "O my Lord,¹ how can I save Israel? Indeed my clan is the weakest in Manasseh, and I am the least in my father's house." (Judges 6:11-15)

Do you sometimes feel like Gideon; helpless in the face of seemingly daunting challenges, and before mountains of threatening difficulties and life's trouble that never seem to have an end? Hear this; *THE LORD IS WITH YOU!* And that means you will defeat that threat, that enemy, that sickness, and you will overcome and have the victory in Jesus Name.

I preached a message once on what I termed as *"The miracle of territory taking"*, and this was based on the text of David's victorious song in 1 Chronicles 16, beginning at verse 17 to 36. My focus was the verses 19 and 20, but I will quote here a good portion of the whole chapter to help you have the full impact of what is happening when it comes to how God deals with and delivers His people:

> *Remember His covenant forever, the word which He commanded, for a thousand generations,* ¹⁶ *The covenant which He made with Abraham, And His oath to Isaac,* ¹⁷ *And confirmed it to Jacob for a statute, To Israel for an everlasting covenant,* ¹⁸ *Saying, "To you I will give the land of Canaan As the allotment of your inheritance,"* ¹⁹ <u>*When you were few in number, Indeed very few, and strangers in it.*</u> ²⁰ <u>*When they went from one nation to another, And from one kingdom to another people,*</u> ²¹ *He permitted no man to do them wrong; Yes, He rebuked kings for their sakes,* ²² *Saying, "Do not touch My anointed ones, And do My prophets no harm."* ²³ *Sing to the Lord, all the earth; Proclaim the good news of His salvation from day to day.* ²⁴ *Declare His glory among the nations, His*

wonders among all peoples. ^{25} *For the Lord is great and greatly to be praised; He is also to be feared above all gods.*

We find in this passage the fact that, it certainly will not require a great deal, nor does it take God a great lot, to do what He needs to do for His children. Likewise, God will not require you to first know great details of His deliverance strategy; having you initially work out all the minute plans and to bring together your best resources, before He moves on your behalf. But, it is about *'remembering His covenant forever, which He commanded... and which He has already confirmed'* without regard for your numerical or financial strength, academic qualifications, geographical advantage, or political affiliations.

More than anything, it is about standing by His own covenant with His people; to ensure that what He has promised, He also will fulfil. Especially for those of us who belong to Jesus Christ, His Son, who is the mediator of a better covenant, not by law, but by His precious blood offered on our behalf; God has committed Himself to make His promises good. That's why I promised that you can, and will certainly have the victory, and triumph victoriously over your present challenge! You belong to that covenant, and that covenant still speaks for you even right now: "*Therefore know that only those who are of faith are sons of Abraham*" *(Gal. 3:7).* And Paul continued to say;

> *But that no one is justified by the law in the sight of God is evident, for "the just shall live by faith."* ^{12} *Yet the law is not of faith, but "the man who does them shall live by them."*^{13} *Christ has redeemed us from the curse of the law, having become a curse for us (for it is written, "Cursed is everyone who hangs on a tree"),* ^{14} *that the blessing of Abraham might come upon the Gentiles in Christ Jesus, that we might receive the promise of the Spirit through faith.* ^{18} *For if the inheritance is of the law, it is no longer of promise; but God gave it to Abraham by promise (Gal. 3:11-14,18).*

> *And inasmuch as He (Jesus) was not made priest without an oath [21] (for they have become priests without an oath, but He with an oath by Him who said to Him: " The Lord has sworn And will not relent,' You are a priest forever According to the order of Melchizedek'"),[22] by so much more Jesus has become a surety of a better covenant (Heb. 7:20-22).*
>
> *But now He has obtained a more excellent ministry, inasmuch as He is also Mediator of a better covenant, which was established on better promises (Heb. 8:6).*
>
> *To Jesus the Mediator of the new covenant, and to the blood of sprinkling that speaks better things than that of Abel (Heb. 12:24).*

You see, the evidence is right there before you. You belong to a covenant keeping God, *who can not lie*, but who ensures that all His promises to you by means of covenant must come to pass. You belong to a new, better and powerful covenant rectified in the victorious blood of Jesus Christ that in fact speaks on your behalf, and also speaks even more powerfully better things on your behalf. It argues for you before God, and against the damning accusations of Satan, concerning your past, present and future. Hence, Romans now says, *"there is therefore now no condemnation to those who are in Christ Jesus,…" (Romans 8:1).*

Jesus, your great Mediator, is speaking even this moment, "you shall not die but live and declare the works of the Lord!" His promises have never failed before and indeed yours will also come to pass. Let Joshua's enduring testimony about the faithfulness of God be an encouragement to you when he said; *"now I am about to go the way of all the earth. You know with all your heart and soul that not one of all the good promises the Lord your God gave you has failed. Every promise has been fulfilled; not one has failed" (Joshua 23:14).*

Walking on Water

The disciples are still battling with their plight at sea. But who will go for the challenge and who dares venture to prove the Word of God; that *"with God all things are possible, and for those who believe, all things shall be possible?"* The sea had, and continued to greatly terrify the disciples.

Yet, the Lord Jesus also knew that this would be the opportunity to help His disciples to overcome their terrible fear for tempest, the sea, other elements, and to help build their faith for the greater works He intended for them to do. It was also a good moment to test spiritual truths in a physical environment, concerning all that the Lord had been teaching His disciples about His authority over devils and the elements. Well, the best way He chose to demonstrate His teachings and His authority was to come to His disciples on a very windy dawn in the middle of a tempestuous sea, walking effortlessly like an eagle gliding over a storm.

Obviously, for the disciples, this way of testing or proving anything through practical demonstration might not have seemed very comfortable, especially if Jesus would try to make them do or face what was proving to be their worst nightmare. But, as a great teacher and coach, Jesus, their Master would not leave them alone to it. Therefore, He made it a point to walk on the water Himself, the waters of the very sea that scared His disciples almost to death.

Of course, while it is a good thing for His disciples to see Him walk on water, it would even be liberating and empowering for one or all of them to walk on the same water also. However, the whole thought of walking on the water was seriously frightening, although Jesus made it seem too easy. We must appreciate that the disciples were all too familiar with the sea and knew, especially in the region they were, how temperamental and dangerous the sea waters were. The sea could suddenly flare up, without any forewarning, causing great havoc, so everyone knew to have great respect for the sea.

No wonder, the Bible says, when Jesus came walking on the waters of the sea, all His disciples were troubled saying *"It is a ghost!"*, and then *"they cried out for fear"*. So much so that Jesus immediately replied, *"be of good cheer! It is I; do not be afraid."* Within no time of Peter hearing that it was the Master, he cried out, *"Lord, if it is You, command me to come to You on the water."*

What an audacity from Peter, but one can almost immediately sense his hesitation as well, as if suggesting, 'this is too good to be true!' Well, Jesus would not disappoint Peter, at least he tried to dare the sea and to help dispel the notion and myth that only a *ghost* could probably subdue the huge power of the sea and walk over water. So, Jesus, in response to Peter's request, commanded him to come, and after he had descended from the boat, he then stepped on the water and walked on the water to go to Jesus.

Peter never thought that could ever happen to him. To walk on water, it had to probably be the *ghosts* who did it. But there's their Master, Jesus, showing and demonstrating that He can do it. And anyone who dares takes Jesus by His word can do it, provided he or she heeds to Jesus' command to *come* to Him on the water.

On the other hand, knowing the nature of Peter, he probably considered his Master's leisurely walk on the troubled sea as a challenge in itself, to his personal faith for believing for the miraculous and the impossible. But, whatever his motive was, the Scripture says that he answered Jesus, "Lord if it be you, command me to come to you on the water" which was rather an extraordinary response to Jesus, who said, *"Be of good cheer! It is I; do not be afraid."* It could have been anything or anyone other than Jesus walking on the water beside the boat, but Peter knew the voice of His Master.

Peter was no fool. Apart from knowing the voice of his Master, he knew how safe, powerful and authoritative it was when Jesus spoke and commanded. He would not rush and jump off the reel until Jesus says so, otherwise, he would be 'testing the Lord His God'. Whatever the case was, Peter knew in his mind that this was a golden privilege, to boldly step over and to conquer the *sea* with all its scary and intimidating power. He wanted to experience a rare miracle by proving God's eternal Word. So it didn't matter the apparent risk involved, his faith in Christ prevailed over his personal doubts, fears, and background.

A quick wisdom note for us from Peter's reaction will be, if you will ever attempt walking on water, do so on a personal revelation of the Lord's command. Miracles are not difficult if you get a precise word from the Master. It is said of the great Apostle of Faith of the 20th century, Smith Wigglesworth, that he never once failed to help, heal or restore a dead person back to life, because he always acted upon a command from the Lord, or a supernatural stirring of the Holy Spirit within his spirit. Of the many great miracles, clearly seen during his ministries are the phenomena records of fourteen dead people that brother Wigglesworth raised back to life by the power of the Holy Spirit of God Almighty. So, it always helps when we hear from the Lord and it always works when we act in obedience to the Lord's commandments and instructions.

Standing on the Word

Upon the beckoning of the Lord, Peter jumped out of the boat and stepped on the water of the sea. He was amazed that he did not sink. Peter then realized after all; the Lord's words and commandments are as solid as rock, providing a solid platform over sinking water. That means, walking on water becomes possible for those who first trust the Word of Christ. My friend, *His Word is solid as a rock when you find yourself in wobbling and sinking places*. It is your solid rock for your feet upon deep, slippery, miry clay. Psalms 40:2 says, *"He also brought me up out of a horrible pit, out of the miry clay, and set my feet upon a rock, and established my steps".*

This very trust and confidence in the upholding, uplifting and stabilizing abilities of the *Rock* of the Word of God is echoed by the psalmist, who cries out to God from the 'end of the earth'. He says, Lord, *"from the end of the earth I will cry to You, when my heart is overwhelmed, lead me to the rock that is higher than I" (Psalm 61:2).* He does not choose his parents, he does not look to his physicians, he does not look to anything he knows except the *Rock* to take away and crush his overwhelming burdens.

My dear friend, the *Rock of Ages*, the Son of Man, Jesus Christ, is that *Rock* according to 1Corinthians 10:4, and He can provide you solid ground to keep you well grounded, balanced and stable at all times. He can save you from what intends to cripple you, by crushing that which is pursuing you for evil. The Son of God is mighty enough to save and to deliver you from all your troubles. Thank God for Jesus, Christ!

I read a riveting story from a great book, the *Apostolic Fathers*[5] about Justus, one of the earliest disciples of our Lord, who literally drank deadly poison and did not die; proving the power, authority and validity of the Lord's words in Mark 16:18. In there, He said that those who believe in Him *"will take up serpents; and if they drink anything deadly, it will by no means hurt them; they will lay hands on the sick, and they will recover."*

Obviously, I am not in anyway suggesting or recommending that anyone should go and intentionally drink anything deadly, or to even pick up a living serpent as such. I am only agreeing with and illustrating the fact of the power, potential, and validity of the words of our Lord Jesus; just how apt, true, profound and applicable it is in and for our trying moments. Although the story does not give the background to why Justus drank, or was made to drink the poison, we can only surmise from the situation occurring around that era, in which Justus became prominent in the Scripture.

This is the same Justus that is mentioned in Acts 1:23, whose other names were Joseph and Barsabbas. After Jesus had ascended to heaven, the original apostles proposed Justus along with Mathias, and prayed that the Holy Spirit may select one of them to replace Judas, whom upon betraying the Lord, saw his eminent death. His death, afterwards, created a vacancy within the original number of the apostles. Obviously, we know from the book of Acts that Matthias became the preferred candidate to replace Judas. However, Justus and the others, apart from the original twelve disciples, who had been with Christ from the day of John the Baptist until the time Christ was taken to heaven, still accompanied the apostles and faithfully served as followers of Christ.

In those early days, they encountered stiff resistance with great threats to their lives, and were often barred from preaching in the Name of Jesus. At times, they were forced to blaspheme and to deny Christ. Some were jailed, others were flogged, and some were killed. For example we see Stephen being stoned to death in Acts 7:59, and in Acts 8:1 we read, *"...Saul (later called Paul) was consenting to his death. At that time a great persecution arose against the church which was at Jerusalem, and they were all scattered throughout the regions of Judea and Samaria, except the apostles."* Later, others, including James, John's brother were killed after Herod the king 'stretched his hands to harass the church' (Acts 12:1, 2).

It might have been under such an extraordinary situation of persecution that Justus was made to take the deadly poison, but amazingly had his life spared by the grace of God. Whatever the circumstances were that made him take the poison, the fact that he did not die was a miracle. And, the fact that he lived to tell his story only proved the remarkable truth and power of the Word of God.

His Word is *"living and powerful, and sharper than any two-edged sword, piercing even to the division of soul and spirit, and of joints and marrow, and is a discerner of the thoughts and intents of the heart"* (Hebrews 4:12).

God's Word is still the same today as it was yesterday, and will continue to be the same no matter the time and circumstances. His Word is still effective and full of power to dissolve your mountains, take away your sicknesses, burn your diseases, remove your burdens, settle your bills, break your limitations, and to render your enemies powerless against you.

Just as 'He is the same, yesterday, today and forever (Heb.13:8)', so are His words in our trying and difficult times. But, someone will have to trust Him, someone will have to believe, and someone will have to act on the promise of the Word of our Lord Jesus Christ, and prove it. That's where power lies, and that is where your miracles are; to take Jesus by His Word and trust that He says it and He will do it (1Thess. 5:24). I have no doubt that anyone who takes Jesus seriously, by trusting Him to come along by their side, even in the face of damming medical report, will surely see and experience His supernatural miracle working power. I have seen and known by experience that it works.

As a pastor, not so long ago in our church, we saw the miraculous healing power of the Lord Jesus, when He caused a life threatening, cancerous tumour in the breast of a young lady to vanish. Today she is still cancer free and has recently married. Another young woman, dependent on a motorised scooter, literally gave it up by the power of the Word and the Name of Jesus Christ. She also is still healed and going about her normal business today.

Just recently, two Indian gentlemen met me in a hospital car park as I hurried to join my wife for her scheduled antenatal scan. One of them was very upset because his lovely mother had suffered a stroke, been completely paralysed on one side of her body, and was in critical condition at the same hospital. Because of her age, and because she could not speak properly, they had serious concerns for her life.

While I hurried from my car and tried to pocket my door keys, I accidentally and unknowingly dropped a British ten pounds note from my pocket. As I paced away quickly from the car park, one of the men, who was obviously heading from where I was going, managed to grab my attention. Then he pointed to the floor, a little distance behind me, telling me, 'it seems you dropped some money'.

I then returned and gratefully picked up the money. But, as I turned to continue on my way, one of the men, the one whose mother was sick, recognised me, because he and his wife had, in the past visited the church where I pastor. In a solemn voice, he told me his story, and asked if I could visit his mother and pray with her on our return from my wife's appointment. I promised that I would, and took his mother's name and ward address. Clearly, the gentleman was wearied, discouraged and upset.

Long story short, I told my wife and she joined me in the hospital ward where this dear woman was being treated. We sought permission from the nurses to pray for her. She could barely open her eyes to see us, and I doubt if she even heard most of what we said. But, God, being gracious as He always is, that same woman is up today fully restored and happy. Her son, the same gentleman who called my attention when I dropped my money, and who was terribly discouraged and worried the day we met in the hospital car park, saw me again recently, and testified to the glory of the Lord Almighty. This time he was smiling, and confirming that his mother was well, totally mobile and independent, travelling places, and going about her normal business at home in India.

My friend, God is so good. What He has done for others, He will also do for you. Only believe, and you too will have a wonderful testimony just by trusting the Lord Jesus Christ and His Word for your healing and your situation, this very moment as you read.

Having a Miracle within a Miracle

Now, let us hear how Apostle John tells his story of the big event and encounter at the sea involving the disciples and their Master, Jesus Christ.

> *Now when evening came, His disciples went down to the sea, [17] got into the boat, and went over the sea toward Capernaum. And it was already dark, and Jesus had not come to them. [18] Then the sea arose because a great wind was blowing. [19] So when they had rowed about three or four miles, they saw Jesus walking on the sea and drawing near the boat; and they were afraid. [20] But He said to them, "It is I; do not be afraid." [21] Then they willingly received Him into the boat, and immediately the boat was at the land where they were going.* (John 6:16-21)

From all good intents and purposes, we see John is squeezing a great deal in a little space and probably in the shortest time possible. These guys, the apostles, had no luxury of time, yet they needed to let us know as much truth as they could about what our Lord both said and did. Their effort was girded toward helping us to believe and to come to the saving knowledge of the Lord Jesus Christ (John 20:30, 31).

Of course, John himself admits in the end that, *"… there are also many other things that Jesus did, which if they were written one by one, I suppose that even the world itself could not contain the books that would be written. Amen"* (John 21:25; also John 20:30, 31). I told you that John is simply hard pressed for time and space, and certainly could not recount the events of Christ 'one-by-one'. He had no need to be too elaborate or dwell on one event too long, since he wanted to bring us as many as possible in the time and space allotted to him.

But, here is what I realised John is eager to bring to our attention from the way he tells his story. That there were actually two great miracles in the one episode. The first being our Lord Jesus *'walking on the sea'*, and the second is that *'immediately the boat was at the land where they were going'*. The first miracle is quite familiar, but the second is strange, and I have not heard anyone give it the worthy attention it is due.

Did you notice how quickly the disciples, who have previously had such rowing difficulties, all of a sudden had their boat thrust on land, immediately after they had willingly received the Lord into their boat? I believe that when the Lord got on their boat, the disciples realised, similar to what took place in Acts 8:39-40, a *Phillip-type transportation,* in which they were divinely caught away in one moment and the next moment they arrived at their destination.

Not only were they immediately thrust to the land, but they safely arrived *'where they were going'*. This means that, the forces that initially hindered and restrained them, forces symbolized by the torrential waves of the sea, which resisted, opposed and intended to stop them from reaching their predetermined destinies, were swiftly broken and removed. They then were made to maintain their course and finally attained their destiny. The disciples definitely got to where they had initially set themselves to go, despite the obstacles and oppositions. They got there safely and conducted their business, and the Lord granted their desires, in spite of the fierce wrath of the tsunamis-type waves which had come against them.

May you attain your life's destiny in spite of the obstacles, my friend! O my Lord, I feel like saying right now, *'Lord Jesus, please step into my boat (I mean, my life) and cause me to safely and swiftly reach my destiny in life. Please do not let any opposition or enemy cause me to have difficulties rowing in life, so as to cause me to abort my purpose and destiny.'* You too can make this your prayer!

For you who are reading this book right now, your story may be like that of the disciples, having extreme difficulties trying to get to where you really intend to get to in life. It may be a career pursuit that might not be going well. Or, it might be a troubling habit and addiction you want to break; or a terrible family situation, a huge financial debt, a burden of a debilitating health condition, or even a need for a ministry breakthrough. I have good news for you. You are coming through and coming out victoriously, and you will attain your desired future, no matter the storm and the raging wave of the seas of life.

Jesus wants to step into your boat, and if you need Him to, then let us agree together in prayer as we pray this prayer: *Lord Jesus, I give you my 'boat', please have my 'boat', and take away my burden right now, and help me to sail safely to my destiny in victory over whatever the enemy had intended against my life. Thank you, Lord Jesus for favour, healings, breakthrough and victory in the areas of my concerns, Amen!*

My friend, that's it! Beginning now, you take a step of faith in God and see yourself as having overcome already. Our God never ever sets up his children for defeat. Satan does, but Almighty God always has the final word concerning your life and destiny. Hear what assurance the unfailing Word of God gives us regarding our Father, Almighty God's assistance in difficult times and moments. Please read, believe, and as much as possible apply them by taking a step of faith in walking boldly in the truth the Word brings to you:

> *You (my enemy) pushed me violently, that I might fall, but the Lord helped me. The Lord is my strength and song, and He has become my salvation. (Psalm 118:13)*

> *The Lord is on my side; I will not fear.... (Psalm 118:6)*

Yes, God is on your side and that is enough. If I were you, I would print and paste the verses quoted above, in visible places in my home and in my car or office, so that I can constantly remind myself: *"God is on my side."* Remember this one thing, that 'if God be for you, who can be against you?' (Romans 8:31), and *"who shall bring a charge against God's elect? It is God who justifies".* (Romans 8:33)

For further encouragement from the word of God, the Psalmists say;

> *For His anger is but for a moment, His favor is for life; weeping may endure for a night, but joy comes in the morning. (Psalm 30:5)*

> *A thousand may fall at your side, and ten thousand at your right hand; but it shall not come near you. (Psalm 91:7)*

> *I shall not die, but live, and declare the works of the Lord. (Psalm 118:17).*

And hear what Isaiah has to say when it seems like all 'hell' has broken loose against you:

> *So shall they fear the name of the Lord from the west, and His glory from the rising of the sun; when the enemy comes in like a flood, the Spirit of the Lord will lift up a standard against him (Isaiah 59:19).*

Your True Identity and Authority

As we draw the curtain on this brilliant story full of peak moments, I quickly want to point out something very significant overall. It regards the actual miracles embedded in the lively 'drama' taking place on the sea. The Apostle John, in the Bible book of John, does not dwell too much on the elaborate happenings and all that is taking place from the time the disciples get on the boat up to when their Master rescued them. Compared to the other gospels, John is very brief. However, I believe that in John's *snap shot* narration of the events, which he gives in only five verses, he is doing something uniquely powerful.

John, under the inspiration of the Holy Spirit, brings to our attention the ultimate testimony of the disciples; that our Lord Jesus Christ is indeed the Son of God and all things, whether quiet or boisterous, whether great or small, and whether animate or inanimate, they are subject to Him and serve Him. I hasten to add that, in fact, all things obey Him. Mark tells us how, on other occasions, the Lord effectively calmed the wind by speaking to it and how it obeyed His command: *"then He arose and rebuked the wind, and said to the sea, "Peace, be still!" And the wind ceased and there was a great calm."* (Mark 4:39)

In fact, the Scripture boldly declares concerning the Lord Jesus Christ that,

> *For by Him all things were created that are in heaven and that are on earth, visible and invisible, whether thrones or dominions or principalities or powers. All things were created through Him and for Him.* [17] *And He is before all things, and in Him all things consist.* [18] *And He is the head of the body, the church, who is the beginning, the firstborn from the dead, that in all things He may have the pre-eminence (Colossians 1:16-18).*

Again, John 1:3 says, *"all things were made through Him, and without Him nothing was made that was made."* Acts 17:28, puts it this way, *"for in Him we live and move and have our being, as also some of your own poets have said, 'For we are also His offspring.'"* This text of Acts ends beautifully and brings a rather special tilt to what Colossians has introduced us to, to include who and what we are in Christ Jesus: *"His offspring".*

I love to hear that over, and over again; that you and I are 'God's offspring', and 'in Him we live, move and have our being'. No doubt; there is something powerful about knowing who you truly are, and your true identity, apart from what others have told you or what you have been forced to become by virtue of your past mistakes, wrong personal choices, or even difficult life circumstances. Establishing our true identity helps us with finding, realising, and utilising our true authority.

To John, Jesus Christ is indeed the Son of the living God; He is the Lord, and He has authority over all of creation. Our lives are in His hands, and Jesus cares about us. He will never leave us nor forsake us.

You Are More Than You Think

Referring to John's narrative of the event at sea already cited earlier, his implicit appraisal of Jesus Christ as the Son of God and the Lord with power and authority both in heaven and on earth, taps into some great truths in relation to the life, nature and situation of believers in Christ. One of those wonderful truths regards believers' true identity and authority as children or *offspring* of God, and how it ultimately impacts our lives and destinies.

An undefined or distorted identity or image is all it takes to *destroy* a person, and to hinder them from realising their true potential and faith. But, we must learn, by virtue of our true identity in Christ Jesus, to navigate our way into God's desired life for us. Yes, sometimes life can be so cruel, to the extent that you become the personal embodiment of your tragic experiences, and sometimes that's all people may name and know you by.

Jesus met many people like that during His earthly ministries and helped them and restored their proper names and identities. For example, *Blind* Bartimaeus (Mark 10:46ff). Do you know *Blind* was not his first name? Also, Simon the *Leper* (Matth. 26:6), obviously *Leper* was not his surname either. Unfortunately, they became tagged, named and described by their misfortune in life. Another example is a lady, that none of us might ever know or call by her actual name, although Jesus healed her later in her life. She is the wonderful lady that is only identified as "*a certain woman with issue of blood*". (Mark 5:25)

Tell me about being unduly bound up to, strapped to and unjustly called and looked upon because of your problem or estate in life, and I will testify. Sometimes, it is not even about being sick or cripple, it's just because you are different, and people will look at you and treat you in a strange manner. But, thanks be to God, whose offspring we are, and who says that it really doesn't matter what people think or say you are. The truth is, you were *made for Him and by Him*.

In fact, He says He loves you and that you are "*fearfully and wonderfully made.*" That's exactly how David saw it when he screamed aloud as if he was rediscovering his true identity for the first time. He says, "*I will praise You, for I am fearfully and wonderfully made; marvellous are Your works, and that my soul knows very well*" (Psalms 139:14).

So, you see how crucial it is that the book of Acts added that very little but significant portion of the entire passage: "*for we are also His offspring*". It is so important because a distorted image and identity would explain the reason for most of the world's troubling problems, whether at personal, social or political levels. That explains why many hate themselves and others as well, and would go to any level to eliminate some others.

I would also add, which is very important, that Satan's main problem was, and still is, the problem of identity! Read the Bible and you will find this to be true. For example Isaiah in giving the background and reason for Satan's eminent and tragic fall, declares:

> *"How you are fallen from heaven, O Lucifer, son of the morning! How you are cut down to the ground, you who weakened the nations!* [13] *For you have said in your heart: ' I will ascend into heaven, I will exalt my throne above the stars of God; I will also sit on the mount of the congregation on the farthest sides of the north; I will scend above the heights of the clouds, I will be like the Most High.'* [15] *Yet you shall be brought down to Sheol, To the lowest depths of the Pit.* [16] *" Those who see you will gaze at you, and consider you, saying: ' Is this the man who made the earth tremble, who shook kingdoms,* [17] *Who made the world as a wilderness and destroyed its cities, who did not open the house of his prisoners?'*

Do you now recognise Satan's real problem? There's an identity issue written all over him, which is mostly responsible for him having an over blotted, self conceited, over exaggerated and misguided opinion and assessment of who he really is. For instance, why would a created being want to exalt himself above his Creator? Such thinking originates from someone who, in complete self-deception, thinks a *world* of themselves apart from what they really are, which certainly leads to one and only one road; self-destruction.

It comes as no surprise that, when part of the manifestation of Satan's contorted identity issues began to show up visibly in some false apostles, and deceitful workers trying to transform themselves into apostles of Christ; Paul quickly linked them to Satan, their *father*, exclaiming, *"and no wonder! For Satan himself transforms himself into an angel of light"* (2Cor.11:14). Satan's *chameleon* like character is part of the manifestation of his image and identity issues, and so are his agents and demons.

Now that you know that the problem of identity is a huge one, involving even Satan, it was then necessary for the book of Acts to permit us into that wonderful truth of who and what we are; *the offspring of God*. And, as a matter of fact '... *as He is, so are we in this world*' *(1 John 4:17)*. Amen. I will say that again '...as He is, so are we (you) in this world'. You've got it. That, in itself, is a powerful and liberating truth of the gospel of Christ; 'we are like Him in this world'. Meaning, we are indeed His true children with a nature that glorifies Him as our Father (cf. 2Pet 1:4).

This truth applies to you, without regard for your racial status, your economic conditions, political affiliation, your bodily state, or your psychosomatic situations. So, Peter was forced to confess that, *"In truth I perceive that God shows no partiality. But in every nation whoever fears Him and works righteousness is accepted by Him (Acts 10:35)*.

That's fair enough, and further more, the logic of Acts and First John are pretty simple. If we are God's offspring, meaning we directly descend and come from Him as our Creator (and not Apes as some falsely allege), it also follows that we must derive our nature, being and identity from Him, and be able to sustain the same through Him, whose offspring we are.

Doesn't even nature teach us the same? The apple fruit bears the characteristics transferred to it, as an embedded biological code from the apple seed out of which it came. Similarly, as a matter of course, we also who are the *offspring of God* bear and contain an embedded code, a spiritual *DNA (deoxyribonucleic acid)* of our Father God, whose *offspring* we are, and so, we become and are like '*He is in this world.*' We are no bastards, but legitimate children of God, with identities that are fully defined in Christ, '*in whom we have been chosen' (Eph. 1:4)*, and not by our temporary setbacks or afflictions.

But, as children of God, who are only like our God in this world, bearing His image, we are called and challenged to overcome, just as our Lord Jesus overcame through all that He went through, by the power He provides through His Holy Spirit. We need to steadfastly keep *"looking unto Jesus the author and finisher of our faith, who for the joy that was set before him endured the cross, despising the shame, and is set down at the right hand of the throne of God"* (Hebrews 12:2).

Secondly, as *offspring* of God in this world, we will certainly continue to be treated as sons and daughters of God. This is clearly the message of Hebrews 12:5-8:

> *And you have forgotten the exhortation which speaks to you as to sons (children): "My son (child), do not despise the chastening of the Lord, nor be discouraged when you are rebuked by Him, ⁶ for whom the Lord loves He chastens, and scourges every son(child) whom He receives." ⁷ If you endure chastening, God deals with you as with sons (children); for what son is there whom a father does not chasten? ⁸ But if you are without chastening, of which all have become partakers, then you are illegitimate and not sons (Children).*

The next time you have someone referring to you as *bastard* or illegitimate, or if that has been any issue to you, know this from today: you are a legitimate child with legitimate rights from the King of kings and Lord of lords. Your earthly parents may have reneged on their God-given responsibilities, thereby becoming 'illegitimate' and irresponsible parents, but your God, whose spiritual *DNA* you bear calls you, *My child,* with great pride. He knows you and has so much confidence in your future. Your God, who is your Father loves you and will continue to do so until heaven. That's your true identity; you are of Christ and *"there is hope for your future, says the Lord...."* *(Jeremiah 31:17)*

Well, this should get any believer excited about life; that in the first place you are no product of chance experiment, nor are you a clone and imitation of another person. Your life on earth is no mistake and evidently, you are not a product of some aggressive and random cosmic accident. But, you have a future and a purpose to live for through Christ Jesus.

You should be excited that you have God's divine nature in you as *His offspring*. Get excited that our Lord Jesus is 'before all things, visible and invisible, whether on earth beneath or in heaven above. Not only that, but He also created all things, and all things have their existence only in Him, thus He has the pre-eminence in all things. This is the truth that sets us free indeed, and this is the truth that any believer desiring a life of victory with consistent peace, must 'buy and sell not' (Proverbs 23:23).

Better Identity and Better Choice for Happiness as God's Will

Most people wrongly believe that to be happy and excited equates to having the next pay-cheque. Some say to themselves *'if only this and that person were in my life, or even if they just care a bit about me, I will be happy.'* Do you really think all that will make you happy if you had a certain contour of your look like this or that; and if your husband or wife were like those you imagine and admire on television screens, and at your office? Certainly, not. All of that has its place, but true happiness begins with what you have on your inside.

True happiness begins when you begin to find your true identity in Christ and allow the image of God in you to truly replace your own made-up image. Let Christ Jesus, by the power of His Holy Spirit shine in you and through you. Allow His grace to take you through each day and be grateful for His gift of life to you. Believe that your Lord Jesus Christ is God overall, rules and has dominion in and over all things, including all that you are facing right now, and you have no need to worry whether there's a way out.

There's always a way out in Christ for your trials. He makes for you a way up into His purpose for your life, no matter how low you've fallen. Your situation is not hopeless, nor is it beyond God's strength that He cannot solve, or resolve it. Know that 'with God all things are always possible' and He is more than willing to help and to embrace you as His beloved child.

Well, let's hear the conclusion of the matter, "*So Jesus answered and said to them, 'Have faith in God'*" *(Mark 11:22)*. "*But without faith it is impossible to please Him, for he who comes to God must believe that He is, and that He is a rewarder of those who diligently seek Him*" *(Hebrews 11:6)*.

Chapter Ten

THE RISER: OUT OF THE ASHES AND INTO LIFE

> *So, Jesus stood still and commanded him to be called. Then they called the blind man, saying to him, "Be of good cheer. Rise, He is calling you" (Mark 10:49).*

> *He raises the poor from the dust and lifts the beggar from the ash heap, to set them among princes and make them inherit the throne of glory. (1Samuel 2:8a). "… to console those who mourn in Zion, to give them beauty for ashes, the oil of joy for mourning, the garment of praise for the spirit of heaviness; that they may be called trees of righteousness, the planting of the Lord, that He may be glorified"(Isaiah 61:3)*

'Rise, He is calling you', is precisely the way to begin this chapter. It vividly tells the emotion and aspiration of the moment, when a man's frantic cry for help finally yielded a desired outcome. He gained the undivided attention of the 'Master', after the disciples had tried to shut him down. The man had cried out, and now, the 'Master' was calling him.

On this famous occasion, the 'Master', who was calling, was none other than Jesus Christ of Nazareth, the Lord and Saviour. Of course, there were good reasons why His disciples referred to Him as 'Master', but according to the Scriptures; *"by Him all things were created that are in heaven and that are on earth, visible and invisible, whether thrones or dominions or principalities or powers. All things were created through Him and for Him. And He is before all things, and in Him all things consist. And He is the head of the body, the church, who is the beginning, the firstborn from the dead, that in all things He may have the pre-eminence" (Colossians 1:16-18).*

Who was He calling? Bartimaeus, the blind beggar, who had joined the multitude in pursuit of Jesus, as He went out from Jericho. Bartimaeus, first called out to Jesus from the depth of his misery and challenge, and then Jesus, with compassion, replied by calling him to Himself. What a privilege; that when we call out to Jesus, whether from the hills or the valleys, He still hears us and responds faithfully.

It is no secret that when Jesus calls out, or calls on a person who is suffering, help is on its way, regardless of whosoever in whatsoever condition. It makes no difference how long or what has been said about your condition, Jesus brings you help when He comes or calls. For example in Matthew 17 (vrs 15-18), when the disciples could do nothing for an epileptic boy, his father became so distraught because they were unable to cure his son. Almost immediately, Jesus came walking down from a mountain and saw great confusion, as a result of an overheated debate between His disciples and the crowd. Apparently, the disciples became embarrassed by the situation, and while the crowd was accusing them, they tried to justify their inability to heal the boy. Meanwhile, the boy's father was as much agitated as the disciples were frustrated, before a waiting crowd. No sooner had Jesus, their Master, arrived, and then He had to intervene to break the deadlock. Moved by compassion for his son, the father of the epileptic boy sincerely pleaded with Jesus, saying;

> *"Lord, have mercy on my son, for he is an epileptic and suffers severely; for he often falls into the fire and often into the water. So I brought him to Your disciples, but they could not cure him." (Matthew 17:15-16)*

Without hesitating, the Lord Jesus commanded, *"Bring him here to Me. ... And Jesus rebuked the demon, and it came out of him; and the child was cured from that very hour."*

I believe the disciples' situation and Jesus' timely intervention prove in every way the power and wisdom of the Scripture that says; *"with men it is impossible, but not with God; for with God all things are possible" (Mark 10:27).* Never give up even after men or women have tried their utmost and failed. God is always greater, and He is ready to help. Always expect something supernatural. Expect a miracle from God when you are before Him, and when He calls on you after you have cried out to Him. Remember, when Israel 'cried out' behind the wall of Jericho, the wall came crashing down (Joshua 6). This time, Bartimaeus, also cried out to Jesus, on His way out of Jericho. Surely, Bartimaeus was bound to see a miracle.

Don't Let Situations Name or Hinder You

Now, here comes Bartimaeus, the son of *Timaeus*. By the way, the meaning of *Timaeus*[6] is *'highly priced; worthy; honorable'*. Supposing that Hebrew and Aramaic names were mostly descriptive of a person's destiny in life or their position in society; *Mr. Timeaus* may have been a 'great' man, given the meaning of his name. Yet, sometimes bad things happen to 'great' people, and *Mr. Timeaus* is no exception in this case. Bartimaeus, *Mr. Timeaus*' son, was blind and a beggar who sat by the roadside to beg from passer-bys. Trying to survive might have been the sole reason why Bartimaeus was forced to beg in the street, and definitely, begging was a tough choice for anyone living with disabilities during the time of Bartimaeus.

Some of the reasons why people like Bartimaeus, who suffered from acute disabilities, found it a much greater challenge to sit in the street to beg or to mix with others, was because, historically people like him were considered the 'accursed' and 'unclean' of their society. Such people, as some cultural cum religious forms had it, did not deserve sympathy, and were unfortunately abandoned to suffer on their own. They were isolated and sometimes publically lynched, presumed to be responsible for the ills of society, and also their own plights, which were often explained to be a consequence for their sins or that of their parents (cf. John 9:1-34).

Our own curiosity could lead us into asking why *Mr. Timaues*, Bartimaeus' father, did not care and provide for him privately and personally. That might be a legitimate question to ask, however the Scripture does not hint at any reason why *Mr. Timaues* could not prevent his son's tragic and distressing situation, but allowed him to sit on the sidewalk to beg.

The truth is, apart from few of our own societies today, that have a vibrant welfare arrangement to cater for physically and mentally challenged people, many still find people with such challenges as needless 'burdens' and frowns at them as if they made themselves so. Hence, it will not be too much to surmise that *Mr. Timaeus* himself might have suffered a level of public ridicule, being the father of a blind child, given what we know today about their culture (cf Jn 9).

In fact, given that *Mr. Timaeus'* name was attached to his son nuances a suspicion, to the effect that he might have encountered some real difficulties, because it was, at that time a common thing to associate or stigmatize an entire family name with 'bad omens'. If one of them unfortunately suffered from what the society considered ceremoniously unclean or culturally unacceptable, their house was named as such. As a result, people could easily be called by their conditions without regard for their true names or true identities.

That's why some individuals, who were healed by our Lord Jesus have their names missing entirely from Scriptures, including those that were simply referred to as the 'paralytic' or the 'woman with issue of blood'. Maybe, by allowing Bartimaeus to get away from the family house and to position himself somewhere along the street corner, was a subtle way of *Mr. Timaeus* distancing himself from the problem, and the pain associated with open ridicule, and family stigmatization.

All of what I have described sound like yesterday's issues, totally a thing of the past and of primitive cultures. However, there are some even in our modern cultures and so-called civilised world today, who are unfortunately still battling with issues of stigmatization and isolation, comparable to the time of Bartimeaus and his family. There are reports of children and descent people who have been bullied and called odd names, causing them to withdraw into seclusion because of their backgrounds and challenges.

Unfortunately, many of today's civilisations have such revulsion for disabilities, and are increasingly becoming intolerant of disabilities. Yet, the truth is that every person alive might have suffered, or is suffering, from some form of disability one way or another. As a result, those who have the means to cover their own disabilities, only use their 'abilities' and emphasize their areas of strength to criticise, condemn, humiliate, isolate, and bully those who are less fortunate; something God hates with passion (see Lam.3:35-37; Lev. 19:14-15).

Instead of our various disabilities being the reason to compete against, avoid or hate one another, I believe they emphasize our individual need, first and foremost for God Almighty, and our collective need for one another; the need for a world of interdependence, undergirded by mutual humility and love, as God would desire for all His children; especially those who belong to the body of Christ. What God would wish that we do with our disabilities and 'abilities' is that we completely submit them in service, and surrender to Him, who alone has all perfection and all abilities. By relying and depending on Him fully, then we can derive His faultless perfection and true abilities in place of our own disabilities (1Tim. 6:15,16; James 1:17; 2Cor. 12:9).

The truth is that, there is no perfection or true abilities anyway, outside of Christ Jesus. This is why our world today, which generally denies and opposes Christ, is full of imperfections and all kinds of disabilities. To pretend that this is not the case, and to continue to use other people's disabilities against them, or to try to make their temporary setbacks permanent by tagging and calling them names, is to practise and to endorse sheer hypocrisy. The kind similar to Simon's, against the woman considered a prostitute, but which was dismissed by Jesus, as ludicrous. (Luke 7:36-50)

Here is what I believe is God's golden rule and prescription for a world of disabilities, the kind symbolised by Bartimaeus' disability, which has great need for tolerance. First of all, like Bartimaeus, we all need, with all urgency, to call out to Jesus Christ by completely submitting to His lordship and saving grace. Then after that,

> ***Let love be without hypocrisy.*** *Abhor what is evil. Cling to what is good.* [10] *Be kindly affectionate to one another with brotherly love, in honor giving preference to one another;* [11] *not lagging in diligence, fervent in spirit, serving the Lord;* [12] *rejoicing in hope, patient in tribulation, continuing steadfastly in prayer;* [13] *distributing to the needs of the saints, given to hospitality.* [14] *Bless those who persecute you; bless and do not curse.* [15] *Rejoice with those who rejoice, and weep with those who weep.* [16] *Be of the same mind toward one another. Do not set your mind on high things, but associate with the humble. Do not be wise in your own opinion.* [17] *Repay no one evil for evil. Have regard for good things in the sight of all men.* [18] *If it is possible, as much as depends on you, live peaceably with all men (Romans 12:8-18).*

Remember, no condition is permanent! The only permanence there is, is *change*. So, there's hope, even for the vilest sinner who desires change through Christ. There's always healing available in Christ for every disability that we bring to Him. If you don't like the *names* or *labels* your condition has thrust upon you; or the *tags* people have deliberately or inadvertently placed on you due to some limitations or disabilities, bring those to Jesus. He has a new *Name* for you: "*...you shall be called by a new name, which the mouth of the Lord will name*" (Isaiah 62:2). "*... and I will give him a white stone, and on the stone a new name written which no one knows except him who receives it.*" (Rev. 2:17)

The Menace of Stereo-typing and Witch Hunting

Very prevalent during the time of Jesus and Bartimeaus, was this strange practice, in which people tried to assign the cause of mishaps, misfortunes and conditions like Bartimaeus', to some ancestral or generational curse and sins of their parents. The consequence of which was to be borne by their offspring. For example, in John 9:1-12, similar situation arose concerning a man who was born blind, who later had his sight restored by the Lord Jesus.

Upon seeing the blind man, the first reaction of Jesus' disciples toward him was nothing near sympathy, or a surprise. They instantly and adamantly assumed that the man's blindness was due to sin. The only one thing they were unsure about and wanted to clarify with their Master was, '*who sinned, this man or his parents, that he was born blind?*' So, then it was never the question of *why* but *who*, because in a stereotypical culture, people insist on finding reasons for blame, which is so easy, because the culture sees reasons as a *given*. Such a society already operates on norms that box things into what their culture supplies as sets of cultural ethos or philosophies, from which judgements of right and wrong are defined and rendered.

Stereotypical cultures and lifestyles are terrible witch-hunt or *blame* cultures, that encourage mindsets and worldviews in which the alibi for an action or reaction are already supplied and given. As such, people who submit to such cultures in any society, find themselves always looking for an object to assign their blame to. Again, such societies nurse grounds for guilt and placing of guilt, usually on an *object* of guilt, a *scapegoat* of their own making, as they find necessary.

Usually, they already have their *culprit* because it's easy to find one, since it is a *given* by the culture under which its society functions. Since the *culprit* is a *given*, the judgement that makes the *culprit* will equally be a *given*. The unique problem that therefore haunts and looms over the head of people in such society is; in essence no one really is safe. But, as usual, the 'powerful' get away while the 'less powerful' bear the brunt of the makings of the culture and their value system, including its ethos, philosophies and worldviews.

In some cases, people have the *why* and already have the *who*, for what they intend to afflict, which is principally informed by their *given* ethos and philosophies. But then, they only need another to affirm their actions and decisions, as seen in the case of the woman caught in adultery (John 8:3-5). The Scribes and Pharisees already knew what the law says about someone caught in adultery. They knew that the person caught must be stoned to death, and in fact, they were ready with stones to kill their culprit, yet they came by quizzing the Lord Jesus.

In such a society everyone is a possible suspect and the tenets of suspicion always reign. Everyone tend to play it safe, and take it 'easy' with others, because they suspect one could be potentially dangerous. Unfortunately, the kind of world and the kind of society that I have just described can be effectively characterised by only one term: *sad*. The people given to the cultural values, ethos, and philosophies of such society, contrary to God's will for us, only end up being terribly unhappy. Whether it is by choice, or one just happened to be found to live their life according to the values and principles of such stereotypical cultures, the end result will always be unhappiness, through a tight and burdened lifestyle. Someone must always be sniffing on somebody, and that potentially saps the juice out of life.

However, one can still be happy, even in the society which I have already described as, *Sad*. Obviously, beginning with a solid faith that is firmly rooted in Christ Jesus will always helps us to overcome. Then, by following the sound biblical principle from Apostle Paul, which I strongly believe will help anybody to mitigate the woes of the menace of a stereo-type and a witch-hunt culture and society:

> *Rejoice in the Lord always: and again I say, rejoice. (Phil. 4:4) Be anxious for nothing; but in everything by prayer and supplication with thanksgiving let your requests be made known to God. And the peace of God, which surpasses all understanding, will keep your hearts and minds through Christ Jesus. Finally, brethren, whatsoever things are true, whatsoever things are honest, whatsoever things are just, whatsoever things are pure, whatsoever things are lovely, whatsoever things are of good report; if there be any virtue, and if there be any praise, think on these things. (Phil. 4: 6-8)*

Chasing Ghosts and Shadows: Why Am I not Happy?

It is so easy to disrupt, and to destroy, what potentially could have been an enviable relationship. Make no mistake, whatever the reason may be, for the sudden or imminent failure of thriving relationships, suspicion will always play a crucial role.

Take David and the young man Hanun, the son of Nahash, king of the Ammonites, who was David's bosomed friend in first Chronicles chapter nineteen. Nahash dies and Hanun inherits his father's throne. David, in sympathy with Hanum and due to his unwavering loyalty to the memory of his late friend, obliges to show kindness to Hanun. But, Hanun would not take David's gesture without suspecting that he had ulterior motives. Hence, Hanum convinces himself that all that David intended to do was a secret enticer to overthrow him, and then he reacts rather awkwardly for defence, to the dismay of David.

Well, whether Hanun's reading of David's intentions was right or wrong, one thing was sure: that clearly dangerous suspicion was building up in minds and hearts. In the end, a historic relationship and friendship, initially nurtured and kept on the basis of genuine trust, suffered greatly. Had it not been for the cruel eruption of suspicion arising from Hanun's distrust for David, as the story later revealed, David was wholeheartedly willing to protect and to support young Hanun on account of Nahash's friendship with him. However, Hanun, eventually and childishly threw away his opportunity for an invaluable friendship. Only to realise that his country and people might be destroyed on account of his treating David the way he did.

We cannot escape Hanun's experience if we choose to handle issues and to go about dealing with people like Hanun. It's good for one to be circumspect, but not so that one becomes suspicious of others in ways that always make us to look for ulterior motives behind people's gestures, actions or choices. This will only lead to unhappiness, and is an easy trap for feeling lonely and isolated, despite the wonderful people and great things we are surrounded by. Living on the edge of checking the hidden motives behind everything, perhaps is the quickest way to destroy some of the best miracle moments that God brings our way. It also spoils the joy and adventure of living.

If we will live and be happy, we need to be free spirited towards the efforts, gestures, actions and choices of others. Just emulate what the legal system or the *Law* is supposed to do; 'presume people are innocent until proven guilty'. Prejudging people and concluding before they have the opportunity to 'prove' themselves, is the product of our own untamed prejudices that cost us a great deal eventually. Among other things, it interferes with our good judgment, our personalities, and will eventually lock a thousand doors before us.

Think about a man or a woman involved in a marriage relationship, but who suspects their spouse every step along the way. Not only would they act toward their spouse with suspicion, but eventually their marriage will erupt into flames for no justifiable cause. Paranoia perhaps, had set in. But, an unfounded suspicion is simply an 'empty vagueness' that erects insurmountable mountains of hindrances on the only path that leads to true happiness, greatness and fulfilment.

It is always the case. Ask most divorcees and they cannot actually tell you, or truly remember the real root and original cause leading to their regrettable divorce. They cannot really say it, simply because it is often too trivial to remember, or too trivial to make any real sense of. Later, they might come up with one or two explanations but very far from the initial cause of their divorce problem. Often, their explanation, no matter how emotional or sincere, is almost always never the primary cause. But because they must explain the reason for why things went bad, the secondary cause becomes primary. This is eventually how things play out when people allow suspicion to have the better of them.

Like the case of David and Hanun, if Hanun were before you today and decided to be truthful, he might not be able to say in truth why in the first place their relationship broke down the way it did. But we know that he suspected what never existed in the mind of David, but only in Hanun's, maybe, fearful and overprotective mind. Influenced by his awful friends, he chased a 'shadow' and caught nothing; he cried 'ghost' and found nothing, and then spent himself, to the detriment of a potentially important friendship between him and David. All of this, was in pursuit of a 'shadow and a ghost' that only existed in his own mind. That's all unfounded suspicion is; chasing a 'ghost' and a 'shadow' that exist only in our own minds.

Consider how many kind and dedicated people walk away from what truly was their God-given purpose and assignments in churches, ministries, and life in general, because of offence that ensued from unfounded suspicion. What about pastors who abandoned gifted and talented men and women in their pews simply because the pastor could not trust them due to his misguided suspicion. In most cases, some of these people, who might have been God's answer to the pastor's prayer for human resources to help build the church, end up being hurt and eventually exiting. Equally so, many decent family relations today become ruined for the same reason. A suspicion toward a relative or a spouse, which was totally baseless, eventually breaks their golden links for a flourishing family future.

The pursuit of Happiness: Dealing with the Ghosts and Shadows

For God has not given us a spirit of fear, but of power and of love and of a sound mind (2 Timothy 1:7).

To reverse the sad trend of 'chasing ghosts and shadows', which only sours, and eventually ruins, our own happiness and other people's happiness, we must put in place a countermotion against the *spirit* of suspicion. But first, we must agree that most suspicions are based on an intolerable *fear* that one has given his or her life to, initially creeping in one's life based on relatively 'bad' past experiences. Other times, the *fear* might be unfounded, just as the suspicion that they bring about. However, whatever the reason or background for the *fear* is, fear and living with fear that controls the life, especially of a believer is not justifiable (see 2Timothy 1:7). Fear is not a lifestyle.

God, in His foreknowledge, knew the destructive tendencies of fear and living with fear, including suspicion. Therefore, He has given us the *spirit* of power, love and sound mind (2Tim. 1:7). These three the Lord has given us to counter and defeat any *spirit* of fear, and of course suspicion, which has *fear* as its root. Obviously, we know that we need the Spirit of Christ who is God's Holy Spirit living in the believer, and the Word of God in order to have and to exercise the *power*, *love* and *sound mind* required for dealing with issues of *fear* and suspicion.

Second, what essentially works for our happiness are a lifestyle and a culture that embrace mutual and individual responsibilities, in which, as a matter of first principle, everyone shows some care, not just for themselves but others as well. This kind of culture and lifestyle say, *one is essentially and actually who they are because of others*: not a blame game that thrives on witch-hunts or suspicion in order to exclude others for one's own advantage. Rather, loving others and helping others to become, when possible, better than ourselves.

> *Let nothing be done through selfish ambition or conceit, but in lowliness of mind let each esteem others better than himself (Philippians 2:3).*

And the reason why this kind of lifestyle is so powerful is that, we humans are much more fulfilled and find fulfilment when we invest in a good cause and the betterment of others. We were built to share and to love, just as Apostle Paul enjoins us by quoting our Lord Jesus Christ, saying, '*It is more blessed to give than to receive*'. (Acts 20:35) Of course there is good evidence that we undoubtedly benefit directly and indirectly, when we look out for the good of others. The bible says, "*The generous soul will be made rich, and he who waters will also be watered himself.*" *(Prov.11:25)* Also, "*Do not be deceived, God is not mocked; for whatever a man sows, that he will also reap.*" (Gal. 6:7) Paul uses his example and says, "*I have shown you in every way, by laboring like this, that you must support the weak...*" (Act 20:35)

The Athenian Gesture: "It is Better to Give than to Receive"

Reading from Thucydides' philosophical History[7], I came across an interesting transaction, regarding the dispensation of political and relational justice, which took place between representatives of former *super power*, Athens and a less powerful and small island called Melos. Athens was suspicious of Melian, because of Melian's decision to stay neutral among competing and rival nations at the time, and thought that in times of war, Melians' neutrality could pose a danger to Athens' homeland security. They could be coerced or solicited, and probably enlisted, by a more influential neighbour against Athens. Hence, the crime of Melos was their neutrality and their reluctance to openly avow support for Athens.

So, when the Melian representative would not yield to the bully tactics of the Athenian envoys to have Melians declare their support for Athens, the Athenian resorted to blackmailing campaigns and threat of open hostility. One of the Athenian envoys remarked, *"But you and we should say what we really think, and aim only at what is possible, for we both alike know that into the discussion of human affairs the question of justice only enters where there is equal power to enforce it, and that the powerful exact what they can, and the weak grant what they must."*[8] This was a clever response of the Athenian envoy to the humble plea for fairness and protection requested by the helpless Melian authority, who unfortunately were locked between a game of bullying 'superpowers'.

Obviously, this was the vile side of Athens, but Athens was equally keen on the principle of helping and relieving others which really sounds like a paradox. Even when the great Pericles of Athens spoke about Athenians democracy and generosity, he claimed it stood uncontested and unrivalled by any other of their time because as he said: *"we do not copy our neighbours, but are example to them. It is true that we are called democracy, for the administration is in the hands of the many and not the few. But while the law secures equal justice to all alike in their private disputes, the claim of excellence is also recognised; ... There is no exclusiveness in our public life, and in our private intercourse we are not suspicious of one another, nor angry with our neighbour if he does what he likes; we do not put on sour looks at him which, though harmless, are not pleasant. ... In doing good, again, we are unlike others; we make our friends by conferring, not by receiving favours. Now he who confers a favour is the firmer friend, because he would fain by kindness keep alive the memory of an obligation; but the recipient is colder in his feelings because he knows that in requiting another's generosity he will not be winning gratitude but only paying a debt. We alone do good to our neighbours, not upon a calculation of interest, but in the confidence of freedom and frank and fearless spirit."*[9]

Athenians' pursuit of 'free spiritedness', against the prevalent human tendency and temptation to use others, was no magic. It hung on their recognition that there was always intrinsic benefit in looking after other's welfare. Seek the good of others and you will find that, in the majority of cases others will look after you. Forget the few odd experiences of breeches of trust; such is life. Even as treacherous as Athens was, they still had the good sense to look after others. '*It is more blessed to give than to receive*'. (Acts 20:35) Also Ephesians 6:7,8.

Kicking 'Religion' and Rising like Bartimaeus

One of the greatest dangers to true faith and the exercise of true belief in Christ has always been 'religion', which is basically human beings' own sets of rules, forms, and practices that are used principally in trying to please God, and the ways in which such rules, forms and practices play out in everyday life. In some arenas, religion may take the form of an over embellished self-styled version of true faith, but hyped up in such a way to serve our own purpose rather than God's.

As it is, religion is very difficult to define, but if there were a simple way to describe religion in this case, I would say, "*going beyond what God says or requires to your own detriment and that of others.*" Within Christian circles, 'religion' or being religious would mean, "serving God only when it is convenient".

The problem is, it is such an easy line to toe; being or getting religious, because the line between practising true faith in Christ and being religious is very slim. Often, even the most sincere believer can be found to be religious about some things; so also were the disciples of Christ, who sometimes were given to *religious reasons or religious spirit*. Although, we cannot say that we know all the reasons why this is so, we know that religion, and giving into *religious reasons and religious spirit*, is something generally motivated and undergirded by subtle pride, selfishness; cultures generally known for encouraging stereotypes, and undetected spiritual blindness, leading to a spiritual stronghold in the life of 'sincere', but sometimes misguided, believers.

Don't forget that it was the disciples, walking along with Jesus, that sternly warned Bartimaeus to hush as he screamed freely to Jesus for help (Mk 10:48). Their prohibition of Bartimaeus was most likely due to the prevalent religious thinking, that the physically blind person belonged to a class of untouchables, and was a sinner (cf John 9:2). It could have also been that the disciples judged Bartimaeus to be in serious breech of their laid down religious codes on how to approach the 'Rabbi', in this case Jesus (cf John 12:20-22).

Just think about the disciples, trying so hard to force on the Lord Jesus a *celebrity's* status for their own *feel-good* sentiments, while being around the *big-man*, as some in our society do today. They tried to conjure good religious reasons for themselves, why a suffering man, blind Bartimaues must not reach out for Jesus the way he did. But the Lord would have none of it. He knew He came for the poor, the blind, the broken hearted, the despised, and so forth (Luke 4:18-19). With all the great religious traditions that preceded Christ and how many insisted on keeping them, and of course thrusting it on others, it was so easy to give in to keeping religious forms and then losing the true essence of God's love, purpose and assignment.

Instead of addressing the true need of God's people, suddenly some find themselves caught up into religious debate trying to, wittingly or unwittingly defend the 'tradition of the elders' through unsighted allegiance, based on *religious reasons* and the influences of *religious spirit*. As a result, such people are unable to endure the truth of the Scriptures, which alone sets people free (John 8:32), and through which the 'stealing, killing, and destroying' works of Satan are effectively dismantled and abolished (2 Corinth. 10:4; John 10:10).

The Lord knew the difference, bringing and giving 'abundant life' to His people without regard for their persons or backgrounds. So, for Him, it was down to the question of saving lives, and not about religious *correctness* or protocol. He made it easy for anyone who had need of Him to approach Him. His approach was somewhat alien to many who had over the years, been schooled and moulded in keeping religious forms, subscribing to *religious reasons* and being dominated by *religious spirit*, rather than addressing the true human needs.

The real challenge for a true believer would be, how do we detect *religious reasons, religious spirit* or religious forms, and how do we respond to them, so that we are not hindered from reaching for our miracles, blessings and purposes? Unfortunately, there's never a hard and fast rule as to how these things work and look. However, because of their huge potential to impact negatively on sensitive areas of our faith, relationships, and purposes, we will touch on two crucial areas, which will help expose how real and systemic *religious reasons, religious spirit* or religious forms are. In the process, we will also look at the Lord's wisdom on how believers can beat this *plague*.

#1. *Religious Reasons, Conflicts and Relationships*

On a more practical note, some of the key reasons why so many potentially rewarding relationships, and especially marriages, among believers fail to attain their best dreams and to keep their initial vows are that, underneath those vows are also hidden, ready-made religious rationales for our imminent actions and exits. In most cases we have already planned our exit strategies and lined up in our minds and in our defence what would be the appropriate religious response against pre-anticipated, preconceived conflicts, situations and things that might go wrong. This is mainly because religion has taught us to be literally the unbeatable 'heroes' in our own *world*, always right in our own eyes, and if anything goes wrong, we must desperately find someone to blame, and not to allow ourselves to be 'walked over'.

In a sense, we've got the *why* which our religion supplies and we only need the *who*, which will eventually come. Because we conceive it in our spirit, we therefore will physically give birth to it. In this context, our religion supplied the *why*, and we make the *who*, usually the culprit and the one responsible for causing our pains and sufferings.

Unfortunately, this kind of mindset about life and way of addressing or resolving issues and conflicts, basically works on the principle that says; 'when things aren't so great then I know someone else, apart from me, must be in the wrong'. This is not Scriptural and is not God's way for true believers. Yes, it is religious, and that's all it is. The problem with this kind of approach tends to be that the one who believes they are always right, and others wrong, will have no desire whatsoever, to take the 'hard road' of trying to make things right even if it means becoming vulnerable for the other person's sake.

When a believer will not see why he or she must take the 'hard road' for the sake of peace and others, more often than not the problem surrounds issues of self-righteousness, normally steeply built and fostered upon a serious *religious spirit*. In many cases, actions or reactions under such circumstances are highly motivated by pseudo-spiritual religious etiquettes and moral codes. Normally lacking, are the Godly ways of love, patience, endurance and forgiveness, which are *"things that are true, things noble, things just and pure, and things that are lovely, of good report, of virtue and praiseworthy"* (Phil. 4:8).

For the sake of peace and others, Paul's best advice must be heeded, when he says in Titus 1:15, *"to the pure all things are pure, but to those who are defiled and unbelieving nothing is pure; but even their mind and conscience are defiled."*

#2. Religious Form and People Agenda

Religious spirit is similar to what I call 'religious form' and basically it seeks to promote and protect empty formalities, without any real deep commitment to God other than that which serves the interest of the person exercising it. Since it is mainly fed by *self-made regulations,* the 'forms' might change, but they do so only when changing serves the secret ambition and agenda of the one who is advantaged, and thus always benefits by it (cf Col. 2:20; Gal 2:11-21). But, the truth is, God thoroughly detests religious forms for what they stand for and the impulsive and reckless way in which they blind the heart and turn people away from God and His purposes.

God has never been interested in religious forms, and if anything at all, He vehemently discouraged them by taking the initiative not to reveal Himself in any 'form'; warning all to *"take careful heed to yourselves, for you saw no form when the Lord spoke to you at Horeb out of the midst of the fire, lest you act corruptly and make for yourselves a carved image in the form of any figure ... to worship them and serve them...,"(Deut. 4:15-19).*

He calls religious forms idolatry, the most familiar of their sort being making a graven image of any kind to look up to, serve or worship (Exod. 20:3:4; Exodus 32:1- 10). But, there are more subtle elements to idolatry which are often overlooked. These include greed, pride, selfish ambition, and the behaviours that encourage and protect them, which really border on and often blend in with self worship or *will* worship. The Scripture is very clear that we; *"Therefore put to death your members which are on the earth: fornication, uncleanness, passion, evil desire, and covetousness, which is idolatry. Because of these things the wrath of God is coming upon the sons of disobedience"* (Colossians 3:5, 6). *"These things indeed have an appearance of wisdom in self-imposed religion, false humility, and neglect of the body, but are of no value against the indulgence of the flesh." (Col. 2:23)*

More specifically, Apostle Paul calls religious forms, *self-imposed religion* and *false humility* (Col. 2:23). Unfortunately these are rampant in today's world; some formal and some informal. However, many people who have masqueraded under formal religious forms for too long might find it difficult, if not impossible, to tell the difference. The truth is that religious forms are all too porous and anyone with an amount of discernment should be able to see through them as soon as they show up. For example, where religious forms exist, there will also be a noticeable lack of true interest in other people. They don't protect people but serve as a good platform for the 'swindlers' and 'conmen' to advance their personal or group agenda, which may be mundane or spiritual.

This is similar to what some politicians do all too often as we see on our television screens. Most friendships or relationships politicians would contract are seriously guarded by what has come to be known as the *Law of 250*. This *Law* works on the principle that says, *the average person influences 250 others in the course of his or her life*. So, first of all when a politician is shaking your hand he literally sees 250 potential voters and the net widens with each person whose hand he is able to shake. That's why most career politicians will easily accept an invitation to attend your church if you have at least on average 250 members in attendance. It gives him/ her a good scope of at least 250, who could each possibly speak to a string or *pyramid* of another 250 within their circle of influence in the very short term, for his /her election just ahead.

Actually, the hard truth is, he/she is not really in love with you, your church or intending to protect your interest and to promote your 'faith' as such; it's all about the politician's votes, and when they see people, they see numbers and potential votes. They might learn and use some religious phrases and a few religious jargons in their remarks to your congregation, but that doesn't make them a true believer. They are caught by and working with a *religious spirit*!

Let me give you a classic example, which happened about a couple of years ago, involving a person who hails from one of our major provinces, who stunned the British public with their hidden gift in music. Not long afterwards the person encountered a great difficulty. Well, the outcome was interesting. Obviously, this person had emerged from a very modest background, totally unknown but bold enough to attempt and experiment with big-screen popularity.

This person was suddenly thrust into a whirlpool of clever games organised by what some consider to be crafty money making schemes in which the participants are the real commodities. The public supposedly choose the winner of this competition with a big promise for the ultimate winner. This person held on until the finals, having already suffered terrible emotional and mental trauma. At the very end of the competition, they lost and, what some had initially feared, unfortunately happened. The person collapsed on stage, due to mental and emotional drains and exhaustion, we were told.

The organizers had already had the best out of their *commodity*, and they in fact won because they held to this person, knowing their presence continually boosted television viewership and potential pay-to-vote audience, throughout the show. This, many believe because there was an unconfirmed theory that a select person or persons are only kept on to arouse and sustain public support for the duration of the competition, playing on human gullible psychology.

But, here's the point I want to make, that some days later, after that competition had ended, our television screen was still busy with different kinds of *competitors* and show *commentators*. It was the turn of the politicians including the head of political parties, to have their go and to score some political points, each taking advantage of the unfortunate situation involving the participant of the actual show. They began to issue what appeared to be stern statement to the organizer of the program to ensure that their 'star performer' was well looked after in a specialist hospital after the incidence. Well, while all this was going on, major nations of the world, including the United Kingdom, were at the same time faced with catastrophic economic recession and political crises of their own.

In fact, we were told this was at the peak of the 'deepest' credit crunch Britain, and other leading industrial nations, had experienced in recent history. Understandably, many were anxious to know what their governments were doing about the economical woes. Many hard working and decent people were suffering and losing their jobs and homes at an alarming rate. Yet the issue regarding the participant of the television show managed to dominate headlines for weeks on our major electronic and print media.

What hypocrisy, what a loss of direction, and what a distraction tactic when people only take interest in others when it works for their personal and selfish ends. The show organizers had undone their 'star performer', and the politicians were now 'scavenging on her carcass,' using the unfortunate situation as their life line to divert attention from their political blunders. Surely, only a few weeks earlier no one really cared who this 'star performer' was.

But, like Bartimaeus, this 'star performer' until they appeared on that show, has been on the *wayside, begging and crying*, until the 'Master called'; so to speak. And all of a sudden, all hands were now being extended to the 'star performer'. That's exactly what religious form does, it excludes you until it can find use for you, and then it includes you without regard for the very tenants of its forms that initially excluded you.

Unfortunately, religious form can only keep you for as long as it has any use for you, and then it abandons you in the end. That is why when our Lord Jesus is dealing with people, He has no regard for their religious forms, because their basis for inclusion and exclusion are flawed, fluid and hypocritical. It only serves their convenience, and their purpose.

Take a look at the 'calling' of Bartimaeus again:

> *Now they came to Jericho. As He went out of Jericho with His disciples and a great multitude, blind Bartimaeus, the son of Timaeus, sat by the road begging. 47 And when he heard that it was Jesus of Nazareth, he began to cry out and say, "Jesus, Son of David, have mercy on me!" 48 Then many warned him to be quiet; but he cried out all the more, "Son of David, have mercy on me!" 49 So Jesus stood still and commanded him to be called. Then they called the blind man, saying to him, "Be of good cheer. Rise, He is calling you." 50 And throwing aside his garment, he rose and came to Jesus (Mark 10:46-50).*

Do you see how the people who warned Bartimaeus to be quiet changed suddenly after Jesus decided to stop and to help, after Bartimaeus persisted? It's so interesting that the same 'mouths' that yelled at a blind man to hush while he was crying out for help, again turned to call him, but at the behest of the love and compassion of Jesus. Were they really calling Bartimaeus because they truly care about him, or they were only calling him because it would help them continue to look good in the eyes of Jesus, and hopefully allow them to maintain their 'position' of importance by the side of the Master.

Well, that's how it works with people of religious form; they will do anything to serve their interest and change again to still serve their agenda. But, like Bartimaeus, persist toward true faith in Christ, cast aside your *garment of* limitations and rush for your deliverance. Just like in the case of Bartimaeus, and just like the Psalmist observed, the voice of the Lord Jesus Christ will overrule and defeat every opposing religious voice, or religious form intended to keep you down for any reason.

> *"The floods have lifted up, O Lord, the floods have lifted up their voice, the floods lift up their waves. 4 The Lord on high is mightier than the noise of many waters, than the mighty waves of the sea" (Psalms 93:3-4).*

Chapter Eleven

THE SPELL BREAKER: OVERCOMING FEAR AND NEGATIVITY

In previous chapters, fear and negativity were identified, to be some of the root causes of suspicion. And, they trigger other harmful behaviours that are in fact, *"little foxes that destroy the vines of tender grapes"* in our lives and relationships (Song of Solomon 2:15). So, what I intend to do in this chapter is to address the problem of fear and negativity. Then, I will suggest some important principles and practical ways of dealing with crippling fear and overwhelming negativity that trouble so many believers today. In some cases, and for practical purposes, I will draw on my personal background, hoping that my experience may shine a light on some of the principles.

I also hope that in dealing with the 'roots' we can also tackle the 'branches' and for our purpose, the *spirit of suspicion*, which we have already identified, and to some extent addressed.

As a result, I will present to you two sets of four principles: the first set to include helpful practical suggestions, purposefully placed at the beginning, to start you off in a good spirit. Then followed by the next set of four principles, to help you identify the nature of fear and negativity; how they play out in our lives on daily basis, and how to get rid of them. At some point, I will bring in what I refer to as, *'the spirit of the overcomer';* discussing the character required to make a difference in a world of fear and negativity.

Understandably, these principles might not initially be easy to put to everyday practice all at once. But, they are achievable because of their crucial and indispensable benefits for addressing the spirit and the bitter roots of suspicion, and their effects, which usually deny people of God's best life and opportunities.

You don't have to live under the *spell* of suspicion, or become hemmed in by the spirit of fear and negativity. You're a *spell breaker*, and God has given you the *spirit* of power, love and sound mind (2 Timothy 1:7), by which you can defy, reverse and defeat the grinding forces of fear and negativity. To ensure your continuous victory, try following these basic practical scriptural ways of life and living:

1. *Put into Practice, 'Rejoicing always, I say Rejoice!'*

Two times, in two separate letters, to two different churches in major cities in the Bible, Paul enjoins his friends to rejoice. They must rejoice and always rejoice. He says to the Philippians, "Rejoice in the Lord always. Again I will say, rejoice!" (Phil. 4:4) Also, to the Thessalonians, he says "Rejoice always". (1Thesa. 5:16) The way out of harmful emotions of envy, jealousy, and other unhelpful thoughts that spiral into suspicion, is to rejoice always when others succeed or seem to succeed. In addition, the Bible offers these clear instructions:

> *Rejoice with those who rejoice, and weep with those who weep.* [16] *Be of the same mind toward one another. Do not set your mind on high things, but associate with the humble. Do not be wise in your own opinion.* [17] *Repay no one evil for evil. Have regard for good things in the sight of all men.* [18] *If it is possible, as much as depends on you, live peaceably with all men (Romans 12:18).*
>
> *Let each of you look out not only for his own interests, but also for the interests of others (Philippians 2:4).*

2. *Put into Practice, this truth: 'You were built for happiness, and learn to be content.'*

To put it more plainly, I would say to you that, the human heart is purpose built for happiness. Therefore, anything less than happiness runs against God's original intention for our lives with detrimental consequences (Proverb 12:25). Let me stress here that the happiness I am referring to is not the same as fleshly indulgence or what some hope to derive from sinful lifestyle. I am referring to true happiness that leads from 'godliness with content', which Paul calls 'a great gain' (1Tim. 6:6).

> *Not that I speak in regard to need, for I have learned in whatever state I am, to be content (Philippians 4:11).*

> *Beloved, I pray that you may prosper in all things and be in health, just as your soul prospers (3 John 2).* What the verse is saying in essence is, may the condition of your life be like that of your soul when you received Christ – renewed, new, saved, and made entirely whole.

> *For I know the thoughts that I think toward you, says the Lord, thoughts of peace and not of evil, to give you a future and a hope (Jeremiah 29:11).*

However, many find their immediate and surrounding communities and associations probably too negative to be able to cope. In some cases many things that surround them tend to bear stains and tags of negativity. Unfortunately, the present state of things tends to work favourably for some politicians, press organizations, and insurance companies. Because, for the sake of gaining votes and making money they can easily capitalize on people's propensity to be found incurably negative and to promote negative views of life. But you have a choice. Choose differently, and practice the truth that you were literally built for happiness!

3. *Put into Practice, this truth: 'God holds a different view of you and your life.'*

God does not want us to live with fear; that things might go horribly wrong with our marriages, our children, our homes, the weather, our jobs, cars, or relatives, just to name a few. For *"the blessing of the Lord makes one rich, and He adds no sorrow with it"* (Prov. 10:22). *"I know that whatever God does, It shall be forever"* (Eccles. 3:14). *"The Lord knows the days of the upright, and their inheritance shall be forever"* (Psalm 37:18).

Similarly, God does not want you living your entire life saving for so-called 'rainy days' – you should be saving for having nice days! God believes in the good things He has placed in you. A lot more people believe in you than those who do not believe in you, or would stand against you (2 Kings 6:16). You were 'fearfully and wonderfully made' (Psalm 139:14), and you are *'God's special work, created in Christ Jesus for good works, which God prepared beforehand that we should walk in them'* (Ephesians 2:10).

4. *Put into Practice, 'Resisting suggestions from the devil'.*

The devil is so cunning that he will take advantage of you if all you think about all day is the fear that something terrible looms over you. For *"the thief does not come except to steal, and to kill, and to destroy…"* (John 10:10). In line with this truth;

> *Therefore submit to God. Resist the devil and he will flee from you (James 4:7). Therefore humble yourselves under the mighty hand of God, that He may exalt you in due time, casting all your care upon Him, for He cares for you. Be sober, be vigilant; because your adversary the devil walks about like a roaring lion, seeking whom he may devour. Resist him, steadfast in the faith, knowing that the same sufferings are experienced by your brotherhood in the world (1Peter 5:7-9).*

The Poisoning Power of Negativity

The crafty schemes and works of Satan remind me of an interesting childhood story about a sly vulture and a feeble cow. Interestingly, it is believed that, from afar, vultures have the ability to sense the hand of death over its unsuspecting victim. Vultures, knowing that any cow that dies provides them with a good feed for a long haul, locate and target a weak and sickly looking cow.

The vultures obviously have no real physical power to kill a cow, but they need the cow to die in order to provide meat for them. What do they then do? One of them comes sneakily and perches on the neck, and close to the ear of a cow it has located among the herds. The vulture then will begin to speak into the ear of the cow, saying, 'do you know you are dying?'

Initially the cow might ignore the enticement of the vulture, but the vulture will persist, 'whispering' into the ear of the cow about its imminent death. After a few more reminders, the cow will begin to deteriorate from bad to worse, and the vulture will chirp again, and again into the cow's ear; 'you are now dead'. With this, the cow's situation deteriorates from being worse to where the cow actually succumbs to death.

What is the moral of the story? It is simply this; that *what you keep hearing you will soon believe, and what you believe you will soon become.* Hence, watch what you are hearing, for it is either inspiring life or subtly brewing death, to which you will soon succumb. Drive away every 'vulture', and resist any voice or chirps of 'vultures' as soon as you hear it.

Personally, I would avoid the company of negative people who fail to recognise that morning comes after the night. I choose to believe that the sun will rise, come what may! It finally rose for Paul and his colleagues during their times of great difficulties at sea, after many days without sunlight. So, it will rise for you no matter how long it takes (see Acts 27:18-26). My wife and I agreed we will do our best to believe and to speak only what lines up with the Word of God. If we find ourselves *eating* other people's words or the devil's suggestions, which are contrary to God's perfect will for our lives, it is our responsibility to quickly identify our mistake, and to immediately shake off such words along with their effect.

Against all Odds - Trying for a Child (Our Story)

We had a very trying and difficult situation, early in our marriage, regarding health issues that potentially threatened my wife's life and any possibility of having our own children. Because of the urgency of the matter, we were referred for specialist advice and subsequent surgical procedure. The report from the surgeon was purely negative, although in all fairness he was concerned. He *overloaded* us with a good dosage of bad news, trying to remain 'professional', without giving us 'false-hope' about our concerns at the time. He almost succeeded in instigating and instilling real fear into us.

He was so determined that he discounted, and did not even give an inch of credit to any other suggestions, apart from what he thought was the way forward. He even insisted at the time that, if he thought we would not return for our appointment with him on a certain date, then he would perform the surgical procedure immediately.

Of course, that played on our minds terribly, because we had thought of other solutions well outside of the doctor's procedure, which he himself admitted had an uncertain outcome for our desire to have children. We wanted to settle for something less traumatic, less invasive, and also still preserve normal biological means of making our own family.

Like most couples, by the grace of God, from the first day of our marriage, we were looking forward to raising a wonderful family. But, our surgeon could not promise us, except that he knew his advice was very urgent in order to prevent a potentially worse situation. Well, we listened, but decided to think and to trust God for the best outcome. We chose differently; to trust and to believe the Word of God. That come what may, we will live in good health and still have and see not only our children, but also our children's children.

We came home and quickly debunked all that the doctor said, and consciously took time to re-interpret most of what he told us, to align with God's Word. I tried to convince my wife that, that 'young man' although genuinely concerned, he was nervous and basically spoke from the position of fear. I said 'believe me, they can be so nervous at times that they say anything, especially when they hear anything in relation to cancer. Let's trust God.' After a time of prayer for healing and some talking things over, we agreed to allow the surgical procedure as God's means for physically finalizing my wife's healing, which we believed had been spiritually settled in prayer by the grace of our Lord Jesus Christ.

Remember 2Corinthians 8:9 says, *"for you know the grace of our Lord Jesus Christ, that though He was rich, yet for your sakes He became poor, that you through His poverty might become rich."* That included our healings also, and Christ has already paid for our healings, my friend! We have to receive it and, in receiving, He provides the means and conduit. Sometimes, it might be through medical processes which He still provides and steers for the desired outcome.

We agreed to the surgical procedure, however, we made up our minds that it is never God's will for us not to have children. So, we refused the doctor's report on that count and looked to God for the gifts of children, despite the medical science report. Surely, we do not always have to accept man's verdict, especially, if it is negative.

Even with the procedure we chose to expect a good and favourable result, and not to be afraid or fearful that things might go wrong. We went in, having faith that 'all things work together for good', seeing God's superintending hands in all that was taking place. And if there were any immediate lessons we learned from our experience, it was that, *sometimes to experience God's miracle, God will allow you to get to a place from where you have no other alternatives but to look to Him alone.*

Of course, contrary to all the worst fears and scenarios initially drawn out for us, the Almighty God glorified His Name by giving my wife an almost painless healing. The surgical procedure went very well, without any complications. After that, we now had to continue to trust God for the blessing of children through normal biological process, as He designed it from the beginning.

Despite the medical odds that the procedure might stop us from having children, we still trusted God. It took a few years of waiting, and persisting; sometimes very challenging, especially in our contexts as *'faith preaching and miracle believing'* pastors. But God was faithful.

During those very challenging days we chose to simply trust God, and one of the key scriptural passages we held onto was Psalms 128, which emphatically says,

> *Blessed is every one who fears the Lord, who walks in His ways.*
> *² When you eat the labor of your hands, you shall be happy, and it shall be well with you. ³ Your wife shall be like a fruitful vine in the very heart of your house, your children like olive plants all around your table. ⁴ Behold, thus shall the man be blessed who fears the Lord. ⁵ The Lord bless you out of Zion, and may you see the good of Jerusalem all the days of your life. ⁶ Yes, may you see your children's children. Peace be upon Israel!*

Glory to God! I can certainly say to you God's report is always better and will always supersede any other report which proceeds, or comes after it. After five 'interesting' years of waiting on the Lord in faith, I am glad to say God is faithful, and by His kind mercies and grace we now have our first son, Malachi, named to the glory of God.

By the way, just in case you are wondering why I described our years of waiting as 'interesting', let me add that waiting on the Lord in faith is not always easy, but it was the best thing to do in our case. Undoubtedly, there were some who took us for 'fools' for trusting in God alone. Also, sometimes, as human beings, other ideas crossed our minds, but we still held on to our belief that one day, and at the right time, God will be gracious in satisfying our desire for children.

God has never failed anyone and He will certainly not fail you if you decide to put your complete trust in Him, even in the face of contradicting evidence. He is the Lord! And, my friend, God must always have the final word in and over your life and circumstances, not men, no matter their status in life. *"Let God be true and all other be liars"* (Romans 3:4).

In hindsight, I can truly say that our experience has helped our walk with God and the lessons learned were, and are still, invaluable. Wait on God, do not fear and He will show up for you, my friend. It doesn't matter what your particular case may be; God loves you and He will not permit you to be made ashamed (Isaiah 49:23).

Being Negative and fearful can be Costly

In the book of Numbers, specifically chapters thirteen and fourteen, we have a brilliant story, in which fear and negativity had great a role to play in what resulted in a terrible outcome for an entire nation of people. Twelve capable men of Israel, chosen from amongst their compatriots, were sent on recognisance, hoping to bring back good news from the place they set out to spy. Unfortunately, ten of the twelve men rather returned with a disturbing and disappointing, negative report, which melted the hearts of all who were expecting them to return with great news of super success.

Immediately, the entire camp of Israel was in uproar, and straight away decided to back down from their original goal of going in, to take possession of the Promised Land, which their God had faithfully promised to them. They fell back onto their own 'plan B'; to return to the wilderness and Egypt, the land of their captivity and suffering. In the end, their fear and negativity grossly cost them the promise and favour of God, and finally their lives; except for two men.

The ten men who brought the bad news, in my view represent a large proportion of people in this world today. These are men and women, who, unfortunately, seem to be plagued by fear and negativity; always expecting something to go wrong. Equally, their entire existence and livelihood tend to be crippled by a, *'I cannot mentality'*. Of most concern, is their ability to unsuspectingly draw and influence a lot of other people, to buy into their way of thinking. They know how to recruit others for their 'army of fearful and resigned band'.

Within the church, such people are the *'nay-sayers'*, so negative, but at the same time wielding such influence over a good number of church members, who tend to come on their side. You will always find them, if nowhere at all, on the deacon board or elder board of the church, usually opposing pastors and the church's vision, because of their own insecurity arising from their fear and negativity filled mind.

Dealing with Controlling Fear and Crippling Negativity

To break free from fear, negativity and their attendant effects, first and foremost, I will assume that you are a Christian who relies on the Spirit of Christ; *"for God has not given us a spirit of fear, but of power and of love and of a sound mind (2 Timothy 1:7)*. Secondly, you will need to avoid the four unmistakable P's, of what I call *crutches*, for victim thinking mentality. Avoiding them will put the spark back into your life and give you some good degree of control. It will positively affect how your day turns out, and will positively impact on your desire for every day victory in areas of your relationship, family, workplace, career, studies, and other worthy areas of life.

These four P's are the ways in which we explain to ourselves what has happened, what's happening and ultimately what will happen as a result of our encounters, transactions, experiences, choices and challenges. They are generally a mindset, worldview or a certain way of thinking or seeing the things that we encounter, and also could be situations that we are involved with almost on a daily basis. They serve as lenses through which we view our own lives, or just life in general. Most importantly, they include the way in which many interpret life and circumstances when trying to make sense of them, and also the means by which people try to provide themselves with a stable niche in a world of constant change.

The four P's represent and culminate into basic assumptions that we make as we go through life, especially when bad things happen or when we encounter difficulties. Identifying and mastering these basic assumptions is incredibly important, because the way we see things makes all the difference. This is profoundly demonstrated by the situation in which Jesus administered healing to a blind man in the book of Mark. After he had a healing touch from the Lord, the blind man was asked if he saw anything. He then answered, yes but *"I see men like trees, walking"* (Mark 8:24).

Depending on how we see it or interpret it, obviously, the blind man's response could have engendered another debate, or even posed a genuine problem, which could have easily led to other sets of problems, possibly to include his treating and avoiding of 'men like trees' along his path. The blind man's peculiar situation educed his great need for a second touch from the Lord's hand for a perfect sight; if he had to see things the way they really appear, to help him relate to them appropriately. This 'blind man' scenario, ironically represent both the problem and the solution, in view of the *crutches* for victim thinking mentality, which is normally induced by crippling negativity and controlling fears.

The Four Costly P's to Avoid

1. *The first 'P' is Pontificating* – People in this category tend to think and believe that they and their challenges are so peculiar, special and isolated, and nothing else compares. In such cases, the person brings themselves to believe, and also wants others to believe, that their present experience or challenge is *god*-given and outside human scope. Even if they thought their experience were human, they intend to set it above all that is common to other humans.

The Scripture that says; *"no temptation has overtaken you except such as is common to man; but God is faithful, who will not allow you to be tempted beyond what you are able, but with the temptation will also make the way of escape, that you may be able to bear it"* (1Cor. 10:13), hardly works or makes 'enough' sense to a *pontificator*. Passages like that, are always for 'other' people but not for them. A common sign of *Pontificating* is found in expressions like, *I understand, but I...* or, *but in my case....*

2. *The second 'P' is Pervasiveness* – people in this category use one bad experience to make a general statement about life. I call them the *Bad Scientists of Doom*, and in my view they are borderline or moderate fatalists. They are most likely to say, 'this is how things are – and everything for them is by and large bad and terrible'. And things are normally defined in black and white terms. For example, if one person of the entire species called *Man* disappointed them, they will invariably reach a grim conclusion about all men. They have no

trouble saying, "All men are bad", just because one chap jilted them. In other instances, just because they suffer one or two setbacks in life, they might conclude that life is unfair and not worth living.

People affected by *pervasiveness* tend to perceive all of life through a very narrow tunnel or an opaque pair of lenses called, '*I can't help it; that's just the way I am and that's just the way life is*!' They can't help but transfer one horrible experience to other areas of life. For example, when they fail in school, they claim they fail in all of life, something that might result in a domino effect on other important areas of their lives, including marriage, business, and the rest.

The way this works is so subtle that you don't even know that it's happening, or that you are using the principle of *pervasiveness* to judge life, others and to interpret your experiences. From our story involving the twelve spies from Israel, although they saw giants in a select area of the Promised Land, upon their return, ten of them immediately concluded that the entire "*land was full of giants and devours its inhabitants*" (vr. 32). How they interpreted to themselves the whole situation regarding the land was with a total sense of *pervasiveness*: "*the land is terrible and we are not able to conquer, or to take and possess it.*"

People who look at things from a *pervasive* point of view usually resign in the face of challenge and consider themselves, '*Victims of Circumstances*' – things always happen to them because they are never in control. Psychologists say that people in this category are people prone to *catastrophizing*, and they are *catastrophizers*. This kind of *catastrophizing* shows up even in their attitude towards saving. They normally addictively save and put monies aside for so-called 'rainy days', because no one knows tomorrow. They have insurance policies for their cats, dogs, roof, car, kidneys, life, and you name it.

My experience while working in the financial services showed me that many remain trapped in this way of thinking – saving or doing things for so-called 'rainy days'. They live constantly thinking and expecting bad things to happen, probably based on past failures; theirs and other people's bad experiences, which they use as reference for their expectations and conclusions.

Hence, most insurance and financial services specialists know now that this is a good tool to use in marketing their products. That is why nowadays, for a monthly charge, banks include with their normal current accounts benefits to cover their customers for 'rainy day' occurrences that might never come. But, customers pay for them religiously, thinking, 'who knows tomorrow... what if...?' Even salesmen, in offering their products, have learned to convince their customers to buy their 'rainy day' products by citing horrible past experiences (true or untrue) of incidences which their 'rainy day' product might cover, suggesting 'it could be you'.

Millicent Maybe – the Chronic 'Pervasifyer' and Catastrophizer

Growing up I read a story called '*Millicent Maybe*' as part of my early reading requirements in grade school. Since I have now lived in the West for a good part of my life, and have also experienced the weather pattern, on a light note, I can safely say without an iota of doubt that the setting of '*Millicent Maybe*' was England. Interestingly, I was schooled in West Africa, however most of the books we had to use for our literature lessons in elementary school were titles like, '*England in Literature*'.

Well, the point of the story was that, 'Millicent Maybe', the main character, acted exactly like her name, never certain or sure of anything. Everything was approached or welcomed with 'maybe' and she therefore took every necessary and unnecessary step in case of any eventualities. She was always unsure of how the seconds, minutes, and hours of her day might turnout. And, being the overly conscious, overly anxious person she was, she always wanted to be prepared for what might happen, and never to be taken by surprise.

So, when she planned to visit the supermarket, Millicent starts first with wondering, maybe it might rain, maybe it might not – maybe the sun will shine, maybe not. And she went on and on, spending endless hours trying to anticipate every possible situation before venturing out of her home. Then, she tried to dress according to what she anticipated might happen during that day. For example, she took a rain coat and an umbrella because *maybe it will rain, maybe the sun will shine.*

When she thought maybe it will snow, Millicent also took her Wellington boots in addition to her umbrella and rain coat. Millicent could go on and on until she could go out no more. If she did go, she was all dressed up for all eventualities in one day. She was a little like the popular comedic character, Mr Bean! Well, 'Millicent Maybe' is definitely a big *'catastrophizer'!* Watch her and don't copy her ways. (cf Proverbs 22:24-25; Proverbs 3:29-31)

Unfortunately, it is believed that people who fall into this category of *pervasiveness* have a short life span because obviously they live all their life worrying about everything, good or bad. They are burdensome to be with and without doubt are some of life's major 'burden bearers', who also end up as chronic worriers. They will certainly worry about whether the day will follow the night, which under normal circumstance should be an unlikely thing for anyone to think about.

With *pervasiveness* comes a dreadful feeling of helplessness, and an unhelpful *'I can't help it'* attitude to life. Such people are most likely to get depressed, paranoiac and to feel isolated and alone. Any real sense of happiness is short lived, and need constant encouragement.

Some good Bible examples with *pervasiveness* tendencies include: (a) The 'Invalid' at the pool of Bethesda, who, in reply to Jesus' question about whether he would like to be healed, chose rather to show himself as a victim saying, *'Sir, I have no one… (John 5:7).*

(b) Also Elijah, the prophet, wailed in despair to God, electing to be a victim by *'catastrophize-ing'* saying, *"I have been very zealous for the Lord God of hosts; for the children of Israel have forsaken Your covenant, torn down Your altars, and killed Your prophets with the sword. I alone am left; and they seek to take my life." (1King 19:10)* Elijah, now the wearied prophet, repeats again exactly the same words in complaining to God about his unfair treatment in verse fourteen of the same chapter, and this time God would not allow him to continue in his 'sorrowful state'. So, the Lord replied to Elijah,

> *"Go, return on your way to the Wilderness of Damascus; and when you arrive, anoint Hazael… anoint Jehu … and Elisha the son of Shaphat of Abel Meholah you shall anoint as prophet in your place. ¹⁷ It shall be that whoever escapes the sword of Hazael, Jehu will kill; and whoever escapes the sword of Jehu, Elisha will kill. ¹⁸ Yet I have reserved seven thousand in Israel, all whose knees have not bowed to Baal, and every mouth that has not kissed him" (1Kings 19:15-18).*

This is typical of *catastrophizer*. They exaggerate and dramatize for special effect, and they mostly feel like *'they have no one'* and *'they are alone'* in this world, trying all by themselves, to struggle things out on their own. Unfortunately, most of what they feel and think about the *'island'* phenomenon is what they only perceive things to be but, in reality, things are not so horrible as they think or imagine.

3. *The third 'P' is Permanence* – This group of people belong to a category I call *'the Impossible people.'* They normally speak in terms of intransigence or obduracy. Things and situations appear to be and are in fact set in solid concrete. Numbers 13:31- *"we are not able" (they speak in absolute terms like can't…there's no way I can…).* They believe that anything negative will remain a permanent feature of their life.

They fail to realize that the only thing that is permanent on earth is *change*. Yes, that's the only thing that is permanent, *change*.

An overwhelming sense of hopelessness does tend to dominate and pervade the world of people affected by, and subject to, *Permanence*. While those suffering from *Pervasiveness* worry if morning will follow the night, those affected by *Permanence* say there will be no morning after the night, because it has not happened and it's somewhat alien to what they are familiar with.

Obviously, this kind of thinking and attitude contravene Scriptures, especially Proverbs 30:5; that *"weeping may endure for a night, but joy comes in the morning."* For example, when people affected by *Permanence* unfortunately experience one set back, through divorce, failure in school, loss of job, or bereavement of a relative, or when sudden sickness comes upon them, that's it! They resign, throw their hands in the air and say things like '*I am going to die, this thing is going to kill me – no need to keep living. No man will marry me again because 'Judas' left!*' As a result, they refuse to see any 'light at the end of the tunnel'.

One distinctive hallmark of people who think in permanent terms manifests in them choosing a name, changing their name, or naming their pets, or even their children, to capture and to permanently reflect, engrave, and remind them of their bad experience. For example, J. *Broke-man*, J. *Hard-Times*, or T. *Sickly*, Miss *Car-Crash*, and so forth (NB: *these names were made up for illustrative purposes and do not reflect any true person I know*).

A perfect example of scenarios of *Permanence* is found in the book of Ruth in the Old Testament. We have in that book a story of an unfortunate tragedy involving the loss of two sons and their father. Naomi, the surviving mother and widow of the family, changed her true name to reflect and to engrave her agony.

Naomi, her name which originally meant *'happiness'*, was changed to reflect her new situation, brought about through the death of her husband and sons. Her name was changed to *'Marai'*, meaning *'bitterness'*, in order to capture and reveal what she now thought to be her permanent destiny. Naomi, who could not see any real solace beyond her immediate problem, turned *bitter*, and to make her experience permanent, the name *'bitterness'* instead of *'happiness'* was chosen, somehow suggesting that was her new identity.

Another typical example involving the use of *permanence* regards Rachel, the wife of Jacob, in Genesis 35:18 in which she named her second son *Ben-Oni*, meaning 'son of my sorrow,' in order to permanently engrave her awful birth pang and difficulties, which eventually lead to her tragic death. Incidentally, Jacob wisely changed his son's name to *Benjamin*, meaning 'son of my right hand', and adverted a potential self-fulfilling prophecy that his original name could have brought about.

4. The Fourth 'P' is Personalizing – This category is similar to *Pontificating*, but the subtle difference here is that, with *Personalizing*, the person really turns on themselves. Talk about self-blame, this group of people take it way too far. They internalise and blame themselves for everything that happens to them or others, no matter the circumstance. I call them *'reckless burden-bearers'*.

People under this category usually overcompensate and do not know when to stop. However, they usually, on the outside disguise themselves under a *'nice nature'*, *'people's person'* personalities, but usually when alone, they look *sombre*, mainly because of their self-analyzing, self-critical activity. For lack of better description, I would say, *'they get lost in themselves'* especially when alone. They normally seek to make everyone think well of them and in the process they may get hurt, disappointed and even depressed, if they think they did not live up to certain expectations.

If you want to know their specialty, it is so easy. In all sincerity people affected by *Personalizing* believe that they are saving the situation by blaming it all on themselves, and so make fools of themselves in the end, but also regret that it happened. One can literally see and tell a person bound by *Personalizing* because it shows in their *'blues'*, and *'mood swings'*, which they often masquerade by overreaching themselves.

A regular character trait that is common to this category is definitely *melancholy*, or a facial expression of a *'deep thinker'*. Such people say things like, *'it's entirely my fault. ...I am only unfortunate, and a person of bad luck. ... I am cursed, they say. I'm used to it, nothing good happens to me....'* For a typical example, when a relationship goes sour, they claim it's because of them.

Grasshoppers Mentality: A Trait of Personalizing

Again, part of our story about the spies sent from Israel hints and describes in a great way what those belonging to the category of *personalizing* would look like. We see *Personalizing* in what I refer to as the *'grasshoppers mentality'*, which shies away from confronting the real situation. Listening to the ten spies who brought back a negative report, they concluded, as part of their overall assessment of the land they had gone to spy, that "*...we were like grasshoppers... If only we had died in Egypt*" (Numbers 13: 33 and 14:1-4). They were in effect saying, "it's all our fault because we listened to, Moses. We should have known better".

The difficulties with this kind of thinking and way of solving problems is that, this approach do not alleviate the actual problems, you only tend to lose the battle in the face of unwavering challenges. It drains all your energy, diminishes your personal confidence and you wake up the next day and the problem is still there.

I will never forget an object lesson the Lord taught me when I had difficult times with one of the prominent universities in England. I found myself in a *catch-twenty-two* situation with tuition fees. Embarrassed because I was unable to continue my studies and also unable to save the situation, I became intimidated when I came across my professors, or university staff who knew me. Soon, it seemed to me that those concerned, particularly, one professor, along with a university credit officer were beginning to enjoy the situation. I began to walk through town very scared and mindful of *'what if…!'* But, on this particular day, as I walked down the street, guided on both sides by high metal street railings, a sudden fear took over me. I became fearful of meeting those who had already caused me a lot of anxieties and worries, in spite of my best effort.

In no time I heard in my spirit, *"Didi - face your enemy!"* I interpreted this to mean, *'face your fear, stop blaming yourself, stop allowing yourself to be frozen because of others, after all you didn't create the situation.'* Until then, I had always blamed myself and exonerated others, saying well, *'it's my education and that's my responsibility no matter what happened.'* This kind of statement and thinking is commonly accepted as a sign of being a conscious and responsible person, but I beg to differ, especially when it borders on, or even becomes a symptom of *personalizing*.

Well, I listened to what I heard in my spirit, and kept going forward along the road. As if someone were encountering *fate* that day, a few minutes later, I came face to face with what I dreaded. Here was the main person I had not wished to see, coming in front of me. And, I heard again, *"face your 'enemy"!* – my enemy, not in terms of the actual person I met, but the mortifying *fear* that had for a long time, robbed me of my self respect and happiness. Sure enough I did and broke the back of fear and intimidation that afternoon.

Who was my *enemy*? Obviously not the professor or credit controller. It was the fear of facing my perceived embarrassment, and of course the *fear of man*. Now, I know so well that's exactly how to handle the enemy called *Personalizing*. Face it no matter how scary it seems, and deal with it, and God will give you the grace to overcome.

The Spirit of the Overcomer

If we take a much closer look at the attitude of two of the twelve spies, we will be able to derive important principles for approaching life's many challenges and adversities. The two, Caleb and Joshua, managed to distinguish themselves from the rest of the spies. They proved that, if one can properly position themselves and put their problems in proper perspective, there will be no need to melt in fear or negativity, before any challenge or an 'enemy'.

What did Caleb and Joshua know about winning over negativity, fear, intimidation, and threat to life? How were they able to maintain their peace in the face of life's adversities and challenges, while others went on uncontrollably?

1. First, in the book of Numbers 13:30, Caleb and Joshua told themselves and others, "we are well able" – What a disposition! Some may call it positive mental attitude. It is the power of faith. They stilled their fellow Israelites and asked them to look away from themselves and up to God Almighty, who promised to give them the land of Canaan. Caleb and Joshua teach us that seeing things from God's point of view is more important than the challenge that you face. Remember, it is said "only obstacles bring miracles, and only trials bring triumph."

Our Faith and Our Confession

Caleb and Joshua's choice, to trust in God in spite of daunting challenges, is not exclusively limited to them; however, the calibre of their trust or faith is surely uncommon for many when face with the same pressure or circumstance.

Such a quality of faith is replicated elsewhere in Scriptures, including the life of the Shunamite woman, when her only child suddenly died. Despite the death of her son, with all its attendant anxieties and worries, she kept a positive attitude; confessing that, *'all is well'* to those who cared to ask. Guess what? She received her child back alive from the dead. Death could not hold her only son captive, and death lost the battle for her son. Her faith in God Almighty to resurrect her only son, through the hand of the Prophet Elisha, paid off fully.

> *...Death is swallowed up in victory."[55] " O Death, where is your sting? O Hades, where is your victory?"[56] The sting of death is sin, and the strength of sin is the law. [57] But thanks be to God, who gives us the victory through our Lord Jesus Christ. (I Corinthians 15:54-56).*

Consider the following text and you will find out exactly why the *process* and *instrument* of death called fear, and death itself hold, great sway over some people, and also defeat so many others.

> *... for whatever is not from faith is sin (Romans 14:23).*

Sounds almost inconsequential, but there you have it. The lack of faith, or not acting from the position of faith might look like a trivial thing to do. But, when it comes to exercising our authority in Christ for tangible results, irrespective of the magnitude of the situation, it has got to be by faith (Heb. 11:6). The Shunamite woman, like Joshua and Caleb, knew exactly what to do. She knew to stand in faith only, and not to doubt or fear because only faith has the power over all that is in this world, including death (1 John 5:4). So, keep your disposition of faith, and maintain your confession of faith, and you will overcome, even when death threatens you.

> For whatever is born of God overcomes the world. And this is the victory that has overcome the world - our faith (1John 5:4).

Unfortunately, *death* thrives on doubt and sin, which belong to the Law (of Moses). Of course, doubt is sin. But faith is not of doubt or sin. Faith is of God and not of the Law. Hence faith belongs to a higher order. Faith comes from above and there is no law against faith (cf Romans 14:23). So, they who exercise their lives by faith, and live by faith, always overcome the world, including all the mundane principles that dominate our universe, and then obtain good testimonies because of their faith (Hebrews 11:2, 39). That's why by faith the dead are raised, and by faith Josiah commanded the sun to stand still. Faith is greater. Faith will move mountains, and faith will change the circumstances, and *"the just shall live by his faith"* (Romans 1:17; Habakkuk 2:4).

Equally so, our confession has huge bearing on the outcome of our situation, and on our life. It certainly is a prophecy of the future, and our present life, in many ways, is the sum total of our confession made in the past. *Our life literally catches up with the confession of our mouth.* In addition, when we become helpless slaves of our feelings, allowing them to dictate to us, we get exactly what we fear (Job 3:25).

It is very dangerous to allow your feelings alone to dictate how you respond to the challenges and opportunities of life. Therefore, when we listen to Caleb and Joshua, they are not only thinking possibilities, but speaking and confessing what they believe, by faith, is possible. They announced to their colleagues, *hey,* "we are well able to take the Land", thereby maintaining a good confession in line with their faith.

2. The second thing Caleb and Joshua knew was to choose their response carefully. In Numbers 14:8, we find that they did not base their response on what they physically saw, heard or felt. On the contrary, they responded in faith saying "if God delights in us...", – that means, the favour of God, like wisdom is more

than ten thousand giants and better than the weapons of war (Ecclesiastes 9:18). And, of course, the weapons of our warfare will always be mighty only through God for the pulling down of every stronghold (2 Corinthians 10:4; cf Jeremiah 21:4).

Let me quote verses 8 and 9 of Numbers 14 in their entirety. Hopefully, they might help you to appreciate the dynamics of faith versus fear, and why it is crucial to choose one's response so carefully.

> *If the Lord delights in us, then He will bring us into this land and give it to us, 'a land which flows with milk and honey." Only do not rebel against the Lord, nor fear the people of the land, for they are our bread; their protection has departed from them, and the Lord is with us. Do not fear them" (Numbers 14:8-9).*

Faith Speaks

Faith says, that *'with* God all things are possible'. Notice it is *'with'* God. It is the same as saying *'if* God delights in us.' This doesn't suggest that Caleb and Joshua are now figuring out whether God will delight in them as a condition for their victory. It is rather a statement of fact, asserting their claim on God and His promises. It is like saying, "if God is for us, who can be against us" (Romans 8:31), which presupposes that God is already for us, and therefore it doesn't matter who comes against us. As long as God is on our side, which is the main thing, nothing shall be impossible. You don't need to fear when you are going *'with'* God or facing your challenge together *'with'* God. He *delights* in you, He is *for* you and not *against you;* therefore, He shall grant you your heart desire.

Sadly, many get stuck at debating about God's will, but the truth is, if *you are 'outside' of His will, you are definitely 'out' of His will.* And, if you are not 'included' in God's will, you are out of His will. For we know certainly that, "*But of Him you are in Christ Jesus, who became* for us wisdom from God—and righteousness and sanctification and redemption—that, as it is written, "He who glories, let him glory in the Lord." (1 Cor. 1:30-31)

Therefore, as part of the revealed wisdom of God's will for His children, *you have got nothing to claim which has not first been willed to you!* The point is, if God *delights* in you, then you must have first been right there in His will. Otherwise, how can He *delight* in you in the first place? That's why Caleb and Joshua, speaking by faith knew not to fear but to plead their victory on the basis of God delighting in them, accepting that they were already in His will.

Faith says do not rebel against the Lord; fear says rebel because things don't feel right nor look good. Fear will push you to doubt God and keep your eyes on what is not possible, but faith says go past your fear, looking away from yourself and the situation, but up to God Almighty.

Faith says God is with us; fear says I am not sure God is with us or with me. If God is not with us, then it becomes impossible for us to overcome. But that's exactly what fear wants us to believe. Thank God that 'He has not given us the spirit of fear but of power and of love and of a sound mind' (2 Timothy 1:7).

Faith says do not fear them; fear says you are better off fearing them. Faith says take charge; but fear says be careful. Hear what Paul admonishes people of faith: *"Be careful for nothing; but in every thing by prayer and supplication with thanksgiving let your requests be made known unto God"* (Philippians 4:6).

The Nature of the Spirit of the Overcomer

Reflected in all the points we have discussed above is the fact that Caleb and Joshua, two of the twelve spies from Israel, had the *spirit of the overcomer*. And such spirit expresses itself in a calm, controlled manner, and makes the wise choice to choose faith over fear. Choosing and exerting a response in the midst of their challenges that reflects the quality of their faith in God.

Caleb and Joshua knew that, as God's people, they belonged to God and served Him. Hence it was God's responsibility and it was in God's power to look after them at all times. This is exactly what apostle Paul knew; not to fear that the sea and wave will destroy him, but on the contrary, that the God to whom he *belonged* and *served* (another expression for God delights in me) would save him as He determined (Acts 27:23-25).

Caleb and Joshua knew that, in all things, at all times the only *permanence* is change and God, who can change any unpleasant situation, delighted in them. Such will always be the grace of God to those who will not give up, but trust in the everlasting arm of the Lord God. That in the times of their need, no matter the situation, He will definitely come to their rescue. Our God is always Almighty, and remember;

> *Every word of God is pure; He is a shield to those who put their trust in Him (Proverbs 30:5). And He changes the times and the seasons; He removes kings and raises up kings; He gives wisdom to the wise And knowledge to those who have understanding (Daniel 2:21).*

Chapter Twelve

THE TRANSFORMER: HELP TO RISE AND POWER FOR CHANGE AND GREATNESS

In Acts chapter three, we are welcomed to a dramatic scene, involving a special miracle of God. It happens to be the very first recording of a physical miracle that was done by the apostles, through the power of God, after the ascension of the Lord Jesus Christ. The miracle was so remarkable, that it caused an instant change in the receiver, and began a spiritual revival among a people who had dire need for one.

The miracle, by itself was a wonderful demonstration of God's ability and man's inability. It showed how the supernatural is possible even within natural spheres. It was about the power of grace to transform life, and how God uses our circumstances to reveal His power and love, even for those who do not trust and believe in Him. Also, the miracle was indeed, God's public statement about how He saves and takes what man neglects, to do with them great things.

This chapter will begin with a little background about the one who directly received the miracle; a man who was born lame from his mother's womb. He was carried and daily laid at the gate of the temple, which is called Beautiful. Now, before digging into the story, I would like, to first of all, consider a few things that are noteworthy, as insights from the actual message of the story.

First, the lame man's issues which were as a result of his paralysis, started right from the time of his birth. Similarly, there are many in our world today, who also suffer issues that would not go away, and their issues seem to perpetually outlast their due course.

Secondly, the lame man had to sadly endure the pain and reproach of his paralysis on daily basis. This suggests that some issues would present themselves for a daily fight, intending to take over one's lives.

Thirdly, he was laid at the *gate*; meaning his paralysis and issues were made public. Well, it's one thing to be paralysed, but it's also another thing to make it public. Because, some obviously can cope with the pains of their paralysis, but not the publicising of it.

Let's face it, everybody has some form of 'paralysis', but most of us, if we can, will spend a good portion of our income and lifetime, trying very hard to dress it up. This is solely to help us cope. Unfortunately, there may be some, including few in the cosmetic industry, who view our effort to hide 'paralysis' as a ready opportunity for their profit.

Nonetheless, the lame man, about whom we are concerned, had his paralysis exposed to the public, and became a public spectacle. Imagine that, he was perhaps, not considered very much, and was reduced to a mere beggar, due to heartless cultural practices of so-called family honour, and religious 'elitism', which discriminated against people with certain paralyses. Or perhaps, due to hardship, he was ostracised as a burden by his encumbered relatives and family.

Of course, thinking about the lame man's situation in the way I have, is not too farfetched, given the culture in which he lived. Even now, such occurrences are still here with us, and are fast becoming a problem. In a world where it seems there's always more to do than time and our meagre resources can allow, some people would do anything to reduce demands on their time and resources. In addition, there are many difficult needs and choices to juggle at the same time, on consistent basis. So, people understandably have hard decisions to make. This ranges from caring for relatives who have great need of daily support, to trying to raise a family of their own, under difficult circumstances. Worse case scenarios include currently constant report about moves toward the general legalization of assisted suicide, sometimes called euthanasia, as a means of ending the sufferings of sufferers and relieving the burdens of those who provide the care.

Whatever the motives might be, it is equally true that, there are cases in which regrettably, some of the decisions to give up on those who need our help, are mainly based on the level of burden, and extra demands caring for those in need, places on our time and resource. Without judging the morality of people's choices, I must admit, for some cases, we cannot deny that, giving up on people who genuinely need us, is a regrettable trend, which must be addressed. There is no excuse for abounding our loved ones, solely for selfish reasons, pertaining to the demands of work, financial constraints, and the need to look after oneself first. We have a God given responsibility toward looking after the needy, and when the individual is unable or fails in this special reasonability, the church and society must not fail. (cf. James 1:27; Isaiah 58:1-14) For instance, abounding or putting our elderly relatives into care homes, must never be based solely on our own selfish priorities, just to mitigate the cost, burden and constraints on our personal time and resource.

So, maybe we have some insights now into why this paralytic man might have been carried daily and laid in a certain place to try and fend for himself. He was 'dropped' in a certain place and left to beg for his livelihood. Those who put him there might have done so, in order to attend to their own pressing concerns, which is not so different from what some of us still do today. Some may want to refer to the lame man's society as primitive, but in terms of most human tendencies and behaviours, theirs was not too different from ours.

The same selfish principle that drove the culture and world of the paralytic man's epoch could well be the same for our modern day era. Without being demeaning, generally speaking, greed and selfishness still unfortunately undermine our claim to true civilisation. The *Adamic nature,* is what is still dominating men and women and their best human attempt to escape this manacle (cf Romans 5:12-21). Our systems largely still promote vanity as virtue, and evil as good. So also do our societies generally detest anyone advocating for the gospel of truth and of Christ, His love and generosity.

We still leave our *'paralysed'* people to battle life on their own in most cases. Somehow, we still 'drop' our *'paralyzed'* people at the 'gate' to be cared for by total strangers, in places where their dignities are eroded; such that even 'growing old' in some societies now, is quickly becoming a great source of worry. Yet, God's answer is always to establish and affirm the dignity of people and to treat everyone with decency, no matter their age or background.

That is why the Jesus does not regard the *'persons'* of man, nor does He show favouritism, in order to measure how He treats one or the other (Acts 10:34, 35). On the contrary, He even physically touched people with leprosy and healed them, when others found them abhorrent and disgusting; excluding them as unclean by religious laws (Mark 1:40-42)

Such is the extent of Christ's love; having compassion, and the power to forgive, restore, heal, bless and grant a favourable future to anyone, who comes to him even in their brokenness. He does not exclude His own, and caters for those in need. 'He is our refuge and strength, a very present help in trouble' *(Ps. 46:1);* and *"when my father and my mother forsake me, then the Lord will take care of me". (Psalms 27:10)* If you have been *'carried'* and *'laid at the gate';* abandoned and forsaken, take heart, because God knows how to come along and help people like you. 'Be strong and of good courage; do not fear nor be afraid; God will never leave you nor forsake you' (Deut. 13:6).

Robbed and Dropped

Remember the story of 'the Good Samaritan' in Luke chapter ten? It is said that the man on the road to Jericho from Jerusalem, was beaten and left to die, having been stripped of all his belongings.

Here again, we have an 'old story', but with great modern sense and moral lesson, that parallel that of the paralysed man, who was left at the gate. We might not have a 'thief' on the 'Jericho Road' today, beating and robbing their victims; however, we've got some 'shrewd' people, posing as business people, specialists and professionals, who 'beat and rob' already poor folks of all they possess. That's what the global recessions and credit crunches of recent history have been about. I believe that, through these recessions or credit crunches, God has some strong messages for humanity, especially for governments and financial institutions; that profiting from a sadistic treatment and cheating of the 'poor' is totally unacceptable (cf. James 5:1-2).

The scenario of the *Jericho Road* still is as much a reality today as when the Lord Jesus first told the story. For example, a former church member once told me how a money lending company took advantage of their desperation. They had desperately needed a personal loan to relieve their temporary sufferings. I heard this family was even renting a television set because they could not afford to buy one. Renting personal television set, one would think this was a practice of distant past; yet, it still exists today, even in England, a *first-world* economy.

In fact, a few years ago, we delivered a television set at a residence of an elderly widow in a similar situation, who lived less than two miles from our house. She was 'over the moon', and with a sigh of relief said, 'now I can call them to take their television away, and I don't have to pay rent anymore'. Thank God for a member of the church, who donated the television set for our charity fund raising event. This gracious elderly widow also got from the church a video player for watching movies of her choice.

Now, back to how the moneylender tried to rip off a member of our church. In fact, it becomes more interesting knowing her son was also a victim of a similar scam. Long story short; the loan company asked the family to do their application via telephone, to which the family agreed. Without any forewarning about a non-refundable application fee, the family went ahead with the application. Later they were conned into issuing a cheque to cover the application fee, with a promise that it would ensure a favourable outcome. Secondly, the agreed loan amount would immediately be put into their personal bank account, once the company had received the cheque for the application fee.

But here's the irony. This family was applying for a token amount as an emergency loan, and the loan company was charging them about a fifth of the amount of the loan in application or 'setup' fee alone. Apart from the fact that they were to pay back the amount borrowed with colossal incremental interest on a short term basis.

Finally, the application was done, but the result? Declined! What happened to the initial application fee of a fifth of the sum that was applied for? *'Sorry, it was an administration fee and is non-refundable,'* says the voice from the other end of the phone. The family threatened to report the matter to the financial ombudsman. But, with no remorse, the loan company exercised their immunity clause in small print, leaving this vulnerable family worse than when they began. With impunity, the loan company warned their victim not to think about taking the case any further, because in fact they were not answerable to any regulatory body including the one the family had wished to report their case to.

No loan, no refund; but that was only half the problem. The initial application fee, which the loan company casually referred to as *administration fee*, like Elisha's servant's *axe head (2Kings 6:5)*, was borrowed from a neighbour who, incidentally, was my relative. What happened? Of course, the woman and her son couldn't get the loan for what they urgently needed it for, and in the end they had to negotiate the payment of the borrowed application fee, which they had initially planned to settle immediately after their loan application was approved.

That's a *Jericho Road*, my friend! Unless God is with you, the *robbers* make it a very dangerous and impossible road to travel, and you could easily be *beaten, robbed and left to die*. But, glory be to God, who, like 'the Good Samaritan', will not let you *die* where wicked *robbers* dumped and left you. Instead, He comes along, picks you up, cleanses and administers His healing to your wounds and afflictions, and restores your true dignity. Guess what? Jesus paid it all, for your healing and your restoration, and you don't have to pay a thing:

> *For you know the grace of our Lord Jesus Christ, that though He was rich, yet for your sakes He became poor, that you through His poverty might become rich (2Corinth. 8:9)*

Struggles at the Gate: Not Forsaken

The man described as the 'lame beggar' in Acts chapter three was said to have been carried by others and laid daily at the gate of the temple, which was called Beautiful. He was there solely to ask alms from those who entered the temple. In verse six of the same chapter, we read that this man, *"seeing peter and John...asked for alms... expecting to receive something from them."*

Alms are defined as, 'gifts prompted by love to help someone in need.' Of course, in truth, only Jesus loves in ways that enable Him to freely give us the right gifts that are tailored to our specific need. But, working with the definition on hand, *alms*, in themselves, imply the presence of a *need*, and someone motivated by love that helps or might be able to *satisfy* an existing need.

The very first problem we encounter in the lame man's story is a man with a *need,* asking presumably those whom he believes could meet his need, one way or the other. However, there's an associated problem with asking, especially with his particular situation of being *'left daily at the gate'*. It would seem, in the eyes of some people that he was trying to make a profiting career out of his disability.

Recent debates surrounding modern welfare states, including Britain, unfortunately reverberates this kind of thinking about those receiving *benefits*. Some continue to make misguided statement about welfare recipients that reduce them to nothing, but beggars and lazy people. Such thinking, sadly blankets in genuine recipients who, for no fault of theirs, must be looked after by the state or others in a loving way. So, in the end, people who cannot help their situations and have to rely on *benefits* or alms, become susceptible to verbal abuse, hardship; loss of personal pride and dignity, and more.

This might have been the case with the lame man, who sat to beg before the gate of the temple; a possible feeling of vulnerability, hopelessness, undefined sense of personal pride, dignity and purpose. He may have been desperate, having to rely on others to 'carry' him, and having to live like a 'scavenger' on daily basis. It was a situation of looking anywhere and to anybody for some form of help, without real consideration for where help came from, or who provided it. His paralysis made him desperate and vulnerable, having to ask for a *love gift (alms)* where and when hate could ensue, by asking people who didn't like him, understand him, or appreciate why he sat to beg.

At this point, the lame man's situation depicts a powerful lesson for husbands and wives, who sadly tend to drive their spouses to ask for love from total strangers, who may only end up deepening their emotional wounds. *Asking for love at the gate,* which is a public space, has many pitfalls, and is even worse for any person with a 'paralysis'. Some of its pitfalls involve the fact that, the 'one asking for love at the gate', faces the danger of negotiating for love from the point of their weakness and vulnerability. In so doing, they are forced to beg to be loved, saying to another, *'please love me..., I know you don't know me or might not care about me; but please love me anyway.'* The 'gate' is simply a vulnerable place and position, to negotiate from, especially in a hostile world of unfriendly culture and practices.

The hard realities about having to be taken to the 'gate', or setting at the 'gate' are that: firstly, the one at the 'gate' is considered needy, weak, dependant, and without help, in a rough world in which they are constantly reminded, that there is no place for the weak, and beggarly. Secondly, taking our problems or needs before the 'gate' is symptomatic of our inner crises and physical challenges with which we are struggling to cope. It implies the presence of a problem that we cannot deny, albeit, we sometime try to pretend as if all is well. Thirdly, taking our issues before the 'gate' is a last result, and a fight for survival. It is a strong statement about the pains and sufferings inflicted upon us by our 'paralysis', and is our desperate cry and search for relieve and solution. Being at the 'gate' is simply a request for assistance, and we are asking if someone would help us.

That means, every time we enjoy acting outside of our Godly character, or even give ourselves over to illicit behaviours, like lies, stealing, homosexuality, lesbianism, prostitution, cheating, and so forth, which the Bible condemns, then it is only a clear sign of being at the 'gate'. We need help, and need someone to help us. There is indeed a struggle somewhere with us, a feeling or state of 'paralysis', which is asking for assistance.

Many 'daughters' and 'sons' today, who sadly find themselves in dysfunctional relationships are at the 'gate'. Sometimes, they try to cover their 'paralysis', and overcompensate as a way of trying to somehow deliver what they falsely believe is required of them, as a prerequisite for acceptance. Indulging in biblically wrong practices is usually an appeasement for acceptance, if no one hears their often long and lonely cry for help at the 'gate'. By using and capitulating to their 'paralysis'; in essence, they have moved into the 'public' to *'beg before the gate for alms'*, so to speak. At the 'gate', they are too willing to exchange their true need for a temporary gain and pleasure; 'silver and gold', instead of a divine healing touch for their 'paralysis', in order to be transformed, and to rise and walk on their own.

Perhaps, part of their own 'paralysis' was due to childhood neglect, a lack of love from parents or even close friends, who were bullies. Or it might have been as a result of failure, ill-treatment, and abandonment from their spouse. Whatever the case may be, the good news for those at the 'gate', who struggle with some form of 'paralysis' is that, potentially, they are God's agents of change and transformation, if they do well by looking to Him. They might be wounded, hurt and despised, but they are not forsaken. God loves them; He can still use them for a great purpose, just like the lame man. (cf. 1Cor. 1:27-30)

Learning from the Lame Beggar's Struggles

There is quite a lot to learn from the life and situation of the lame beggar, who was left at the *gate*. Hopefully, we can glean a few things that we can appropriate as practical lessons for our own wisdom:

First, the lame man, without doubt, had to deal daily with total strangers whom he had never met or known before. Yet, the Bible says he still asked them for *alms;* maybe as many people who passed by the place where he sat daily.

Here's what happens when we neglect our own in the *gate* or in 'public entrances'; we leave them to the *mercies* of strangers. That's why the Church must never abandon her own people, so as to not push them into places where they should not be looking for help. It is a shame to hear stories about Christians who spitefully throw out other Christians, because of their 'paralysis', only for them to fall into the wrong hands, wrong places, and of course the evil traps of Satan.

Second, when you've been so abused and neglected by some of the very people you depended on, then you turn to settle for less than what you really deserve and need from life. Imagine, the paralytic or the lame beggar, given that all things were equal, what would be his most immediate need? Of course, any well meaning person will tell you straight away, it's for wholeness or healings; to be able to rise up and walk. Surely, walking gives a degree of independence that allow a person to go out to fetch for daily needs like food, water and shelter.

So, for a 'paralytic' to be asking for alms, in this case *money*, when in fact they could be healed and should be asking for healings, means that somehow, this person has resigned to their plight and confused their priorities. It often happens this way; mainly because they see no other hope of being able to rise up. Their world and daily experience, unfortunately, framed their paradigm and shaped their worldview.

In this world, most people choose things and stuff over real solutions for their pressing 'paralyses'. Many are quick to treat the symptoms of their 'paralyses' than would treat the real problem, or the root of their 'paralyses'. Some say, 'if I just get more money I will be fine, or if I just get to be more popular, I will be happy.' But we now know as a proven fact that this way of tackling and addressing our problems are mere window dressing, papering over matters, and are most likely to spiral into even more difficulties.

The third crucial lesson in wisdom that we can glean from the lame beggar, at the *gate* is the fact that, when people mean evil against you, they will also go the next step further to ensure you actually live out their predictions, expectations and opinions – a kind of self-fulfilling prophecy, so to speak. The reason is simple; they want to be able to say in the end, "yes, we said it so, that s/he was not going to amount to anything!"

I am sure this is not exclusive to me alone; that on occasion, in my time of true need and during sensitive transitional period, I have been denied possible opportunities, because I simply was not in the favour of those at the helm of affairs. People had used such opportune times either for settling scores, or for perpetuating their own selfish agenda.

I remember quite well a few such instances, because they occurred during some of my most difficult years in high school and college, when I could have done with assistance. However, I found out that certain people, who were in the position to put my name forward for scholarship for further studies deliberately refused and recommended others instead. And twice, I was made to forfeit certain important meritorious awards and positions.

Now, looking back, I count it all blessings to know that God's choice is not necessarily people's choice and people's choice is not necessarily God's choice. *('Our ways are not His ways and His thoughts are higher'- Isaiah 55:9)*. It is a principle in God that when people drop and ignore you, as they did to the paralytic man in our story, God will always pick you up. The psalmist says, *'when my father and mother forsake me, then the Lord will take me up'. (Psalm 27:10kjv)*

Know this; when people drop you and discount you for no apparent reason, you do not have to be discouraged or disappointed. God has a better placement for you. Those who drop you do not qualify for the grace and gift you contain and carry over your life. You are better off allowing them to make your decision and choice easy, through disqualifying themselves in their unwise attempt to disqualify you.

Little did this paralytic, or those who dropped him and abandoned him daily before the *gate*, know that by letting him down in the same place, they were 'dropping' him right into the gracious hands of Almighty God, who is ever so compassionate. *They let him down but God picked him up.* Think about Jacob en-route to his uncle's village, having had a death sentence passed against him by his own brother, Esau. The Bible says that after covering some distance, he became terribly exhausted; I believe also frustrated, at what could be the betrayal of the trust and love he had for his brother. (I understand he did cleverly 'negotiate' his brother's birth rights, but to threaten to kill him was more than just a settlement).

Weighed down by the enormous burden of not knowing what to expect and the anxiety of starting a new life with his uncle, he lay down to sleep. Real deep sleep came over him and, all of a sudden he began to dream about angels who were very busy descending and ascending a ladder. At the top of the ladder, was the Lord Himself. So, Jacob became awestruck, and his reaction was that of amazed surprise, and he said, *"Surely the Lord is in this place and I did not know it". (Gen 28:16).* Let me paraphrase that. Here is what Jacob is truly exclaiming; "So, after all, the Lord still cares about me and knows where I am. He has not abandoned me through all this hardship and struggles of my life. Will He care about the whereabouts and the welfare of a helpless fugitive?"

It certainly will make a world of difference to know this for a fact, that somehow *where life's challenges take us and drop us are the very places appointed for our divine encounter with the Lord.* Next time when life troubles come your way, just pray for it to pick you up and drop you were the Lord will meet you. Many times life's troubles and challenges can be the only vehicle prepared by God to transport us on the highways and, to the destinations of God's supernatural blessings.

The fourth lesson in wisdom from the lame or paralytic man's life and situation is that; it is so natural for people's bitter unrelenting sufferings to make them accept their lot. Worst of all, the treatment, especially meted out to such people through neglect and abandonment, particularly enforces on them a strange apathy to resign in despair instead of rising, to the challenge to request from life exactly what they truly need.

This is comparable to what happens to a slave who, because of his years of cruel treatment, becomes institutionalised, so much so that freedom is no more a priority. He would rather work at becoming a better slave than attempting to be freed, because his humanness has not only been distorted by his experience, but his entire sense of purpose and personal fulfilment has now been programmed and redefined. If you told him a way of escape, that slave might regard you as a trouble maker, and try to remove you from his presumed peaceful world.

Similarly, the same is true for battered women in traumatic marriage relationships, who tend to cope under repeated circles of abuse. Of course, this is not God's programme for our lives, neither is divorce. The Lord will always challenge us to rise to the challenge of life by using His wisdom, *"for we have the mind of Christ."* Christ is not a victim, but victorious; He is not conquered, but He is more than a conqueror. These women get so used to their undeserved plight that some even accept 'beating' as an expression of love.

Hence, the day their macho-men begin to treat them humanely, they begin to think that they are no longer loved. It's a kind of reversed or negative programming that makes a person enjoy pain and crisis, something usually described as *tragic-pleasure*; like the pleasure people strangely derive from watching movies or plays categorised as a 'tragedy'.

They might first resist, then learn to cope, and finally accept that such is life and it's normal. Sadly, reversed programming is not inborn but the doing of one human being to another human being, or society to the individual, which the individual now accepts wholesale as their destiny. Under such circumstances, one is not only now the victim but also a self-doubter, a self-afflicter, because he or she has bought into an idea, a system and definition of things and life that has been systematically ingrained, over a period of time.

For example, when I was growing up, I couldn't see anything or any further beyond our little township we interestingly called a city. This was all I knew then. It was the best thing that ever happened to me. Mind you, no one sat me down to force it into my head, I grew to know it that way, because that's the way it was. But here's the irony; you know it didn't matter to me that we didn't have safe drinking water, or electricity, nor properly planned streets, flush toilets, and so forth. I was not uncomfortable with the way things were in my 'city'. In fact, I felt better privileged than some in my area, because we had a few amenities more than they had. Of course, others, mainly foreign expatriates also had more than we had. But then, through the most unlikely of events, civil war in my country, I found myself thrust into other nations that were more developed than mine.

In those countries, I found it initially difficult to fully enjoy their facilities and social amenities, which were now at my disposal. I had ingrained philosophies and strange survival ideas to explain why I couldn't, and it was all profoundly convincing and gave me some moral high grounds for thinking the way I did. I saw 'wastefulness' in the lifestyles of my new host countries simply because, compared to my situation in my initial country, for a lack of a better term, we were natural 'recyclers and preservers'. And, here I was thrust into societies that 'dispose' of any and everything. Almost everything was 'disposable'. You can guess what I immediately began to do, 'gather and keep' what others would happily dispose of!

Of course, "Brain Damage" is the worst nightmare a man can ever have – it's a nightmare that makes its way into real life. This was exactly why God allowed the generation of Israel from Egypt to languish in the dessert, because they couldn't understand that they were no longer Egyptian slaves, but God's chosen people. Not only had they been brain drained, they were 'brain damaged', to remain subservient and to 'enjoy' unpleasant circumstances, even after they were liberated from Egypt.

A Victim of Reversed programming?

The man in our story is most likely a victim of what I call *reversed programming*, having become used to people daily picking him and dropping him before the 'gate' to beg for his livelihood. How could he ever get out of what his situation, society and people have made him to become? Or did he ever think it was possible to change his unfortunate plight? What resources were available to him?

What about the man at the pool of Bethseda in John 5? Jesus asks, "do you want to be made whole? His answer, "Sir, I have no man". Pretty interesting, since right there before him stood, not just a man, but more than a man, the Man, Jesus.

The bible says about the lame man, *"when he saw Peter and John about to go into the temple, he asked for alms...expecting to receive something...."*

Here's a lesson of spiritual wisdom and significance: *Don't always give people what they expect. Give them what God desires them to have.* Don't even give them stuff because they are accustomed to it. Hear from God and do as He designs and designates, and the result will always be unparalleled. That's how miracles happen. Let a man expect, but you give him such as you hear and have from God, in the Name of Jesus Christ of Nazareth.

It pays, as Christians, to discern and to know what a person's true need entails, and not necessarily what's most apparent, or what they ask just for the sake of it. Philippians 4:19, *"my God shall supply all your need according to His riches in glory by Christ Jesus"*. It is *need*, and not *needs* that God supplies. God supplies your significant need, like the Japanese will love to teach you to fish rather than give you fish, and hopefully you might own the entire fishpond someday. God will go to the root of your issues and grant the important need that you have, so as to sufficiently change, or amply enhance and impact on, other 'needs' which might have arisen as a consequence.

Frankly, tossing a few *coins* to a man who is acutely disabled never solves his problem, when you can instead give him back his health. It only tends to keep him coming to the same spot to do the same thing, begging for *coins*. However, to heal the same man of his paralysis would certainly grant him the ability, not only to rise up, but also grant him his independence, perhaps to go about earning his own *coins*. With his healing, I believe he will begin to give 'legs' to all the great things he has always only dreamt about, and which were impossible because of his disabilities. Once the lame man before the 'gate' receives his healings, it would permit him to be able to join the crowd inside the temple for worship. By the way, after he was healed, he immediately entered the temple before which he had only sat.

Possibly, every time the lame man saw people walk past him, going into the temple for worship, the lame man's greatest desire was what he told himself; that "I pray, one day, I too can straighten up, walk and worship, or simply just have a feel of standing with the crowd, raising my own hands to God in surrender" (cf vr8).

Tell you what; God will always answer sincere prayer like that. Especially when the prayer is not based on covetousness, envy and the need to compete unnecessarily. Historically God has always delighted in freeing people from their bondage so that they can serve, worship and glorify Him (Exodus 4:22 and 5:1). If your motive is right, and your priorities are right, raise you voice in prayer to the Almighty God, and He will send from heaven to deliver you (Psalms 57:2, 3).

> *"Then you shall say to Pharaoh, thus says the Lord, Israel is my Firstborn…let My son go that he may serve Me"* (Exodus 4:22 & 5:1).

The Lame Man's Healing: How and Why

To glorify and worship God, the paralytic, or the lame man, is made to rise up in the Name of Jesus Christ of Nazareth. He gets healed and completely made whole. Some things emerged right away as great wisdom and inspiration on the back of the healing miracle that took place:

First, it is the fact that the man is restored to true purpose. I didn't say he was given purpose, but he was restored to purpose. Why? Because purpose has always been there, waiting to be discovered and harnessed for all its usefulness. The lame man has always been potentially great, but sadly trapped in a paralysis that hindered him from coming into true greatness.

Are you being trapped by your *paralysis* young man? Woman, is your potential trapped because you decided to yield and succumb to the result of some bad choice? Shake off the dust of despair and rise up in the Name of Jesus. Go and glorify your Maker in becoming what He wired you up for.

The *second* thing about the healing of the lame man: it was done in no other name than the Name of Jesus. Remember Philippians 2:9 and 10, "therefore God also has given Him the name which is above every name, that at the name of Jesus every knee should bow, of those in heaven, and of those on the earth, and those under the earth (hell)". Yes, this cripple, this bent and tied-up man, this paralytic, jumped to his feet simply at the mention of the Name, Jesus Christ of Nazareth.

Third, it is evident from Acts 3:5 that, like on other occasions when religious folks had come by and streamed into the gorgeous temple, whose gate was called *beautiful*, this lame man was certainly expecting something when Peter and John came by. However, he might have not been specifically expecting a miracle of healing at that moment.

No, read verse six and you will see that the lame man was asking for silver and gold coins (money). At least that's what Peter implies in his response. Some people will settle for and negotiate for perishable things instead of the true healing of their soul and body.

They tell themselves, 'if only I had some more money, I should be fine.' To some people, some more money means driving their body to the limit, sleepless nights of working day and night through another job. For others, some more money entails putting in more time into over-time jobs for over-time wages. Well, if you have good cause for doing that reasonably, like most are likely to presume, that's okay.

But, for most reasons, running your body down through over-time jobs is the suggestion of the devil my friend. There's nothing better than being the wholesome person God intends you to be. Hear this, *"It is vain for you to rise up early, to sit up late, to eat the bread of sorrows; for so He gives His beloved sleep" (Psalms 127:2)*. And *"Unless the Lord builds the house, they labor in vain who build it; unless the Lord guards the city (you), the watchman stays awake in vain" (Psalms. 127:1)*. It is folly to trust in one's own strength. Hence, work, but work wisely in Christ, and have time for God, your family, church, and good friends.

> *Yours, O Lord, is the greatness, the power and the glory, the victory and the majesty; For all that is in heaven and in earth is Yours; Yours is the kingdom, O Lord, and You are exalted as head over all. Both riches and honor come from You, and You reign over all. In Your hand is power and might, in Your hand it is to make great and to give strength to all. "Now therefore, our God, we thank You and praise Your glorious name (1Chron 29:11-13).*

Fourth, always expect something good.

> *So he gave them his attention, expecting to receive something from them ⁶ Then Peter said, "Silver and gold I do not have, but what I*

do have I give you: In the name of Jesus Christ of Nazareth, rise up and walk" (Acts 3:5-7).

Most times my friend, when we don't know what to do and feel overwhelmed by our own struggles, all we can do is to expect something good in the process of applying all we know to do. Even when we don't know what exactly it is to expect, just stand and wait in expectation. And here's the point of my fourth tip, in the wisdom of God from the lame man's life and situation: *expecting something is better than expecting nothing at all!*

Some come to God expecting nothing and say, 'well God knows'. Have you not read Matthew 7:7 which says "ask and it will be given to you, seek, and you will find; knock and the door will be opened to you"? Jesus puts it this way, "ask *anything* in my Name and it shall be given to you" (*Matt 7:7*).

I believe this text overflows with desire and expectation across the board. Ask, and seek what? The answer is; *anything*. Knock at what? The door. What kind of door? Any door that holds God's blessings and your desire. But, you must come *asking, seeking, knocking* and let God work the detail along the way. Because when He has finished, it will be exactly what you needed but probably didn't even know. The point here is; *keep asking, seeking, knocking until such a time when your expectations are realized and your desires are granted.* The secret is persisting consistently, and *persistence always breaks resistance.*

Some people no doubt have some expectations, but sometimes they might also need to give their expectations some direction while they wait on God. May I suggest that for whatever reasons or expectations that you have, for which you decide to wait on God, the primary goal should be that you expect Jesus Christ to change your life for the better. Someone has said, "*when you take care of better, bigger will take care of itself*". There's a lot of powerful and transformative truth in this way of thinking about life as a whole. You really don't need that next raise in salary to make you happy if you are already unhappy with your own life.

You need Jesus first, for your joy and eternal happiness (*Mtt.7:7 "Seek first the kingdom of God, and all these things (monies, clothes, etc) will be added to you"*. The truth is; the Kingdom of God has no supply problem, there are only people with a direction problem. For this very reason, we need kingdom knowledge for kingdom provision. We need kingdom direction to attract, and to tap into the wealth of the kingdom.

> *My people are destroyed for lack of knowledge. Because you have rejected knowledge,... (Hosea 4:6). Beloved, I pray that you may prosper in all things and be in health, just as your soul prospers (3John 2).*

From Healing to Revival

Something dramatic and brilliant takes place in verses six and eight of Acts chapter three. Do you see the once lame man freely jumping and yelling at the top of his voice? Do you hear him praising God for the good things He has done? I hope that you can feel his joy. He is electrified! He is ecstatic and full of joy beyond believe.

One of my favourite portions of Scripture actually is Acts 8:6-8. Verse 8 says, *"and there was great joy in that city"*. One man, Phillip, using the Name of the Lord Jesus Christ, brought healing to countless sick, and freedom to demonically possessed people. All of a sudden, the blind are seeing, the crippled are walking and unclean spirits are violently exiting the lives of their victims. But also the people are hearing the Word of God preached with power, and Christ is being preached right in the heart of Samaria. The result; great joy fills and filters through that great city, which was noted for spiritual apathy but renowned for debauchery and immorality.

Put plainly, when it comes to God's dealing with us, our destinies are definitely hooked to others and vice versa. In this case, the healing miracles of God, the multitude being moved to believe, and the joy that dramatically filled the entire city of Samaria, culminated into one great occasion at the same time. The passage says,

> ... *Philip went down to the city of Samaria and preached Christ to them.* ⁶ *And the multitudes with one accord heeded the things spoken by Philip, hearing and seeing the miracles which he did.* ⁷ *For unclean spirits, crying with a loud voice, came out of many who were possessed; and many who were paralyzed and lame were healed.* ⁸ *And there was great joy in that city (Acts 8:5-8).*

What is happening in Samaria is what I consider to be the equivalent of revival and spiritual reawakening. It's clearly an *Auza Street* of the first century.

Samaria is on *fire* for God, my friend, and there's healing and there's joy throughout the city. Here's an interesting bit of a passage that will interest you. It says, *"when the righteous are in authority, the people (city) rejoice..." (Proverbs 29:2).* What that means is that the righteous have a way of bringing and putting joy back into people and places where they were once lacking. They *re-vive* (bring alive again), and they re-awaken what has slumbered and died. That's exactly what this one man, Phillip, full of the Holy Spirit did to slumbering Samaria, as the joy of the people overflowed.

I had to intervene with the Samaria story just to bring you to this point. Did you know that, by healing the lame man, Peter and John caused an unsettling stir in that nice, quiet, and all-propped religious temple? It was unprecedented. They were not used to loud, roaring noise in their services, because they were not 'Pentecostals'. These well trained theologians, and their 'middle' and 'elite' class religious systems always managed to keep a tight lid on folks that were considered 'untrained' and 'unlettered', in order to preserve the peace in their organized religious meetings.

But, the sudden drama of what had just taken place, right before their temple's gate, was so tumultuous that they took note that the rather eccentric fellows joining them that morning were certainly not members of their 'church'. Peter and John had fire in their bones, untamed and not intimidated by social orders. They attempted what the fellows of the temple had only sat around and probably ignored for religious reasons.

Yet, it's interesting that it took the situation of the lame man, who had always sat outside and before this temple, to bring revival inside the same temple. I believe their temple might have had revival sooner, had the original 'members' exercised a little bit of faith to invite the lame man into their midst for a simple prayer of faith, in the Name of Jesus, rather than keep him outside before their gate.

Shortly afterwards, in verse ten we hear, *"then they knew that it was the man who always sat before the gate begging alms...."* First, this is a clear and an unequivocal acknowledgement of the truthfulness and reality of the miracle that had just been performed on this lame man. They all knew him, that he was physically crippled or lame, and recognised he was the same man that sat before the temple day-in and day-out. No one could deny that he was healed; neither could any suggest that the miracle of healing was fake and a forgery.

Here is the real point, and I dare say point of embarrassment for the 'church'. Do you know that all the while this man had been at the temple gate with people daily flowing and trooping in and out of the temple? They did not even know who he was, except that he was a cripple. *"But God has chosen the foolish things of the world to put to shame the wise, and God has chosen the weak things of the world to put to shame the things which are mighty..."* (1 Corinthians 1:27).

One truth emerges from this incident; that the 'church' didn't know the name of the lame man, although he had always been there right before its gates; but God knew him. Jesus knows, not necessarily those who hide under the guise of religious elitism or who even claim to be His, but those who are His sheep, who know His voice and follow Him (John 10:27).

Therefore, my friend, while it seems like for now no one knows your name, no one cares, or even wants to bother with you, know for certain that God, whose child you are, can locate you for a great work from wherever people have *dropped and left* you. He will touch you and He will heal you, *but first, wait until God raises you.* There's always a supernatural lifting and blessing for God's people and a time appointed for God to comfort His own. We know and understand *"that the Lord, He is God, it is He who has made us, and not we ourselves; we are His people and the sheep of His pasture" (Psalm 100:3).*

> *Then he showed me Joshua the high priest standing before the Angel of the Lord, and Satan standing at his right hand to oppose him. ² And the Lord said to Satan, "The Lord rebuke you, Satan! The Lord who has chosen Jerusalem rebuke you! Is this not a brand plucked from the fire?" ³ Now Joshua was clothed with filthy garments, and was standing before the Angel. ⁴ Then He answered and spoke to those who stood before Him, saying, "Take away the filthy garments from him." And to him He said, "See, I have removed your iniquity from you, and I will clothe you with rich robes." ⁵ And I said, "Let them put a clean turban on his head." So they put a clean turban on his head, and they put the clothes on him. And the Angel of the Lord stood by (Zechariah 3:1-5).*

> *Now the Lord had said to Abram: "Get out of your country, from your family and from your father's house, to a land that I will show you. ² I will make you a great nation; I will bless you and make your name great; and you shall be a blessing. ³ I will*

bless those who bless you, and I will curse him who curses you, and in you all the families of the earth shall be blessed" (Gen. 12:2-3).

Other People's Opinion

To draw the curtain on this chapter, I'd like to touch on a few things, using my personal background to illustrate how important it is to be discretional about what people think and say about you. Anyone seeking a 'lift' or help from God, regardless of your physical or spiritual challenges and circumstances, it is so important that you learn to listen to and rely completely on God's opinion about your matter, and not necessarily what people say, unless you are sure that they were sent by God.

It is most certain, given our normal human tendencies that people who walked by, whether of those going in or out of the temple where the lame man sat to beg, including the people who might have used the same route as they went about their business, had something to say openly or in private about the lame man's condition. Whether for good or bad, people tend to explain to themselves or others the reason why things are the way they are, and without exception try to assign some alibi and causes.

Sounds strange, but the human species understandably live in a world of causality, and we can't help looking until somehow we make or find a 'cause' for every 'effect'. Hence, our world and ourselves value, and are addicted to, 'opinion' judgement. But, as God's people, the sooner we free ourselves from other people's opinion, the freer we become to pursue and live out God's agenda and purpose for our lives.

My personal experience and background regarding the opinion of people leads to a few helpful conclusions. First, we need to free ourselves from what society imposes on us and from people's costly opinion, cultural deficits and stereotypes. Only in this regard I would say with caution, *you don't need people*. You only need God's opinion about who you really are.

Secondly, most times, most of the things people say to hurt you and to make you feel belittled, especially in conflict situations, I truly do not believe they mean or intend what they say. What they say really only becomes a problem for us, if we take them to heart and muse over them continuously, allowing them to hinder us. Because, by musing over such things, we inadvertently empower them.

Let me illustrate this by an example from my personal background. One of the most cutting things I heard as a teenager, intended by Satan to destroy my personal confidence and self-worth came from someone whom I still hold in great respect today. In fact, the irony is that before I had this unfortunate situation with that person, they gave me the very first complete bible with concordance, during the initial stages of my decision to follow Christ. This person helped me in Sunday school and bible studies, and also helped initially when I learned how to share my faith with others.

So, this person was not mean or bad at heart at all, and in fact I still believe that the same person is a very good Christian, who meant well. But on this occasion, they just goofed like all of us sometimes do. Unfortunately, life can be strange and we all make mistakes, sometimes hurting those we love, and are sometimes hurt by those who love us as well.

This person hastily misjudged a situation which happened in a very stressful environment, and ran their conclusions before my side of the story was ever heard. As a result, I was openly and sharply rebuked among friends and peers, with damnable remarks been made against me and my future.

Apparently, all that this person said regarding my future could have easily been believed because, back then, things didn't look promising. I came from a little town, had never travelled, and had little knowledge of the already sophisticated world of technology outside my realms. At the time, my country was at war. I was then a refugee with no educational qualifications, or a specific job skill. Worst of all, although God had been so good to me, even up to delivering me from imminent death a few times, I *played* church, and did not love and commit to Him as I really should have.

However, having heard all that was said by this individual, somehow I took no offence at all, and I am so glad the Lord did not permit me to answer back in anyway. But, to their credit, after those damning remarks, a few people wisely intervened, and the individual graciously recanted the careless words and remarks that were passed against me.

Now, I know that some of what was said and thought about me spurred and motivated my initial drive to make something of my life. And although at the time I didn't retort, nor respond verbally, something rose up in me; a huge flush of great energy, not for physical fight, but a quiet assurance that none of the words spoken would negatively impact my future. The fact that my response was measured and the fact that the pronouncement of this person did not elicit the normal kind of hostile response that it would have in many cases from a teenager, diffused the situation right from the outset. The person had clearly over reacted, but I remained surprisingly calm.

Can I just add, as a fact of life in general, that the thing about life is, usually, *greatness intimidates the not-so-great, and greatness lying low and buried in other persons can be perceived by the intimidated ones. So much so that they will fight you, even though the fruit of greatness is not yet fully manifest.* This is not about me saying that I am great, or that my greatness spurred the regrettable remarks that we made about me. I am only saying, this is what I have observed about life: that when people are actually claiming to be talking you down, they are only trying to talk you out of your greatness, that they've already perceived, but which intimidates them, and which is in the first place the hidden reason for them trying to talk you down.

Some of the damning remarks I have heard throughout my life, I believe, were used by God to make me who I am today. I decided not to chew on such words and not to resign to lack and poverty. That would have made people *gods* over my destiny. So, I became very determined (with some terrible mistakes too) to forge a life with purpose against the odds of my background and extreme financial lack.

In the midst of all these, God has been so good to me and He blessed me beyond my weaknesses. By His grace, I have seen many good things and encountered many good people as well. He continues to show me that no matter our present challenges, there's hope in our future (Jer. 31:17).

Here's what I am trying to convey to you; *if you don't chew on the ungenerous things that people say to you, but choose to rather trust God with and for your life and future, you will succeed.* Quite often the hurtful things that people say, they really don't mean to say them and even if they do, they are just what people say. Find out what God says and you'll know that you're hearing the truth. It's to your advantage to decide what you hear and what you listen to, and to equally decide what you do with what you hear and listen to.

Unfortunately, some will hear and listen to what others say and it will become their *ladders* for descending, but hopefully, you will use those as your *ladders* to ascend to the place of greatness that God intends for you to occupy. Keep rising, and keep going forward; be a *spell breaker*! Go on, live out your purpose; be a catalyst for change, and transform your world! 'For with God all things are possible.'

Chapter Thirteen

THE BREAKTHROUGH: CAPITALIZING ON GOD'S MIRACLE MOMENT

> *You brought us into the net; You laid affliction on our backs. You have caused men to ride over our heads; we went through fire and through water; But You brought us out to rich fulfilment. (Ps. 66:11-12)*

Most times, I believe, God, in His own wisdom and for reasons best known to Him, would hide us for a period. Sometimes, He may even allow people to name us based on our temporary set-backs, only for Him to raise us up gloriously in the end. And that's a miracle! Consider *Joseph*, the forgotten brother of the sons of Jacob. Only later in life did he realize the true impact of God's wisdom in allowing him to be separated from his brothers and to be sold into Egypt.

There, in Egypt, he was lifted and crowned a prime minister, in the same land of his enslavement. In acknowledgement and celebration of the wisdom of God in directing his life, and for orchestrating events at different stages of his life, he tells his fear griped brothers who considered themselves liable for a possible reprisal, that, *"But as for you, you meant evil against me; but God meant it for good, in order to bring it about as it is this day, to save many people alive"* (Gen. 50:20).

Consider also *David*, the shepherd boy, totally unknown, 'faceless' and overlooked by his own father. Although his family did not think much about him, and relegated him to be the least and the most unlikely for any meaningful purpose in life, so much so that he was made to follow sheep and to chase away wolves and bears in the forest, God had a better plan for David. (The psalmist has said, indeed, *"when my father and mother shall forsake me, then the Lord will take care of me." Psalms 27:10).*

David, despite his odds with his father and family, God still chose him to be the king of Israel, the only king hand-picked by God Himself. Later, God referred to him as 'the man after my own heart' (1 Samuel 16:1-3; 18:12-16).

What about *Moses*, a man thrown and forgotten at the backside of the desert? He was a fugitive and a murderer, who was on the wanted list of the Pharaoh of Egypt. He had a price tag on his life; "Moses, wanted dead or alive for a handsome reward". But later, God raised Moses from his hideout in obscurity to champion the cause of Israel. God does not normally choose the purest and brightest person, but people like Moses, the 'runaway', to stand before pharaoh to demand the freedom of the children of Israel from their long captivity of about four hundred years.

The most intriguing thing about all this is that Moses himself was all too aware of his personal weaknesses. He knew, more than everyone else, that he definitely did not qualify for the assignment, which was thrust upon him (Exodus 4). In Moses' reckoning, God's special assignment required a proper man, and most likely, some 'Harvard professors with honors', well groomed and nurtured specifically for the task of liberation. But what *'Mo'* failed to realise was, that when God Almighty calls or sends, it simply means you can. It means He will be with you, and He will execute the job through you; only make yourself available. (cf Exodus 3:12; 4:11,12).

Now, consider the *lame man at the gate* of the temple in Acts chapter three. The 'church' had never, not one day, taken the trouble to share fellowship and to minister to this man's true need for healing, except that they threw a few coins to him every now and then. But, sitting outside that church was a miracle ready to happen by divine design, the very catalyst for God's special revival in that very church, which I suppose was lacking in relevant supernatural authority and powers. That lame man was the *occasion* and *opportunity* prepared by God, the potential material for indoor crusade, but which was ignored and left sitting outdoors for all that time.

The church had blatantly avoided their moments for breakthroughs. Their very acknowledgement of the fact of the miracle which took place by the hands of 'visitors', Peter and John, surely also implied a sad recognition of two things. First it was a missed opportunity. Second, it represented their personal and collective, inane unbelief in denying the possibility of true miracle, and Jesus Christ being the true Son of God with power to set captives free. These facts become the basis for Peter's vehement rebuke and discourse later on in the same chapter, beginning at verse eleven.

I said, 'missed opportunity' because, the 'church' or temple could have probably been appointed for doing the miracle, if they had chanced it by tuning down on their religious tradition. Had they received the teaching of faith that Jesus delivered, in their very city and most likely from the same temple, they would have ventured in faith exercises with the paralytic; a clear opportunity to put faith to work. Because of their doubts and unbelief, they effectively cut themselves off from a *"new and living way which Christ consecrated for us through the veil, that is His flesh" (Hebrews 10:20).*

Unfortunately, many individuals, as well as churches, are similarly missing out on such great dynamics of spiritual reality and the opportunity for miracles, signs and wonders. This is because they have rather chosen to stick to archaic tradition that they won't relinquish. They fail to recognize the new things God is doing and wants to do for and through the lives of simple, and I dare say *weak* men and women in our time. But, the result will always be the same for those who fail to appreciate that God's power is still very dynamic and strong today. They will live to regret how they sadly missed such a great opportunity that was set right before them at their *gates* of life.

Could it be that the reason why the invalid was positioned in no other place than before the temple, was so that God could reveal His power to this temple by healing the lame man? Or could it be that God wanted them to see the other side of faith, when it is truly and rightly employed for God's glory? Or, was it intended to provoke their faith for God's healing gift and the exercise of it? It might have also been the answer to prayer, to see signs and wonders and for revival in the temple. But the *raw material* for the sign and miracle was provided and was regrettably overlooked, for reasons only known to the people who attended the temple. Whatever the mind of God was concerning the temple and the lame man, the fact remains that they soon found out how great a chance they had but lost, probably because of religious hard-headedness.

Very often, just like in our own times, and even like the days of Seymour's Azuza Street revival at the turn of the twentieth century, God will use seemingly foolish and unassuming persons and things to do His great works. Seymour, himself with paralysis in his eyes, was ignored, and subjected to racial prejudice, even by the church during his day. Also, the lame man before the gate of the temple, most probably subjected to religious and cultural prejudices, mainly because of his paralysis, was totally ignored until, God miraculously thrust him into His preordained purpose.

By this, it is easy to appreciate the wonderful truth and relevance of what James, the apostle says about the callings and workings of God; His choice of seemingly and physically undesirable people who look unequal to the awesome assignments of God, but whom He chooses by His divine knowledge and wisdom. James (2:5, 6) says, "Listen my beloved brethren, has God not chosen the poor of this world to be rich in faith and heirs of the Kingdom which He promised to those who love Him? But you have dishonoured the poor man…"(cf Matt 5:3). This same position is further buttressed by the apostle Paul in 1Corinthian 1:26-29, in which he boldly declares,

> *"For you see your calling, brethren, that not many wise according to the fresh, not many mighty, not many noble, are called. But God has chosen the foolish things of the world to put to shame the wise, and God has chosen the weak things of the world to put to shame the things which are mighty; and the base things of the world and things which are despised God has chosen, and things which are not, to bring to nothing the things that are, that no flesh should glory in His presence."*

Does that sound like you? Do you wonder if you will ever amount to anything? Is your strength disappointing you in the face of what you thought God designed and anointed you for? Then, it's time to rise up because you have no idea how good people like you are in the hands of God. Hear this; *your awareness of your personal weakness is the acknowledgement of your need for God's all-surpassing and supernatural strength, which is granted in time of your need.* God's promise in our weakness is straight forward; "know that you are weak, but I am almightily strong, and when you need Me, partner with Me, and draw on My strength, then you too become strong for your tasks and assignments".

That was my paraphrase of 2 Corinthians 12:9 that says, *"My grace is sufficient for you, for My strength is made perfect in weakness.…"* A word of further assurance for those who are weak is offered by Paul when he says, "And God is able to make all grace abound toward you, that you always having all sufficiency in all things, may have an abundance for every good work" (2 Corinthians 9:8).

'Savour' the moment. Your time might just be around the corner, for that long awaited breakthrough you've been seeking and desiring. You may have thought that those desires were impossible, because your own strength was woefully small and failing; and that you didn't have the required pedigree for the height that God wanted you to climb. But, none of those actually matter when God's grace locates you, and then selects you for greatness according to His purpose. Your part is to obediently take that all-important step, to capitalise on the divine moments that God has already arranged in your life, for your breakthroughs. Like the lame man at the gate where Peter and John showed up, he 'expected to receive something from them', and according to Peter, they gave him what they had; a miracle. Expect a miracle today, and you shall receive it! Let God be gracious to you, and bless you even above your expectation. He is a miracle working God.

Chapter Fourteen

THE PROOF: HE IS ALIVE AND MIRACLES STILL HAPPEN

> *And seeing the man who had been healed standing with them, they could say nothing against it. [16] saying, "What shall we do to these men? For, indeed, that a notable miracle has been done through them is evident to all who dwell in Jerusalem, and we cannot deny it. (Acts 4:14,16)*

The episode involving the healing miracle and the response of those in the temple, somehow presented another enigma in itself. It stood as a clear witness and a great challenge against the intractable position of the congregation, about the works and testimonies of Jesus. How could they deny that a man who was above forty-eight years old, and who had been lame from birth, was healed by the power in the Name of Jesus? How could they refute Jesus is the Lord, and He was the Messiah who walked among them?

Primarily, many of them had blatantly denied and continued to deny the messiahship of Jesus. In fact, He had been crucified not long before, because they claimed that He made Himself equal to God by calling Himself the Son of God. Their ultimate goal was to refute all claims that Jesus was and is the Christ. So they didn't want to have anything to do with Jesus and His teachings. Yet, they have had and witnessed what, in every respect, was the greatest proof of what, in my view, is the most authoritative evidence of the sonship and messiahship of Jesus. He is the Christ and He is the Lord our saviour!

Here is the proof in Jesus' own words while physically present on earth, given when He answered those who doubted if He was the Son of God:

> *"When you lift up the Son of Man, then you will know that I am He... (John 8:28)*

What a terse answer, and what a clearly brilliant way to put it. In contemporary parlance, we say things like, 'the proof of the pudding is in its eating'. The Lord Jesus was simply saying, *'you cannot doubt that I am the Son of God after you've killed me and then I do what no human can do; rise again' (cf John 10:17).* That in itself was no human feat, only God could do that for Himself and others. And yes, Jesus rose again after He was crucified, proving that He was and is the Son of God, and that 'death could not hold Him captive' (Acts 2:24).

However, some, and I believe most worshippers and leaders in the temple where the lame man was healed did not believe in Christ. To prove that most of the worshippers and their leaders in the temple did not believe in Christ, you only need to know that, had they truly believed in the Name of Jesus, then there would have been a record or a testimony of their attempt, at least, to pray for the lame man who daily sat at their temple's gate. Such record or testimony of a *major* effort, especially when a successful miracle later occurred even in another context, would have been present as we have with other good attempts by people including physicians, the disciples and ordinary men and women (see Mark 5:26, Luke 8:43, Mark 8:19, Acts 9:36-40, Acts 19:13-15).

Secondly, Peter and John had to caution their *disbelief* in seeing the invalid healed, as if the worshippers thought it was impossible to heal so easily and quickly what seemed to clearly be an impossible problem. After this, Peter and John had to now do a good job of educating the entire tempt or 'church' about how all this is possible in the Name of Jesus, the Son of God.

Even when Jesus told them He is the "*way, the truth and life, and no one gets to the Father except by Him (John 14:6)*", most of them didn't believe Him. Now Jesus is crucified and, all so soon, the things He taught and claimed while He was alive and walking among them are being confirmed and fulfilled. Now, their thoughts are taking them on a trip back into the days Jesus was with them in person, probably when some of them could have easily touched Him physically, asked and received answers to their questions.

Just imagine them literally beating themselves mentally, saying to themselves, "how stupid I was. Could I not have followed this Man and have Him do some things for me, probably heal me. Or, I could have now been a healing evangelist, like Peter and John, helping people in my cities and communities, but how stupid I was standing there in doubt and unbelief!" If we had the opportunity to sample their mixed reactions regarding the healing miracle of the lame man, those could have been the feel and sound of them – obviously, some believing, some still in *limbo*, others standing in denial. But, in the end, just like other times in the Scripture, the temple might have been left with a congregation divided in opinion.

Further on, in the book of Acts, this very temple became a central point for future evangelistic activities through the disciples, because it was possibly still full of 'unbelieving' Jews who opposed the message of the gospel of Jesus Christ.

Without doubt, the state of the temple with 'unbelievers', can be likened or transferred to some contemporary churches today, that might need to be evangelised again. The reason is that, most churches today are full of 'unbelieving Christians', who pride themselves in "*having a form of godliness but denying its power… always learning and never able to come to the knowledge of the truth (2 Timothy 3:5-7).*

I came across a brilliant story in one of William Barclay's New Testament commentaries. In my view, the story is an excellent answer with dynamic illustration, for all who oppose and deny the claims of the Lord Jesus and His power to heal and deliver all who are bound. The moral or the whole essence of the story in a way mimics what I believe to be the greatest proof of the sonship and messiahship of Jesus when He said, *"When you lift up the Son of Man, then you will know that I am He..." (John 8:28).*

The story goes like this:

> *A man who had been a reprobate and a drunkard was captured by Christ. His workmates used to try to shake him and say, 'surely a sensible man like you cannot believe in the miracles that the Bible tells about. You cannot, for instance, believe that this Jesus of yours turned water into wine.' "whether he turned water into wine or not", said the man, "I do not know; but in my house I have seen him turn beer into furniture."* Barclay adds, *"no one can argue against the proof of a changed life".*

Can you, or are you going to argue against the 'proof of a changed life'? In view of this, it would be most unwise to resist the evidence of an outstanding miracle like Jesus rising from the dead, as He said He would. Similarly, it would be unwise to even try to deny the possibility of a mangled body being straightened up, if it took place right before your eyes, in the Name of Jesus. With God, 'all things are possible" (Mark 10:27). Miracles happened then, and miracles still happen today because Jesus is alive!

Miracles are still Possible

Now, how does all this relate and apply to you who are reading? It's pretty simple and straight forward. Miracles are still possible today and yours is a possibility with God. Our Father knows best what you really need and, in your miracle, He also is glorified. He will do what you ask but remember that it's always for you to glorify and to serve Him who gave you your miracle.

For you who desire to do miracles, it's also possible. Like Peter and John, you too can be a useful *instrument* or servant in God's hand, to bring joy to your slumbering church and neighbourhood. You are no different from Peter and John, but you need to recognise God's scheduled opportunity and plunge in by faith. I will put it as it is; '*take the risk*' and let heaven back you.

And to you who might have all this while been in doubt, and have failed to recognize that Jesus is still in the miracle business, but now you've read and seen that surely God is merciful, gracious, compassionate and powerful - well, this is your moment. Only believe and have faith that God can touch you and bring you wholeness. You don't need to go way back to where you missed that opportunity. Christ, by His Holy Spirit, is at work right now, right where you are. The good thing is, "*He is the same yesterday, today and forever*" *(Hebrews 13:8)*. Now is your time of salvation, and now is your time of visitation.

Miracle Delayed is not Miracle Denied

A striking thing about our odd life experiences is that many things we go through, which the devil intends for evil, will in the end fall to the glory of God, who delivers us and then brings us into His safe refuge. Consider Psalms 34:19, "*Many are the afflictions of the righteous, but the Lord delivers him out of them all*". Also the evidence in *Romans 8:28*, "*that all things work together*", agrees with the psalmist's assertions. Another passage puts it this way, '*for it is God who works in you both to will and to do for His good pleasure*' *(Philippians 2:13)*. Only God knows the timing, the occasion and place; and how to turn things for our victory and, ultimately His glory.

Sometimes, some of the things we face and go through seem to go on forever, as if to outlive their due term. However, through all of that and behind the scenes, God's wisdom is not absent. Of course, God loves His people, and He's great, and all-powerful, and all wise at the same time. He loves us and always wants to take care of our needs. He is all-powerful so that He can do for us 'even far more exceedingly abundantly above all that we ever ask or think of' (Ephesians 3:20). Nothing we desire is too difficult, neither is His hand too short, but God is also so wise, and wiser than men, that He will do and only permit that which is best for us in its proper time *(He has made everything beautiful in its time, Ecclesiastes 3:11).*

So, while in our view our situations and circumstances may seem to outlast their due time, God is never late. He is the *on-time* God. For example, the timing of the healing of the paralytic or lame man was so ideal. Everything and everyone connected to his miracle had to be in that place, and the occasion had to be right for his miracle to have the desired impact, designed by God, in His perfect wisdom.

We can read about the episode and account of this miracle today and be encouraged, challenged and changed, because it happened the way it did. Those who saw it, those in the temple and everyone who knew the lame man, equally benefited from the powerful outcome of God's supernatural work done in his life, because God allowed the time, place and event to come together.

Let's hypothetically surmise that the healing miracle took place at a different time or place. Things might have been different then. Obviously, the number of people who witnessed the miracle and became impacted by it may not have been of the same configuration. At best, the occasion could have been different. Probably, the make-up of the worshipers also different. Peter and John might not have had the same opportunity to be seen or approached by this lame man before the temple gate. Maybe the lame man, after he had been healed, might have just quietly left and gone home, without running into the temple for people to behold what a great thing the Lord had done in his life.

However, a situation like that could have effectively meant that there would have availed no occasion in the first place for the gospel to be preached with power and authority in the temple, as it happened. Only God made it possible that through this healing miracle, a whole new way could be opened, for those who had denied the very basis of the faith; ' believing in the Name of Jesus and being saved as a result'.

It is so amazing that God's ways and thoughts take into account the total picture of things. *His view about what we face is so comprehensive and so are the solutions He grants, which are meant to be comprehensive and total as well.* His views always look from and over a distance, and because He knows the beginning from the end, God does a great work of complete salvation. God is not into temporary measures or first aid. His touch is permanent and His grace is forever (*Eccles. 3:14 –whatever the Lord does is permanent, and the gifts and the callings of God are irrevocable Romans 11:29*)

Prayer

It's time to pray. Let me have the privilege to pray for and with you right now. You may connect to this simple but powerful prayer for you my friend, by responding at the end, 'Yes, Lord Jesus I believe and receive, Amen!'

> *Father, I pray that you will reach out in love and power and touch my friend right now, restoring to your child health, strength, wisdom and your blessings. Bless, anoint and use your child to show forth your glory O Lord Jesus, and grant exceptional grace for my friend reading this book to demonstrate your good works and miracles in the life of others. If my friend has any need for any miracle, please Lord Jesus heal my friend*

and grant perfect soundness in every area as you did for the lame man at the gate. Thank you Lord for answer to prayer in Jesus Name, amen.

The Wisdom of God's Wisdom in Your Trials

Something outstanding took place beginning in Acts chapter three and verse eleven, which once again shows that God is so wise and that the wisdom of God far surpasses anything we know right now. Just as with His chastening, for God's wisdom to make any real sense to us, it has to always be afterwards. Only then, can we appreciate the full benefits, mainly due to our humanness. For *"no chastening seems to be joyful for the present, but painful, nevertheless, afterward it yields the peaceable fruit of righteousness to those who have been trained by it"* (Hebrews 12:11).

All of this is the workings of the divine wisdom of God, which Apostle Paul, with great relief, celebrates in two of his epistles when he declared, *"Oh, the depth of the riches both of the wisdom and knowledge of God! How unsearchable are His judgments and His ways past finding out" (Romans 11:33)!* Paul, elsewhere continued further to bring to us the nature of this wisdom, declaring, *"but we speak the wisdom of God in a mystery, the hidden wisdom which God ordained before the ages for our glory, which none of the rulers of this age knew, for had they known, they would not have crucified the Lord of glory"* (1 Corinthians 2:7-8).

So, there we have it. The wisdom of God has *depth of riches*; it is seldom spoken in plain speech or language, but in mysteries, and is hidden, and was ordained before the ages. This does not necessarily make it unknowable. Only that the wisdom of God's wisdom, or its raison d'être, can be known mainly afterwards when it has borne its fruits, or unless the Lord, by special divine revelation, makes it known beforehand through the Holy Spirit of God. Even then, we still often have real difficulties trying to appreciate exactly what God is saying or what He is doing, until we see the actual *'fruit'*. It has nothing to do with our faith or ability to believe God is true and able; it's mainly the exercise of our humanness and limitation, when it comes to our relationship with God, who is omniscient and almighty. For example, Abraham, the father of faith, "believed God, and it was accounted to him for righteousness." (Gen. 15:6) However, about thirty 30 years into the promise of God concerning which he first believed God, we read in Genesis 17:17 that, *"Abraham fell facedown; he laughed and said to himself, "Will a son be born to a man a hundred years old? Will Sarah bear a child at the age of ninety?"* In verse 18, Abraham instead, suggested Ishmael for God's promised blessing, although the promise was actually for Isaac.

You see, it was easy for Abraham to put Ishmael forward for the blessing, not because of unbelief, but understandably, Ishmael, was already physically born. Humanly speaking, that made sense for a one hundred years old man and his wife, who was also ninety years old. Although they believed God, it was seriously difficult to appreciate the wisdom of God's wisdom in choosing Isaac, and the whole process of the long wait, and all they had to endure at their age.

Normally, we, like Joseph, can hardly tell the wisdom of God while being *churned, brewed or refined* through life's sometimes unpleasant, unsolicited situations (Ps. 105:17-19). But afterwards, you can stand at the end of it and say, like Joseph, "you meant it for evil but God meant it for good...." (Gen. 50:20). At this point, the wisdom that was hitherto hidden in that problem, or in that life challenge, becomes known. The veil is removed and it all makes sense.

At this point, that which was unspoken and inexpressible in the regular language of human speech, begins now to be put into intelligible words of human expressions. Until now, your challenge has literally been speaking, but not in the language you were able to receive. It was just too coded and shrouded in mysteries for you to be able to break it down. But, now that you have experienced it, gone through it and come out of it, you now have sufficient knowledge and skill to unravel the coded messages of your trials and challenges.

Soon you'll begin to realize and appreciate how your own experience has deepened, and also how deep the riches of the wisdom of God were through all that you had to go through. Sometimes it is amazing how the experience gained from one event could be so deep in *the riches of God's wisdom*. That out of that one experience, God and life qualify you for greater heights, and through your one trial, other things and other people, stand to benefit immeasurably.

This was Paul's confession after he had been schooled in the wisdom of God's wisdom through human trails.

> *Blessed be the God and Father of our Lord Jesus Christ, the Father of mercies and God of all comfort, ⁴ who comforts us in all our tribulation, that we may be able to comfort those who are in any trouble, with the comfort with which we ourselves are comforted by God. ⁵ For as the sufferings of Christ abound in us, so our consolation also abounds through Christ. ⁶ Now if we are afflicted, it is for your consolation and salvation, which is effective for enduring the same sufferings which we also suffer. Or if we are comforted, it is for your consolation and salvation. ⁷ And our hope for you is steadfast, because we know that as you are partakers of the sufferings, so also you will partake of the consolation. ⁸ For we do not want you to be ignorant, brethren, of our trouble which came to us in Asia: that we were burdened beyond measure, above strength, so that we despaired even of life. ⁹ Yes, we had the sentence of death in ourselves, that we should not trust in ourselves but in God who raises the dead, ¹⁰ who delivered us from so great a death, and does deliver us; in whom we trust that He will still deliver us, ¹¹ you also helping together in prayer for us, that thanks may be given by many persons on our behalf for the gift granted to us through many. (2 Corinthians 1:3-11).*

Paul even takes his appreciation and understanding of the wisdom of God's wisdom in our trails further in his Romans' epistle when he says;

> And not only that, but we also glory in tribulations, knowing that tribulation produces perseverance; *4* and perseverance, character; and character, hope. *5* Now hope does not disappoint, because the love of God has been poured out in our hearts by the Holy Spirit who was given to us (Romans 5:3-5)

Another Apostle, whose invaluable contribution on the same subject is worth hearing, is James. He is so clear about the unparalleled value of the wisdom of God's wisdom in our tests and trials. He is a real veteran, and an encourager without precedence in this area, and so he puts it so plainly. He wants us to know that the profits are huge for staying put and not being shaken because of our trials. So he commands that we 'take our trials in our stride and to enjoy them. Don't complain because they will make a total woman or man of you in the end!' Here it is in James' own words:

> My brethren, count it all joy when you fall into various trials, *3* knowing that the testing of your faith produces patience. *4* But let patience have its perfect work, that you may be perfect and complete, lacking nothing. *5* If any of you lacks wisdom, let him ask of God, who gives to all liberally and without reproach, and it will be given to him. *6* But let him ask in faith, with no doubting, for he who doubts is like a wave of the sea driven and tossed by the wind. *7* For let not that man suppose that he will receive anything from the Lord; *8* he is a double-minded man, unstable in all his ways. *12* Blessed is the man who endures temptation; for when he has been approved, he will receive the crown of life which the Lord has promised to those who love Him (James 1:2-8,12).

It is amazing that James mentions wisdom when he is talking about trials and testing. Somewhere between the lines he sees a connection, between what we go through and the embedded wisdom within what we go through, and of course the wisdom also intended for ourselves, which we derive in the situation. This wisdom is not only necessary to help strengthen us to 'thrive' in our prevailing and on-going trails, but it also teaches us about life, in the end, making us better people.

One distinct peculiarity of James' approach to our sufferings and trials is what he mentions as the *'testing of our faith'*. In other words, while we think about our situations as odd and will do anything to get out of them quickly, James is actually saying that the wisdom of God's wisdom in our pressing trials, is actually not about us as individuals, but the faith we claim to have. *So, it is rather a trial of our faith than it is about us being on trial!* Question; will your faith pass the test? Will your anchor hold in the midst of the storm?

It was over forty long years in testing, so to speak, for the lame man, who sat at the gate called Beautiful, in Acts chapter three. Invariably, we all will have our testing of faith, some long, some short, and some tougher than others, but each in certain areas of life. Unfortunately, none of us can determine the when, why, where, how, or length of it. But one thing is common to all; the wisdom of God's wisdom in all that He may permit us to go through, and which profits greatly in the end. It will also be a source of peace to know that, in all that we go through, He is there with us. *"He promises never to leave us or forsake us" (Hebrews 13:5)*, and He also said *"When you pass through the waters, I will be with you; and through the rivers, they shall not overflow you. When you walk through the fire, you shall not be burned, nor shall the flame scorch you" (Isaiah 43:2)*.

Sometimes I wonder, as others do, why it took so long for this lame man to finally get his miracle. Was he not around when Jesus was going about healing the sick? Did he not hear about Jesus, or were there no relatives who knew and heard what was happening at all the healing crusades the Lord conducted? We may not be able to find all the ready answers to our questions, but in all, the wisdom of God will always prevail. As we saw earlier, sometimes the destinies of others are so tied to our miracles, that until the time and seasons are right, nothing actually happens.

Or, again, like in the case of Esther, there is always bound to be such a thing like *"yet who knows whether you have come to the kingdom for such a time as this?" (Esther 4:14)*. Or even, as we saw with Joseph's own confession to his brothers, whom in the physical he thought had done him so much evil, but upon hindsight understood the wisdom of God, and therefore he was able console his fearful relatives. He told them, *"but as for you, you meant evil against me, but God meant it for good, in order to bring it about as it is this day, to save many people alive" (Genesis 50:20)*.

Ultimately, we see how Joseph's situation with his own brothers impacts on him, sets up Joseph for God's promotion, and then changes the lives of his brothers for good. They stuck together, were delivered from envy and hatred, and also saw and experienced God's grace and miracles through the life of Joseph.

Joseph, in the end, was a powerful embodiment of the message and beauty of God's grace to his bothers, who thought they deserved only worse treatment and death, for the wrong they did to their little brother. Who else could have represented and communicated the message of God's unlimited grace and love, except Joseph himself, who was ill-treated, and had to suffer the consequences of his brothers' erstwhile, selfish decisions and choices. At least, Joseph learned this truth in the end, that his experience was purposeful and was the wisdom of God's wisdom in his trials.

Evangelising the Church

Interestingly, present, within that gorgeous temple, were a group of 'unbelieving' and religious Jews, whose lives were to soon be greatly impacted upon through the whole scenario with the lame man who received his healing. Through this miracle, an occasion presented itself for the living gospel of faith to be preached to those who might have otherwise remained securely cocooned in their errors and shady traditions.

They had to listen, because they had seen the proof of the power of the gospel, which alone is able to save and to deliver those bound for hell. With such a powerful demonstration of the Word of God, and seeing a healed cripple leaping, jumping and shouting in their midst, all ears might have been tingling to hear how it all happened, and what must they do to receive the same grace.

By the way, religious gatherings serve as some of the best occasions for the glory of God to descend with utter amazement. No wonder Peter and John took advantage to preach the good news of the Lord Jesus Christ.

You mean Peter and John went to preach to the sophisticated Jews and to evangelise a whole temple or 'church' of God? Yes, I believe God had in mind to convert, and to restore to Himself, this glorious temple built in the Name of God, but which had over time slipped into practicing 'religion', instead of sincerely *'seeking God in truth and in spirit'* (John 4:23, 24). This temple might have been full of religious showmen who didn't have faith. Think about it, we have modern equivalents of such giant temples in our day.

We built huge and gigantic religious monuments, full of unbelievers – and it's terrifying how much goes on *around* the people but not *inside* them. Often a good number of them come for all the wrong reasons, not to seek God, but to meet friends and to clap themselves happy. Some come simply for business networking, and others come for the songs and music. While they sing aloud, many times there's little going on by way of change in their personal lives, or even obedience to the Word of God.

In fact, it has been said that our generation is the only one that sings worship songs dried to their early death at the same rate at which they are being produced. You know why? The answer is simple. We live in a disposable era, in which almost anything in our societies is deemed to be disposable. Everything is disposable. 'Faith' unfortunately for some is disposable, and I am afraid even life itself is fast becoming disposable. In some western societies now, although it's frowned upon, sadly, elderly people are deemed as economic burdens that should be 'disposed' of; and selfishly, unborn children are legally 'disposable' under the guise of 'abortion rights'.

We swap and shift by the minute. And because most of our modern worship songs are really not Holy Spirit inspired and born out of a true heart of worship, but made to excite the flesh, they are more prone to being neglected, compared to our older traditional hymns, which have stood the test of time. Unlike those hymns that were born out of true, and in many cases, personal encounters with God, some modern artists roll modern 'praise' songs out of the factory of entertainment houses, purposely engineered and arranged for people's 'itching ears', and popularity. The idea is for people to 'fall in love with the song'; but how about falling in love with God first?

Our once fiery and sincere preachers have turned into motivational speakers, mimicking great antics of salesmanship. In some cases, not much of it can move a fly, let alone change lives or drive a den to promote change or even present a little challenge to the hearers. We've made of our preachers men and women who focus more on styles and clever use of words with enticing rhythms of music. We have now great funny storytellers and entertainers behind some of our pulpits.

Why have preachers suddenly turned from the 'lively and burning coal' of the Word of God, which is 'sharper than any two edged sword'? This is a good question that begs an answer. Instead of *"contending for the faith once bought by the precious blood of Christ and faithfully delivered to us by the saints"* (cf Jude 1:3), some preachers are rather contending for the ways of the world against the church; arguing that the church of God must adapt to the world in the name of being trendy, modern, and relevant.

Obviously, I am for modern forms, story telling and all that But let's get back to the *meat* of it; the matchless Word of God, the power and presence of the Holy Spirit, the love of God, faith, prayer, the longing for righteousness, holiness, and all the things that make for true godliness. They are right there, richly in the Word of God, and the Lord Jesus is our true model when His brothers, then unbelievers, tried to persuade Him to *contend* for worldly fame rather the faith, He refused. Jesus told them that the world hated Him, because He testified against the works of the world that they were evil (John 7:3-7). Similarly, Jesus said that those who will take exception to the evil works of this world, in order to follow Him fully, will be hated and persecuted by the world (John 15:19-21).

Therefore, we, His disciples must consider, and even get wearied if need be, about the kind of testimonies we champion. Are they contending for worldly fame, speaking for the evil works of the world as opposed to speaking for the faith? Are we asking and arguing for the church to lower and modify its high spiritual and moral standards so as to accommodate the evil works of this present world? Or we are lowering our standards because of worldly gains and popularity? Don't forget, *"godliness with contentment is great gain. For we brought nothing into this world, and it is certain we can carry nothing out"* (1Timothy 6:6,7).

While I am writing, I have in mind, places where we have situated some of the best buildings Britain had ever built in the Name of God. Most of them have now been turned into nice tourist attractions, that provide great sights for on-lookers, but nothing really of true spirituality. The only thing 'religious' about them now are the names, steeples and style of the buildings themselves with predictably well rehearsed music and chants delivered to a very few, who collect and gather in the centre arena of the buildings. O, that God will revisit us again, and revive His works, and restore His glory in those buildings!

Recently, a self proclaimed Freemason relative of a member of our church, who attended a service, boastfully told me how 'Christian' and charitable their Freemason group were, because they paid for a renovation work on one of the falling towers of a huge cathedral, that has become a relic and a UNESCO protected site. That's not just shameful but disgraceful, and stands as a bad reminder to the body of Christ in Britain, indicative of how we've practically neglected, and have been sidelined from our core position and responsibilities as true believers in Christ, in nations that are in dire spiritual turmoil.

What does all this point to? Are churches in our time needing to be 'evangelised' also? I will be the least surprised if the Lord instructs some to begin to think about something along that line. Probably, we are losing, or have lost, our 'first works' (Rev. 2:5) from the looks of things. There's never been anytime in history when the church has been so sucked-in by the world and its debauchery and wantonness, so influenced and lured by the dodgy practices and principles of the world in the name of *being all things to all men*. Gone are the days when the true church was mostly persecuted for its beliefs and stands on faith and morality.

Unlike the historical church, most of what we see today is now mainly just a fight for mere identity and social status. This is often symbolized by erecting vast multi-million edifices and conducting big advertising drives to 'recycle' existing Christians, through mounting programmes with flimsy titles like 'fresh fire'. It wouldn't matter even if the title were 'cold fire', and the people still had the Word of God preached with God confirming His Word by signs, wonders and people being saved by the power of the Holy Spirit.

But, the opposite seems to be the case with those who drum up big titles with no substance, a wonderfully styled and staged conference in which great 'orators' argue in favour of worldly trends under the guise of church growth strategies. This is exactly what happens when a people or movements lose their focus, fervour and purpose.

Is there hope for the churches? I believe, there is. But, it will come from God Almighty, and through the power of His Holy Spirit. He will cause us to be revisited by His *Day Spring from on High*, to revive and to refresh His people once again. It will be sooner than later!

Dealing with Establishment Mentality

I believe the Jewish temple, with its magnificent and beautiful gates, somewhere along the line temporarily side stepped its main focus and purpose. As a result it had begun to enforce and to celebrate its weak past and tradition. Hence, it simply became a place harbouring, maybe some very sincere 'seekers', but people who were now trapped in 'establishment' mentality.

Unfortunately, most people who are trapped and encircled by this dangerous mentality don't look beyond themselves. They are not those who 'come and to save those who are lost', but on the contrary, they want to save only themselves. They are about 'name' keeping not God seeking. They are more concerned about what people think about them than what God thinks about them.

They make rules and thrive on rules and authorities to entrench themselves. Most of their time is spent on propagating, elaborating, strengthening, and protecting the rules that they make in the Name of God. Remember Jesus with the Pharisees and Sadducees and their laws. He said to them, 'you spent all your life making rules that yourselves don't keep, all because you want to exclude others' (See Matthew 23:13).

That's exactly the case, the one with 'establishment mentality' is intent on excluding others, but in very subtle ways that selfishly provide protection for themselves and their pursuits. That's why the Son of God had no patience for the unrepentant Sadducees and Pharisees. He told them, *'your fathers killed the prophets (the voice of God and of Justice), and you built beautiful sepulchre for their bones'* (Mtt. 23:29-32).

Well, it is almost tempting to say, 'thank God for the invalid or lame man, and his faith to be healed, which allowed the true light of the gospel of Christ to enter and pervade a dark, dying temple, and to challenge its nonchalant religious 'congregation' to a new hope.'

This is the point; that the things that happen to us, big or small and the things that we go through, harsh or painful, most often bear within them the subtle wisdom of God's wisdom, plans and purposes. God may not cause those situations but, regardless, He may use them for greater purposes, even beyond ourselves.

Most often, like Apostle James says, it is not even about us, but our faith, and where it relates to us, the Lord is with us in it, working through it to bring us out of it. While He is glorified, we turned out much wiser, and others of course are inspired, blessed through the experience and wisdom we gained. It is just absolutely amazing how the miracle of God brings good out of terribly bad situations.

> ... *"Fear not, for I have redeemed you; I have called you by your name; you are Mine. ² When you pass through the waters, I will be with you; and through the rivers, they shall not overflow you. When you walk through the fire, you shall not be burned, nor shall the flame scorch you. ³ For I am the Lord your God...* (Isa. 43:1-3).

Part III

POSITIONING YOURSELF FOR BLESSINGS AND MIRACLES
[*More Possibilities in the Mysteries of God: Possessing, Recovering and Enjoying Your Blessing and Inheritance*]

Chapter Fifteen

THE GAINT KILLER: GOD'S SECRET WISDOM FOR ATTAINING HEIGHTS

Commit your way to the Lord; trust in Him and he will do this (Ps. 37:5)

In Numbers 14:1-12, we have such a brilliant word about how our challenges ought to serve, in helping us to get to where God desires for us. This understanding is so critical for believers, and we need to know that our challenges are more than just what they appear to be. Actually, they build and set us up for the victory that we require for attaining God's prophetic destinies and promises.

If you were to browse the immediate context of the story, of which the book of Numbers belong, you will realise that God, willingly spurred by His love, justice, and faithfulness, took it upon Himself to deliver the children of Israel, during the period of their great suffering in Egypt. God was under no duress to execute deliverance for Israel. Just that the time came for His promise to Abraham to be fulfilled. So, He decided that the time had finally arrived for Him to respond to the *cry* of Israel. Through His wisdom and the strength of His might, He did something that had never been done in history.

God moved with great terror and vengeance against the Egyptians and their pharaohs, with only two things in mind; to liberate His people and to bring them into a good land that He had prepared for them. If He took them out, He had to bring them in.

May I therefore suggest to you that whenever God takes you out from an initial address, or a situation, He certainly will bring you into a new address and into a better place and condition. For the Israelites this meant taking them from their captivity in Egypt to a beautiful land of promise, prosperity, and a land which flowed with 'milk and honey'.

The Lord liberated His people and brought them through many difficulties. But, at the banks of Jordan, the very ground next to the promise, and at the verge of entering the Promised Land, a challenge arose. They received bad news, and became very discouraged. They imagined and saw a steep challenge of gigantic proportion.

Have you been there before? When it seems all was set for taking and having that which you've desired and waited for, prayed about and in some instances sacrificed for, only to realise it was not what you thought? Sometimes, it's only days before the full manifestation of the good you had expected, and then the devil shows up in a big way with a bad report, least expected.

The Israelites received a bad report, delivered by men they trusted, their hand-picked representatives. The men would have been the best crop of their military specialists, ingenious leaders, and of integrity amongst their tribes. Hence, when they spoke, their people listened and acted. When the men delivered their report about the land which God had promised, instead of inspiring the rest of the Israelites to move quickly into the land, they became dispirited, and asked to return to Egypt, the land of their captivity.

As you read Numbers 13:27 to 33, you get a sense of the full impact of the report on Israel, and the kind of atmosphere that the report engendered through the spies, their assessments, conclusions, and the reactions of the entire camp of Israel after they heard the report. Let me attempt a brief analysis of the situation, by picking on some of the salient points in their report, in order to render some important observations for our purpose.

Initially, all the spies who returned claimed that *'the land is good, but!'* Does that sound familiar husband or wife? Yes, in some respects we are all like those spies. God gives us His best but in our limited understanding, we meanwhile always find some form of fault, one way or another. It may not be the case with you, but quite often you hear folks say things like this about their spouse, *"she is beautiful, but,* or *he is caring, but."* Beware of *buts*, and don't throw all the *good* away with, or because of the little *but*. Treat the *good* and the *but* as you would the *baby and the bath water scenario*. Appreciate the *good*, and work on the *but*. Don't abandon the '80%' for the '20%'; that's the whole wisdom of the *Pareto* or *efficiency principle* in my view.

Secret Wisdom for Facing Giants & Attaining Heights

There are at least five important lessons for attaining the heights we desire, which we can learn as God's secret wisdom from the lives and situation of the spies and the Promise Land.

Lesson #1: Good things never come easy, and even if they do, it involves some degrees of uncertainty (the buts), and there is no easy way to the pearl.

Whether it is about pursuing your faith in Christ, freedom, wealth, a successful life, excellence in your profession, a university degree, or getting your desired wife or husband – you've got to battle and to overcome a certain degree of challenges, including disappointments, discouragements, betrayals, and uncertainties.

The reasons for this are many and varied, but can be surmounted.

1. *Other People's Challenge:* Bad reports are bound to come in some forms and at some levels. They might be news of discouragement from well meaning people. It could even be a seeming failure in our attempt to go for our dreams, or to fulfil a desire. It's quite normal no matter your faith.

   Having escaped war in my own country, I tried to enrol into a university in one of my host countries then. The first real challenge I had was fighting the discouragement battle. Some friends, who had earlier attempted to enrol but failed, told me I was attempting a mountain I could not climb, and that it was virtually impossible to enrol for a tertiary education at that time, with the foreign high school qualification that I had.

   When I finally managed to get enrolled, the same people raised new concerns with me about the question of accreditation. However, my major challenge then was always economic hardship. I couldn't afford tuition fees, or funds for daily living. But I learned that, *every good opportunity for fulfilling our dreams presents equal challenge, with sometimes tougher odds and options.* I had to push on, trusting in the grace of God Almighty.

2. *Personal Challenge:* Apart from bad reports from others, you yourself may lack the required confidence, skills or abilities to pursue your dreams and desires. Something inside you actually affirms and concords with you that you surely cannot become or do whatever God wants you to do and become.

   Nothing ever frightened me more than the thought of being called by God into ministry. Right from the outset, the very awareness of my personal limitations and weaknesses always gave me away, and I tactically avoided any opportunity to speak to anyone, or to preach in morning assemblies in Bible College.

Personal challenge; this to me is the greatest enemy and biggest challenge and obstacle that could befall any person just beginning, or following up on their dreams or promise. It has the potential to lead to other serious issues including the derailment of your future. So, deal with it!

Lesson #2: Our Challenges have the tendency to cause us to give up on God, question His integrity and to become cynical about His ability and faithfulness.

Have you ever encountered anyone who, due to unfortunate or tragic experience in their background, ask questions like, *"if there was truly God, then why did He allow such and such to happen?"* We all fail, at some point in our lives, to recognise the fact that human beings on earth take definite actions with consequences, whether immediate or deferred. Hence, we really should be asking that question the other way round, *"if there is God why not?"*

For the Israelites, in the wake of their challenge concerning the Promised Land and the bad report they received, their overall reaction turned out to be the most tragic move, which was to decide to reject God and the leaders God had given them. They ignored Moses and Aaron, who had been with them all this while, and chose to elect new leaders. At least Aaron had always been their man, made to prepare *golden calf* for them, yet they dismissed him.

By the way, Preachers, watch out, and take a clue from Aaron. Even if you 'sin' for them in appeasement, it won't stop them from 'sinning' against you when the time comes. *If they can 'sin' against God, they will definitely 'sin' against you.* It is therefore always better to be found to please God, than to please man against the will of God.

This means that challenges have the odd potential for blinding their sufferers. We are told in the verses that God found the behaviour of the Israelites, not only appalling, but punishable, by giving them over to the consequence of their careless pronouncements. Apparently, their resentment for God at the time amounted to rejecting and despising the Almighty God (vrs 11, 12). Had Moses not interceded in a timely manner, God would have allowed them to be immediately stricken.

Lesson #3: Every challenge presents you with an unequal opportunity to birth your dreams, depending on what you make of it. (vrs 6,7)

Caleb and Joshua could not wait to see and to inhabit the Promised Land, knowing it would change their lot for the best. So, despite the many other voices of fear and discouragement, they rose and spoke differently concerning the same land they had helped to spy out.

Caleb and Joshua teach us to choose our response carefully, teaching us that, every time you hear the majority say what they always say and are used to, for example how things are so impossible, you must choose to see things differently as God would have you see and know them.

Caleb and Joshua were therefore motivated and driven by their perspective and interpretation of the Promised Land, while the rest were driven, frightened away, and even frozen by the same land. I have always wondered, how people, including a relation, because of 'challenges', chose to return to our then civil war ravaged country, claiming that our country of refuge, with its relative peace and more favourable quality of living, was impossible and deplorable.

In my mind, their decision to return to our country at that time was more like *'running from the frying pan into the fire.'* And truly in the end it proved to be so. But they had made their decision to return, mainly because of similar reasons as the Israelites had; a bad report about the Promised Land. The Israelites chose to return to Egypt, the same land that devoured them along with their children, turning their backs on Canaan, the Promised Land.

Lesson #4: If only we'll consider well, we will realize that the opportunities in our challenges far surpass our greatest challenges. The only thing is we don't know.

Let's consider the analogy of a pregnant woman. Out of nine months of having to daily bear under the challenges of pregnancy and the final birth pangs challenge, she brings another life into the world. Ultimately, the result is that, a man becomes a father, she a mother, others grand parents, and brings honour to the father, joy to others, and the child of course becomes a potential husband, or wife to someone, among other things.

The same child might become a leader with potential to influence the world remarkably. All this becomes potentially possible just for a single price of nine months of endurance with pregnancy.

Now, consider the children of Israel, a people without a country, who were now at the verge of having one for themselves, their children and posterity. Besides, with their new country they had a promise of greater freedom and liberty, which they had never known all their lives in Egypt. But they chose to fear the single price of moving straight on into the Promised Land, and that generation of Israelites lost their opportunities and privileges.

Lesson #5: The greatest challenge in life that we face is how to overcome our immediate challenge toward our opportunity or dream. Because, every challenge leads us closer to the opportunity and the promise.

Those who did not make it to Canaan died at the banks of the River Jordan, only a stone throw away from their permanent inheritance (vr. 26ff). Regrettably, many of those who usually give up, do so right in the middle of their miracles; some also fail before they begin, and still so many stop at their very last challenge, immediately close to their miracles, having successfully overcome every previous challenge.

I will close this chapter, with six, Bible inspired suggestions based on the life and experience of the spies and the camp of Israel. The intention is to help you make your challenge to work for you, and help you to ride on the wings of your challenge to great heights.

The suggestions themselves were thoroughly gleaned from Numbers 14:7-24, on a verse by verse basis, and I believe they will help you to turn your challenges into stepping stones that will work for you instead of working against you.

   a. Always see things from the perspective of God. Or see your challenges from the point of view of God. The way God sees them really matters. Don't attempt your challenges relying on your own feelings and emotions or physical strength (Vr. 7).

   b. Always endeavour to know God's will concerning whatever your challenges or promises are. If God promised you, then it means He will move mountains just to help you obtain the promise (Vr. 8).

   c. Never become a rebel nor join those who rebel against God's purpose because of their own lack of understanding, fear and insecurities. The number one aim of the devil through your challenge is to make you rebel against God, and thus lose out on God's supplied favour and help for coming through your challenges. Surely, without God's favour toward you, your challenge is a stumbling block instead of a stepping stone (Vr. 9).

   d. Remember that it is easy to throw stones (criticize) – so people (even the greater number of them, including your family) will criticize you especially when you decide to act on God's words or promises. But don't be deceived by numbers and the logic and intensity of their criticisms. Continue to keep your eyes on God and 'go forward', which is the only way out of your challenge (wilderness) into your promise (Vr. 10).

e. Remember that your past good God, the God of your little valleys and 'Egypt', is the same good God of your present and future challenges, and indeed your God of the mountains as well (Vrs 22 – 23).

f. God's approval and victory in every challenge is gladly obtained by those who choose to be different by following Him fully. Being different in a world of indifference is to adhere to God's voice and seek to please Him alone. How do you please Him? Don't doubt Him, go forward and act in faith (Vr. 24)!

Chapter Sixteen

THE GOLIATH CHALLENGE: ANTICIPATING YOUR DIVINE OPPORTUNITIES

The story of David and Goliath in 1Samuel 17:20-24, 33-37 is quite intriguing and also very revealing for anyone who is looking forward to a great life with God. The way forward is actually to begin to anticipate and prepare for possible future challenges, which in truth are your divine opportunities in disguise.

Understandably, for the 'pragmatic' person who thinks the best way to live is just getting on with it, I know it might sound a bit 'pessimistic' and burdensome, to ask them to think about preparing for future challenges. But, without you being conscious of it, that's exactly what you are doing right now; preparing.

Believe it or not, God asks that we *"write down the vision for it is for an appointed time and would speak in the end" (Habakkuk2:2-3)*. So, all I am trying to do is to remind, and to encourage you to take your present preparation from the unconscious to the conscious realm, giving it all your best, because a lot more depends on what you are doing right now.

You know how we tend to go to school and make every effort to finish successfully, so that we can become employable or be able to start up something in a chosen specialty, and to be able to afford good living? That's similar to preparing for future challenges. It gives us some leverage and some degree of control over how our future turns out. It also helps, in that whenever an opportunity avails itself, we are already ready to take it on.

Let me simply define 'preparing' as *getting ready beforehand*. It is a pre-activity in view of a prospect or an expectation, and a desire. Or, it's just something done in advance.

Challenge, on the other hand stands for a competition, a battle, a task, a reality, or a problem that needs to be faced and hopefully resolved. Yet, in the light of our Christian faith, a *challenge* connotes an opportunity, a 'faith builder', and a process, in some cases necessary for the victory we will have at the end. And interestingly, there are so many challenges that life presents to us. Even the desire to enter into marriage comes with its own challenge, and one must always prepare if indeed they expect to have a good and successful marriage.

However, not many people realise that, in fact, we are born into challenges, and to begin with, the very circumstances that surround our conception and birth involves great challenge. We have challenges as children and challenges as adults. Life is full of challenges. But the major question we need to confront is, asking ourselves if indeed we are prepared to handle our challenges as God gives us the grace?

How prepared are you to discern the divine opportunity for a life of purpose that lies within your challenge? And what will it take to prepare for your challenges especially those of us seeking great things from the Almighty God? Are you ready *'to turn your lemons into lemonade'*?

Giant Problem – Giant Solution

Goliath represents a form of challenge; a battle, and a task that the children of Israel had to face or confront. Their challenge and the way it was attempted provides a lifetime wisdom, and crucial lessons for people who intend to effectively face their own challenges and to overcome victoriously. Let's consider a few of these lessons from this great story:

Lesson #1: The challenges of life will either lift you up or sink you. You can either ride on the wings of your challenge to greatness, or your challenge could become a stumbling block to stop you from reaching greatness. The difference is preparation.

Just for a while, imagine surfers, who aim for and mount a huge wave of the sea to propel their surfboard for a terrific surfing experience. The greater the wave of the sea, the better they lift and surf. How majestic!

The entire story of David and Goliath is a wonderful soul lifting experience, and a great story involving challenge. Although his name is not mentioned, the first time we encountered David was after God had rejected Saul as a king, because of his regrettable disobedience and arrogance towards God's commandments, in 1Samuel 13. Upon rejecting Saul as king before Him, God revealed to Samuel, His prophet, in verse 14 of chapter 13, that He has already "sought for Himself a man after His own heart, and has commanded him to become commander over His people." Soon afterwards, the prophet, under God's instruction, was sent to anoint with oil God's chosen king for Israel.

The prophet had only been told about the family of this prospective king but not the name or description of the person himself. He was only told to locate the family of Jesse, a relatively insignificant Bethlehemite family. In that family, God found and anointed for

Himself a king for Israel in waiting, a young lad and a shepherd boy, David, whom God referred to as a 'king after His own heart'. Then, after that, David returned to the bush and to keeping his sheep.

Meanwhile, a time came when Israel, along with their existing king, Saul, was faced with a growing and daunting battle against their arch enemy, the Philistines. Israel as a nation had seen and experienced different kinds of challenges and battles; however, this one was totally different and very intimidating. In fact, they were taken by surprise when no other person but the great giant and veteran, referred to as Goliath, took his position and roared from the brow of the rocky, high hills.

Let me intervene with few quick wisdom references from the life of Israel before going further:

> (1) The challenge or battle you fail to overcome today will definitely surface as a big giant before you in the future. My own childhood experience with bullies taught me, that I either face my challenge squarely now, no matter how intimidating or fierce it might be, or avoid it as an easy escape and continually live under duress and fear, with possible catastrophic outcome in the end.
>
> The same is true for people who try to cover their weaknesses in some form without learning to conquer them now. In this case, it will work like a bad prophecy, causing greater harm and shame in the future. Israel unfortunately failed to annihilate, or to summarily defeat Philistine when they previously had the opportunity and, with Philistine being spared, Philistine later produced a giant opposition called Goliath, who was now firmly poised to annihilate Israel.

(2) In life, there's one natural promise; we will always face new challenges, with the potential to surprise us if we are not prepared.

Now, the armies of the two nations have been set in battle array on both sides of opposite hills along the valley of Elah. The call into battle of those days was mostly trumpeted from hill tops and mountains amongst valleys. The battles themselves were held down in the valleys, as armies descended down the adjacent hills of the valleys.

This time, something strange happened. The Philistines changed the rules. The Philistines knowing that they had the upper hand, because they had Goliath on their side, decided to change the rules of the battle. Instead of the army meeting at the bottom of the valley to fight, they decided that the outcome (victory) of the battle should rather be decided by a contest of *champions*; one representative from Israel and one from the Philistines. Naturally, Goliath, the giant became the champion of the Philistines. But Israel had no one to go for them. Why? They had not prepared for this kind of challenge before. Little David, just stumbling into the battle field, would later come to their rescue.

Let's size the two champions as they do with heavy weight boxers. First, Goliath was too intimidating. He was a giant, 9'9" tall. His armour was 125 pounds and his spear had a fifteen pounds iron head. He had a javelin, a bronze helmet, and He was a veteran and a skilled warrior (1Samuel 17:33).

David, a youth of about seventeen years old, who had only been keeping his father's sheep in the bush, not knowing what Israel was going through at the battle front, was sent by his father to take some food for his brothers in the camp of the Israelites. He got there, and then he heard Goliath again throwing a challenge to the Israelites, to send a representative and a champion to face him. Goliath even threatened to destroy any representative that they would choose.

Of course, David was enraged by Goliath's threat and insults against Israel, but especially Goliath's blasphemy against their God. So, he first asked some of the soldiers of Israel, and then his own brothers what would be done for the one who kills Goliath.

David's insightful question to the Israelite army, and then to his brothers, pre-empts two important wisdom principles in the lessons of challenges:

Lesson #2. Challenges present unequal opportunities for the fulfilment of our dreams. Ask the right questions – know the reward.

Lesson #3. Your rewards in life are directly related to the kind of challenge you are prepared to face and to conquer.

David's brother, Eliab (*Meaning, God is father*) heard him when he inquired about Goliath and also what would be done for the one who kills Goliath, and takes away reproach from Israel. Eliab immediately got angry and shut David down, accusing him of being arrogant. But you see, while Eliab, Saul and the rest of the army of Israel considered Goliath a ferociously huge and unconquerable challenge and caved away, David saw a good 'recipe' and an open door for handsome reward and promotion. This fact, undoubtedly represents a major difference between champions and losers.

David's reaction to Eliab's scrutiny and comments was swift and decisive. The Bible says about David, *"then he turned from him (Eliab) toward another"* asking the same question about rewards for killing Goliath and removing reproach from Israel. Unlike Eliab, those David asked confirmed that *"it shall be that the man who kills him the king will enrich with great riches, will give him his daughter, and give his father's house exemption from taxes in Israel."*

Imagine all that for solving only one problem, which involved facing and defeating Goliath on behalf of Israel. Of course that was more than enough incentive for a young man, whose sole occupation had been watching over his family's entire life-time assets of only a *'few sheep'* in the wilderness. It couldn't have been any better than that, a great door of opportunity had just opened and David's prayer for breakthrough was being answered.

Unfortunately, there aren't many people who would see *Goliath* as a means for their breakthrough and an answer to their prayers, but David did. He saw a divine opportunity in the challenge of Goliath. Eliab didn't see a *cause* and a good reason, or motivation to rise to the challenge. His *cause* and motivation were not strong and compelling enough to dwarf his fear, but David had a *cause* to live and to die for.

Along these lines, the young David teaches us, again, three great lessons in the wisdom of challenge, and how to use them to our advantage, no matter the price and our temporary oppositions. At the same time, David also brings us into *the behaviour of a champion*, a man with a *cause*:

Lesson **#4**. *In the battles of life, you will definitely find good and well-meaning people who will advise you to be careful, and cause you to lose your opportunities and blessings. They don't understand that great blessings are born out of great risk and certainly from great challenges. It is a strange mathematics but the result is always highly gratifying. The greater the risk and the challenge, the greater the rewards.*

Like David *turned* from his brother Eliab, who sought the easy path with the rest of Israel's army, Jesus sharply rebuked Peter and *turned* from him, saying he was an offence, because Peter tried stopping Jesus from going to Jerusalem where He would ultimately face the cross for the ultimate redemption of humankind (Mtt.16:23). Thank God He *turned* from Peter and continued to Jerusalem. David saw a good cause for facing Goliath, and the Lord saw a good cause for going to Jerusalem, knowing He would be crucified there (Hebrews 12:2; 2:10).

Lesson #5. Eliab tried to stop David and David replied, *"is there not a caused?"* When it comes to facing challenges in life, you've got to be resolute, forceful and persistent. Before you do, first know the cause and insist on it, or find a good and compelling cause, then do something about it.

You have got to, with God's help take, your destiny into your own hands at some point, instead of waiting for people to first endorse you. The vigorous reaction of Eliab could have easily gotten David discouraged, had he not seen and known the *cause* for which he stood. He was ready to defend and redeem his nation, and of course, take the opportunity for him to break from poverty, and to change his family's destiny for good.

Lesson #6. Always consider the reward of your challenge and not the report of your inability as others perceive them to be. Stand up firmly for a good cause and your difference will soon become apparent from the rest.

Which Battle Outfit?

When David insisted that he had what was required to defeat Goliath and to save Israel, he was taken to King Saul, and Saul, after a brief conference, wisely agreed for David to become their champion. In addition, he offered David his complete war armour; his helmet, shield and sword, which David found to be too heavy. He hardly could walk in them, so David immediately took them off and explained to Saul that he had not tested those before.

> *Lesson #7.* Know your strength, and choose your battle outfit wisely. Often, when we face our battles, people offer a whole lot of possible expert views and suggestions, except those we really need. Some present a quick way out with counterfeit labels. But know that genuine solutions are usually long-term and have been tested.

Lesson #8. Get rid of anything you haven't tested before. Don't let people put their *suits* on you. David said, I will go in the *Name of the Lord,* and, with his sling and stick, which he had tested before, he killed Goliath. The truth is; every "Goliath" is killed in the 'Name of the Lord' and with a weapon that has been tested by the user.

The name of the Lord is a strong tower, the righteous run to it and are safe (Proverb 18:10).

Qualities for Anticipating Divine Opportunities and Greatness

David faced his challenge because he was prepared. Even becoming a king, he was prepared, that is why he was chosen by God. Becoming the king of God's people, Israel, was no chance game as people would want to think. The Scriptures make it abundantly clear that David had always been in preparation, awaiting his opportunities. It might not have been specifically for kingship or killing Goliath, but indeed for greatness, when the time came and the opportunity availed itself. This was almost an open secret to some of the people who knew David privately in preparation (see 1 Samuel 16:18). And when the time became right, David was not just the choice of God, but also the people.

Gleaning from 1Samuel chapter 16, a compilation of the qualities that David gained in preparation that endeared him to God, his people and king Saul can be made. In verses six and seven, God, who does not see as humans see, affirming His absolute ability to assess above all humans, provided for Himself a king amongst the sons of Jesse, the father of David. That meant, God had thoroughly looked all over Israel, and the only one that satisfied His 'high' standards for a king over His people, was one of the sons of Jesse, the young man David.

While it is apparent from the reading of the text that some were judging David from flawed external human measurement and criteria, God was seeing more in David than was immediately visible to the human eyes. It seems to me that it was David's personal character, his attitude and acquired skill, that 'impressed' God for him to be chosen. Of course, that would entail and mean that David had also cultivated deep and rich spirituality towards God as a basis for all he knew and did.

Other people, who knew David privately, located and recommended him. When King Saul had his rare vexing and troubling issues with a distressing and evil spirit, a servant of King Saul, without hesitating put his neck on the line for David; highly recommending him as the best person to help the King. Here is what he said about David in 1Samuel 16:18, *"Look, I have seen a son of Jesse the Bethlehemite, who is skillful in playing, a mighty man of valor, a man of war, prudent in speech, and a handsome person; and the Lord is with him."* There we have it, need we improve on that?

This certainly describes a man with a mission and purpose in life, who has put some time into preparing himself adequately for life's opportunities. David, from what the servant of King Saul said about him, was a good man, but also very versatile, the kind of person any top boss or company would love to employ. He was the kind of person that could easily create opportunities instead of waiting for one. David, in brief, worked hard to make himself indispensable in every way, and remember, apart from man's recommendation, he had God's and *"the Lord was with him"*.

When David finally met his potential employer, the King, Saul loved him greatly and immediately gave him a job as his armour bearer (vrs 21). Having greatly impressed the King, through his contribution in refreshing and providing respite for the King from his affliction of the distressing, evil spirit, David found favour with the King and was requested to stay in the palace with the King (vr 22).

Well, that sounds like promotion, and a great change in destiny for a young man, who has before now been following sheep in the wilderness and confronting bears and lions. David here is already living the reality of Bible truths, *"a man's gift makes room for him, and brings him before great men"*, according to Proverbs. 18:16.

Lesson #9. Opportunities will always come to those who are prepared. Our attitude and skills are everything we need to face our challenge, no matter our position or location. Most people miss this important truth and only concentrate on their appearance, and delight in outward adornment.

Work on your appearance, but you've got to kill your 'lions' and 'bears', as David did. Love God, be resilient, be versatile and climb every mountain, and also work on your character, the lack of which greatly hinders and betrays all of one's hard work, skills and good appearance.

Things to Know and Do before Goliath Appears

Still dwelling on the life of David, we can gain some more valuable insights into his plans and strategies, to inform and to enrich ours, for seizing life's opportunities and for facing our 'Goliath' when he eventually appears. Trying to keep things systematic, we will do a modest trace on David's life, looking at 1Samuel 17:33-37 on a verse by verse basis, and then derive the essential principles for life's application, concerning what we need to know and to do before Goliath ever appears.

(#1) *Vr. 33.* Always remember, it is not your age, but your attitude within the challenge of life, that makes the difference. If you ever intend to rival 'Goliath' and overcome then:

(a) Seek that the Lord is with you and delights in you (cf Number 13:27-33)

(b) Develop a positive attitude no matter what other people say (cf Number 13:27-33).

(**#2**) *Vrs 33, 34.* Begin from where you are. Don't wait for big opportunities before you start. Where you are is the road that leads to where you are going. Your present experience is your most valuable asset for your future battles.

(**#3**) *Vr 36.* Don't avoid the *lions* and the *bears*. They are your faith, wisdom, knowledge and experience builders. Your mastery of your present challenge or task should eventually make you prepared for overcoming greater challenges. For a moment, think about Proverbs 24:5; *"a man of knowledge (not muscles) increases strength."*

(**#4**) *Vrs 37.* (a) Remember your God. Have faith in God's ability to help you. Your past good God is your present and future good God.

(b) Take a step of Faith and the Lord will back you up (cf Numbers 14:5-12). 'Without faith it is impossible to please God' (Hebrews 11:6)

(c) Remember that the challenges of life are not necessarily designed to defeat you, but to prove you; perhaps you know what to do. In Judges 3:1-4 we learned that the Philistines were left to be a test of Israel's obedience and their confidence in Yahweh.

Chapter Seventeen

THE MAGNETIC NATURE: PROVOKING AND POSSESSING MIRACLES

The official name of the woman that we intend to consider in this chapter and the next, for some unknown reason, was not given. However, she is the woman in 2 Kings 4:8 to 37; simply referred to as the Shunammite woman, and specifically described as a *notable* or great woman.

Based on her story, she could also be portrayed as persuasive, because she, with a great tact, was able to convince a reluctant man of God to accept her offer of a 'purpose-built' upper room apartment, for himself and his disciple. Most importantly, she belonged to a place called *Shunem* and thus her description as a *Shunammite*.

Shunem means *'uneven'*, and if the use of the reference, '*Shunammite* woman', has any relation to the quality of the woman's nature or character, then one could surmise that, there was something special about her. Why would the one telling the story specifically prefer to call her a *Shunammite woman,* instead of using her true name, if it were known? She certainly must have earned herself the description, as a *Shunammite;* supposing that there was something quite peculiar, and in a positive way, 'out of balance' or 'uneven' about her. I would like to think that among other things, she was very assertive and forceful. So, making use of what in theology, and in particular homiletics and hermeneutics, is considered as a *preacher's liberty*, I would take it that, the reference to the woman as a *Shunammite* in this context conveys a certain point of view from which she is seen.

But, without being offensive or derogatory, let's consider right from the outset that this woman was not a 'regular' or 'normal woman'. And here are my reasons: First, she needed a miracle, and second, against all odds, she went all out to get it. The eighth verse of chapter four says that, she actually imposed on the man of God to stay in their house. No wonder the bible calls her a 'notable woman', because she did unusual and extra-ordinary things.

The Mark and Power of True Nobility

Remember, every person the Bible designates as truly 'noble' did something unusual and notable. Cornelius, the Roman centurion in Acts chapter ten, because of his unfailing faithfulness to God and his consistent generosity to God's people, he was exclusively picked to become the foremost gentile believer, through whom other gentiles had opportunity to freely partake of the gospel of Jesus Christ.

The people of Berea, who were considered most 'noble' among their contemporaries for receiving and carefully searching the Scriptures, earned themselves the praise of the apostles in Acts chapter seventeen verse eleven. Also, the Roman Centurion, whose servant was healed by the Lord Jesus in Luke chapter seven, was also deemed 'noble' because of his kindness to the Jewish community in building their synagogue and for exercising great faith.

Similarly, Hannah, the woman who persistently stood in faith for a child from God in first Samuel chapter one was a 'noble' woman. She sought her miracle with such 'bitterness of soul', immense pain, and a great faith, that Eli the Priest even thought she was drunk with wine.

Our present world will find it almost absurd to think that true nobility is a virtue for provoking and possessing miracles, and in some cases resurrecting a lost miracle. They use the term nobility vaguely, for what is falsely called 'class status' and status symbol.

However, in Scriptures, nobility was used sensibly, to describe the character and life of 'ordinary' men and women, who distinguished themselves through the exercise of 'extraordinary' faith towards God. Their nobility was also found in their reverence for God and the things of God, often translated into their good deeds, during times when such qualities were generally in short supply. In so doing, the same people, by virtue of their nobility, or noble character and deed also attracted God's benevolence in various measures and ways.

True nobles did not necessarily belong to a privileged class, or the high-ups and people who had to toe the line of self-imposed bigot's trend that was then prevalent in their societies. They only went beyond what was normal and ordinary when it came to faith and their trust towards God, typified by taking 'extraordinary' steps in obedience to the Word of God and proving, by their actions, that they truly believe God.

To put it more plainly, one would say the 'nobles' acted 'abnormally' and probably upset the majority, who followed the average way of tradition, religion and customs of their societies. That is why, most noble people experienced, sometimes, exclusive miracles and true divine encounters, because generally, *they were ordinary people acting in extraordinary ways in faith.*

Often, people who expect miracles, and who wish to provoke and possess those miracles, must become *noble* in the biblical sense. The same is also true for those who intend to resurrect their lost miracles. Expect to go contrary to what a good number of people ordinarily believe and do. For by faith, *"women received their dead raised to life again"* (Hebrews 11:35).

You will have to sometimes be ready to be called 'abnormal', eccentric and extreme in the eyes of many. Like the disciples of Jesus Christ, you may turn the 'world' of many people *upside down,* so to speak, by changing the 'order of their world' and probably how 'their world is ordered'. The disciples on their part refused to follow the existing order of things as witnesses of Christ. They simply did not allow rigid, manmade tradition to hold them back from God's true purpose; preaching the gospel and bringing healings to God's people.

Most often, Christians fall short of experiencing God's miracles because many prefer and embrace the existing order of things and come to be bound by them. And as a result, many fail miserably. The reason why they fail is because no true child of God should desire or even belong to this present 'world order'. The Christian belongs to a greater order, called the supernatural order of spiritual principles, meant to turn around things in this physical realm; *'for whatsoever is born of God overcomes the world. And this is the victory that has overcome the world – our faith'* (John 15:19).

Indeed, those who are the nobles, are people who actually know and appreciate the supernatural order of things, and allow such order to command, control, and to saturate their dealings here in this present 'world order'. Obviously, such people are *in* the world, but like Jesus says, "they are not *of* the world, just as I am not of the world" (John 17:16). And He continues to say, "I pray for them. I do not pray for the world but for those whom You have given Me, for they are Yours" (John 17:9), and such are those whom Jesus "has chosen out of the world" (John 15:19), for a kingdom mindset (Matt. 16:19) which is a totally a new "world order" for commanding God's supernatural favour, miracles and blessings on earth.

> *And I will give you the keys of the kingdom of heaven, and whatever you bind on earth will be bound in heaven, and whatever you loose on earth will be loosed in heaven (Matt. 16:19).*

Secrets of true Nobles: Wisdom from the Shunammitte Woman

Those who, in the real bible sense, are nobles, possess qualities that set them apart from others, including those who steal nobility and those that envy the nobles. What makes them true nobles are the very secrets that bring them into God's favour and cause them to experience the measure of blessing that others can only dream about.

From the life of the Shunammitte woman, we might be able to glean some of the secrets of the true nobles by answering the question, 'what did she know?' This is in the hope that we too can benefit from her knowledge for provoking and possessing our miracles.

1. *Honour has Rewards.* The Shunammitte woman discovered how to provoke the miracles and blessings of God. There is nothing superficial or gimmicky about coming into the blessings and miracles of God. It always will be the same, for every person who desires something from God, but lacks the natural abilities or resources to obtain their desire in the physical. Follow obediently the principles or divine laws God has put in place for provoking His supernatural blessings and miracles, and you will get a good result.

In the case of the Shunammite woman, one could argue that she literally stumbled into her miracle because she had not intentionally set out to do what she did in order to receive a miracle from God. But, that's the very point of the power behind obediently following God's set principle on earth for heavenly intervention. That, it works even for the most unlikely people, the 'unintentional' and the intentional, with the same kind of needs that are governed by divine laws or principles for their fulfilment.

This is consistent with how anyone who truly repents of their sins, accepts Christ's forgiveness, and submits to Him as Lord and Saviour expects to be fully saved, because they've done what is required and lawful before God (cf Ezekiel 33:16,17; Romans 10:12). For example, if a baby should unintentionally drop a mango seed onto a fertile ground that supports the growth of mango trees, it will grow and flourish and bring forth mango fruits, just as the farmer would intentionally plant a mango seed for the purpose of harvesting mango fruits in their due season.

The Shunammite woman provoked and attracted a miracle of a boy child by honouring the man of God, Elisha, with his servant, Gehazi. Here is the principle: *Honour has rewards. Honour attracts and brings rewards to the honourer.*

> *Ephesians 6:2-3 "Honor your father and mother," which is the first commandment with promise: ³ "that it may be well with you and you may live long on the earth."*
>
> *Matthew 10:41- He who receives a prophet in the name of a prophet shall receive a prophet's reward. And he who receives a righteous man in the name of a righteous man shall receive a righteous man's reward.*
>
> *Ezekiel 44:30 - The best of all first fruits of any kind, and every sacrifice of any kind from all your sacrifices, shall be the priest's; also you shall give to the priest the first of your ground meal,* <u>to cause a blessing to rest on your house.</u>
>
> *Esther 6:9 - Let them robe the man the king delights to honor, and lead him on the horse through the city streets, proclaiming before him, 'This is what is done for the man the king delights to honor!'(NIV)*
>
> *Mark 6:4-5 - But Jesus said to them, "A prophet is not without honor except in his own country, among his own relatives, and in his own house." ⁵ Now He could do no*

> *mighty work there, except that He laid His hands on a few sick people and healed them.*

It is an established divine principle that one way to attract and establish God's miracle for your life is to honour those whom God honours, including men and women of God.

Mary of Bethany was restored and remembered for modelling such great honour (Mark 14:3-9; Also Luke 7:37-50). Mary demonstrated what, in my view, is an uncommon quality of honour linked with value appreciation.

First of all, to honour someone you must find them *valuable,* otherwise it will be impossible to honour them. What you can do without, you are most unlikely to find valuable, but your honour will always pursue and appreciate what you find valuable, because you cannot do without it.

Secondly, you will pay any price, including honour, for what you find valuable.

In Marks narration of the anointing in Bethany, two groups of people emerged; those who did not think the Son of God deserved to be anointed with a flask of costly spikenard oil; and only one woman, who thought He deserved that and more. We see here two different attitudes toward the same Person, under girded by the principle of value.

The question that was implicit in that passage, by those who opposed Mary's anointing of the Son of God was; '*is He worth all that much, so as to be honoured in such a way?*' Well, you run your own judgement, but a Man who has spent all His life healing sick men and women, forgiving their sins and taking away their guilt, restoring a widow's dead child to life, casting out devils and raising men and women from the dead; I can not tell if you could even begin to put a price on

Him, because not even the whole world can buy Him. Yet, it all boils down to value and honour.

Unfortunately, in our current circle of Christianity, and even society at large, many people seem to have lost the good sense and decency of *'giving honour to whom honour is due'*. Take for example, how pastors, who spent all their time sacrificially looking after the welfare of the people whom God has entrusted to their stewardship, most times with great sacrifice to their own family, in the end turned to be greatly dishonoured by those who continuously rain down damning allegations against them, without any justification.

The pastor prays and teaches the congregation most things that help them succeed spiritually, as well as in the physical arena, including their businesses, family, health and so forth. The congregation then drives the best of cars, and lives in the best of houses and earn enough to support their life styles, which is a good thing, especially when the flock flourish by the Word of God.

But, as soon as the very pastor who has been of great help to them buys, or gets a little gift of a decent car to drive, he will be criticised in every way. No, I am not arguing for pastors to live scandalously, but the question is, do we value our pastors enough so as to honour them in the manner that reflects who and what they represent to us? This is not just about pastors, but also our doctors, our school teachers, our parents and anyone that deserves to be honoured as a matter of sound, Godly principle.

> *Romans 13:7 - Render therefore to all their due: taxes to whom taxes are due, customs to whom customs, fear to whom fear, honor to whom honor.*

> *1 Timothy 5:17 - Let the elders who rule well be counted worthy of double honor, especially those who labor in the word and doctrine.*

> *Ephesians 6:2-3 - "Honor your father and mother," which is the first commandment with promise: ³ "that it may be well with you and you may live long on the earth."*
>
> *1Peter 3:1,7 - Wives, likewise, be submissive to your own husbands, that even if some do not obey the word, they, without a word, may be won by the conduct of their wives... Husbands, likewise, dwell with them with understanding, giving honor to the wife, as to the weaker vessel, and as being heirs together of the grace of life, that your prayers may not be hindered.*
>
> *John 8:49 - Jesus answered, "I do not have a demon; but I honor My Father, and you dishonor Me.*
>
> *Acts 28:10 - They also honored us in many ways; and when we departed, they provided such things as were necessary.*
>
> *Romans 12:10 - Be kindly affectionate to one another with brotherly love, in honor giving preference to one another*
>
> *1Timothy 5:3 - Honor widows who are really widows.*
>
> *1Peter 2:17 - Honor all people. Love the brotherhood. Fear God. Honor the king.*

Honour and Gratitude

Honour also involves showing respect and gratitude. Gratitude in the sense of simply appreciating and reciprocating kindness in ways that demonstrate sincere indebtedness for a favour received. It is more of this kind of honour that our society and churches very much need.

Many tend to be unashamedly ungrateful toward God, and others from whom they receive some form of favour. Most often, it's due to sheer misinformation, that when it comes to God or servants of God, we are entitled to everything we receive, big or small, from God, the church or a pastor. *But the thing is, wherever dishonour exists, favour ceases to exist as well.*

We can literally stop the flow of favour towards us by purely being ungrateful. Hence, *gratitude is the hand that opens the tap of favour and keeps it flowing.* The depth and extent of gratitude also literally determines the amount of favour that flows our way. Continue to regard favour as your right and your most recent favour might be the last from the same source, but be grateful and you will be established in favour continually.

Only one of the ten lepers who were healed returned to give thanks. He understood the principle and power regarding favour, and Jesus affirmed him before other men, which was in itself an added favour.

> *And they lifted up their voices and said, "Jesus, Master, have mercy on us!"* [14] *So when He saw them, He said to them, "Go, show yourselves to the priests." And so it was that as they went, they were cleansed.* [15] *And one of them, when he saw that he was healed, returned, and with a loud voice glorified God,* [16] *and fell down on his face at His feet, giving Him thanks. And he was a Samaritan.* [17]
>
> *So Jesus answered and said, "Were there not ten cleansed? But where are the nine?* [18] *Were there not any found who returned to give glory to God except this foreigner?"* [19] *And He said to him, "Arise, go your way. Your faith has made you well."(Luke 17:13-19)*

Like the Shunammitte woman, I had a fellow bible school colleague who exercised the principles of honour in most ways, without consciously realising that he was doing it, but benefited greatly from the rewards of honour. He told me how, while in seminary, he made it a point of giving me money and provision because he learned from experience that every time he offered me things, almost immediately, his own needs were taken care of supernaturally. Those were the days when I could not have afforded to return the same kindness in material terms even if I wanted to. I lived from day to day!

Well, he did not particularly set out to give me money or things hoping to also get things back, neither did I know God was taking care of my friend's needs, because he shared his money and provisions with me. I don't even think he had his need met because of me – it's far from that. I believe that *he was blessed because he was honouring God by honouring one of His servants, and by his action activated the divine laws of honour that bring about blessings*. My friend told me his testimonies of favour and blessings only after he had proved it time and time again, and because, on one occasion, I insisted that I was concerned that I was becoming a burden by accepting money or provision from him.

The rewards of honour are not only limited to or associated with people in ministries, including pastors of churches. It extends to what the book of Hebrews refers to as honouring strangers, which might unwittingly result in entertaining angels (Hebrew 13:2). I believe the book of Hebrews had in mind the episodes in the Old Testament, including Abraham and Sarah in Genesis 18:1-9, in which men, appearing as strangers and passers-by turned out to be angels of God with good promises of miracles for them afterwards.

This brings us to the second principle that this Shunammitte woman knew and applied:

2. *Divine duty is established by physical gesture, and physical gesture does attract divine favour.* This woman did, by nature and inspiration, what the Lord Jesus Christ was to later affirm in the New Testament as an important prerequisite for entering into eternal life. *(Mtt. 25:35 – "I was a stranger and you fed me…")*.

She knew to do her divine duty with a physical gesture, and she knew that physical gestures derive divine favour. A spooky area for any well meaning Christian, centres around great spirituality without the accompanying works of love, or works of faith, an issue that Apostle James argues, requires always a good balance. He says, *"but someone will say, "You have faith, and I have works." Show me your faith without your works, and I will show you my faith by my works" (James 2:8).*

Our works, especially those done in Christ, in most instances are expressions of our silent, but great faith in the Word of God, His commandments and abilities. Without shouting about the extent or greatness of our faith, we can choose and act in accordance with our unavowed faith, and that will still be counted in the eyes of God as faith. So, to say for instance that I love God, whom I don't see, it doesn't matter my sincerity in faith regarding my love for God; that's just the starting point.

But, coupled with my love for God, if I also honour a man, woman, or child of God whom I see, then that definitely translates into honouring God. My honouring God this way will still be in harmony with faith, and is indeed faith and the expression of faith. To this concept James had this to say, *"if one of you says to them, 'Go in peace; keep warm and well fed,' but does nothing about their physical needs, what good is it? In the same way, faith by itself, if it is not accompanied by action, is dead" (James 2:16,1; cf 1John 4:12).*

In a sense, we can be doing everything right, especially praying hard and believing God for our desires, but the very thing which is the key can be ignored. The physical actions, to go with our hard earnest prayer and strong belief, should be in place. It's easy to ignore the fact that faith is not always carried out by the conventional things that we all love to do, but sometimes a good gesture, even unconsciously done for one of God's children, which comes before God as a memorial that causes us to be remembered during our own time of need.

A powerful illustration of this is found in Acts 10:4 (NIV). Cornelius, the gentile, was told by an angel from God, *"Your prayers and gifts to the poor have come up as a memorial offering before God."* One might argue that the Shunammitte woman or Cornelius was not really a believer in Christ as we are today, but that's the very argument of faith under or without the Law:

> *"(for not the hearers of the law are just in the sight of God, but the doers of the law will be justified; ¹⁴ for when Gentiles, who do not have the law, by nature do the things in the law, these, although not having the law, are a law to themselves, ¹⁵ who show the work of the law written in their hearts, their conscience also bearing witness, and between themselves their thoughts accusing or else excusing them) ¹⁶ in the day when God will judge the secrets of men by Jesus Christ, according to my gospel (Romans 2:16).*
>
> *But be doers of the word, and not hearers only, deceiving yourselves. … ²⁵ But he who looks into the perfect law of liberty and continues in it, and is not a forgetful hearer but a doer of the work, this one will be blessed in what he does* (James 1:22,25).

This brings us to the third principle that the Shunammitte woman knew and applied:

3. *The Law of Recognition (the ability to discern right from wrong, good from bad, the temporary from the permanent, truth from lies, and real from counterfeit) governs behaviour, and those who are so led see more than the ordinary sight (vr. 9).*

A significant part of what the Shunammitte woman knew and did was not to focus on personality or appearance. She literally went past the person of the prophet to focus on the office he occupied and the anointing of the man of God, Elisha. Because Elisha, by virtue of his office and anointing, did not belong to himself or serve himself, she tells her husband, '*I know* that this is *a holy man of God*'. So, her honouring the man of God was simply based on her discerning the One to whom he belonged and whom he served, God Almighty.

Her motive was never to entice the man of God, but to honour him, because it was right to do so. Unfortunately, there are those who honour people because of personal ties or other ulterior motives, which are easy temptations for most people.

When it concerns marriages, some have married the wrong people just because they believed the person had well polished language. And unfortunately, they soon find out that they hung an important lifetime decision on a fragile string, like facial looks, or good accent. People forget that even the devil, will come glistening like an angel of light, although he's not (2 Cor.11:14). It's better to focus on permanent values like character, and the testimony of God over a man's life than fleeting things like hair style.

It will certainly take more than a common look to go beyond the physical person. The Shunammitte woman said, *I know*. She was *thorough* and *discerning*, otherwise she would have missed her golden opportunity to have what she had always yearned for in private and in public. Remember, Elisha was not a very physically impressive figure. This was a zealous farmer who received God's call and barbecued all his cattle using the very yoke sticks for wood on his grill.

It's good to look good, but I believe the prophet had no time for our present day 'makeover' obsessions, but God still called him. His appearance might have been so old fashioned that even young people found him a laughing stock, to taunt and call him names, but he was God's messenger and prophet (see 2Kgs 2:23). Notice, *very often God places and connects our miracles to unpleasant people and in seemingly unpleasant situation.* You must be discerning not to miss your miracle.

4. Compassion and spontaneity work like a miracle. Learn to be driven by your inner convictions (vrs.10). The Shunammitte woman was spontaneous and compassionate. She, at her own volition, saw a need in the life of the man of God and quickly moved to meet his need.

That, in my view, was about one of her greatest strengths. You don't wait to be asked, let your giving or whatever you desire to do, be spontaneous and voluntary, in other to touch God's heart. The secret is always *be moved by inner conviction rather than external compulsion and coercion* (see 2 Cor. 8:12;9:5 Also see James 4:17).

To have been able to convince her husband to build a little extension on their house for the man of God, is no doubt indicative of a woman who of course was a good wife to her husband, and largely a good woman by nature, because men don't normally expect, or honour such big demands from their wives, unless the woman has been exceptionally respectful, and good. Building the extension for the Prophet was one thing, but having to have him and his protégé as part of their family meant a long-term commitment.

The humorous side of things would involve, having to cope with outrageous ear-drum perforating snores, coming from two gentlemen, obviously wearied and tired from a long distance walk on dusty roads. There may have been nights when the husband of the Shunammitte woman woke her up at night saying to her, *'honey, your prophets at the top are snoring and 'driving' at the same time, won't you do something about it?'* (Just my imagination). All I am saying is that, considering how involving this woman's gesture would have been, she had to be a person of true compassion and generosity.

5. *Favour is entreated* (vrs. 12, 13). It is so natural that every thoughtful move toward another will excite and attract a reciprocal gesture with spontaneity. The Shunammitte woman's experience teaches us that a quality gift or offering is so magnetic, not only with the ability to attract, but to also determine the quality of favour it pulls toward the giver. We learned from her that favour can be entreated and is definitely 'entreat-able' (cf Malachi 1:8-9).

Make and give quality gifts, for favour begets favour, and the quality (not necessarily the quantity) of your gift will determine the quality of your reward. *Also, look away from yourself if you want others to look to you.*

6. *Favour speaks compellingly even amid impossibilities (vrs 14, 15)* - here's the miracle: The woman actually needed two major miracles. First of all, her husband was too old and probably both of them, because of their ages, lacked the required biological strength and capacity for child conception and birth. Secondly, they've gone childless throughout their marriage. So, for the prophet to speak of them having their own child, he seemed to be virtually promising the impossible.

He must first heal their biological capacities to make a child, and then pray a child into the womb of the Shunammitte woman, if we were looking at things physically. No wonder then that the woman spoke in a way that has always looked like she was trying to shut the prophet down from arousing what seemed like 'false hope', as if it was too good to be true. But the prophet insisted, 'you will embrace a son by this time next year', because the 'favour' she had caught with the prophet was speaking compellingly on her behalf.

7. *Faith can move mountains (vrs 16).* "No my Lord. Man of God, do not lie to your maidservant!" People have always thought this was an expression of doubt and faithlessness from the woman. Quite to the contrary, it wasn't. Knowing the character of the woman in this whole story, she expresses doubt at no point.

Here, she was agreeing with the prophet, like we would usually do when we are so full of joy over a good news about a long expected, long awaited, wish that comes suddenly when we are least prepared, and when prevailing circumstances don't even support any evidence of such breakthrough. This is like saying with exclamation, "is it true? I am going to have a baby!" – Note, she says, "man of God do not lie to your maidservant", which, when transferred into our situation, sounds like the very next logical expression to follow would be, "I can't wait to see this happen." The very next verse will clearly buttress my observation, that the woman believed the prophet.

Further on in verse 17 of the same chapter, the text says – "But the woman conceived." Now, do you know if she hadn't believed the prophet, she would not have bothered her 'old man' at all (cf. Heb. 11:11). After all, he had no strength. Now, there's the proof that she believed when the prophet said she would embrace her own child, specifically a son. There it is, every true prophet speaking from God will give you a sign, so Elisha says she will have not just a child but more specifically a son.

8. *We need 'conceiving faith' for conceiving our miracles.* Finally, the Shunammitte woman teaches us a lesson in faith for provoking and possessing our miracle. She was a woman of faith, teaching by her life how to receive your miracle; by believing and exercising faith concerning 'whatever you ask from God, or are promised from God, by a man of God'.

Faith is always necessary for conceiving every miracle of God (Heb. 11:6). Even Sarah, with a very similar situation as the Shunammitte woman, it is said that "*by faith, Sarah herself also <u>received strength to conceive seed</u> and she bore a child when she was past age, because she judged Him faithful who had promised*" (Hebrews 11:11). This kind of faith is called *conceiving faith.* It moves you to do things, not only differently, but to attempt things above your personal strength and ability (Rom. 4:17), using God's strength, which He supplies as you put your faith in Him.

Chapter Eighteen

THE POWER OF FAITH WITH PERSEVERANCE: RESURRECTING LOST MIRACLES

*By a prophet the Lord brought Israel out of Egypt,
And by a prophet he was preserved. (Hosea 12:13)*

The second half of the Shunammitte woman's life with Elisha the prophet, shows us how it is possible for the devil to attempt to steal, kill or destroy what God has blessed His people with. But, more than anything, she also teaches us how resilience and perseverance in faith towards God can cause God's blessing in our lives to be preserved. I would like to view all that is taking place in this half of the Shunammitte woman's life, as a lesson into *'resurrecting our miracle when the enemy kills it'.*

We find in 2 Kings 4 verses 18 to 21 a scenario in which Satan might attempt to 'steal' or 'kill' a God-given miracle, as his agenda has always been (John 10:10). At that point, that's no time to despair or to succumb to his cunning schemes. If he touches anything of yours, like he intended with the Shunammitte woman's child, striking him dead with sun stroke, you know exactly where to go.

Martha and Mary sent for the Lord Jesus Christ when their brother whom He loved, suddenly succumbed to death by sickness, having been afflicted by Satan. The widow of Nain suffered the loss of her only son, but she encountered the Lord of life, Jesus Christ, coming into their city when they were on their way out of the city, and He immediately restored him back to life.

What do you do when your miracle suddenly leaves you? The Shunammitte woman teaches from her experience that, no matter how difficult the situation might be, it is possible to get your miracle restored, by following the proper course of action through the power of faith with perseverance. And there are basically nine things that we can derive as a course of action from the experience and encounter of the Shunammitte woman in *resurrecting* her miracle.

Nine Principal Stations to Resurrecting your Miracle

1. Remain calm and don't be anxious (2Kgs 4:21). About how to remain calm and not be anxious, Apostle Paul puts things in words more profoundly than anyone can present or say them. First, Philippians 4:6, 7 says, *"be anxious for nothing, but in everything by prayer and supplication, with thanksgiving, let your requests be made known to God, and the peace of God which surpasses all understanding will guard your hearts and minds through Christ Jesus."* Second, 1 Thessalonians 5:18 – *in everything give thanks; for this is the will of God in Christ Jesus for you.*

The wisdom here is that our thanks go toward the God who knows and sees everything, not necessarily the giving of thanks for the problems, or troubles that confront us. That, as such, is not what constitutes the will of God for you; rather, it is giving thanks to God in everything at all times, which is the will of God for His people.

In a sense, we don't glorify our troubles by allowing them to take over us completely, as if they are bigger than our God. Obviously, Satan wants us to believe that God has left us and forsaken us through the challenges and troubles he visits upon us. But, giving of thanks is an expression of faith in our God, that the Lord is able to take care of the situation. It helps you to remain and maintain your calm, and not to be anxious, knowing that your God will act on your behalf.

2. Return to the source of the miracle (2Kgs 4:22). The woman ran to the man of God not her husband. Elisha as the servant of God represented his God of miracles in this case.

3. Retain good confession of your faith (2Kgs 4:23). Revelation 12:11 says "and they (we) overcame him (satan) by the blood of the Lamb (Jesus) and the words of their confession…."

4. Resolve to be quick (2Kgs 4:24). Time is of the essence. The more time elapses, the more likely discouragement and the temptation to slack in zeal might take over, and then you easily quit on pursing your miracle, or desire for it to be restored. Not to be quick may also introduce other factors, including the devils own overwhelming feats of complication. Apart from everything, the woman does not want her husband to return home to find their only son dead. He may just also die. So her speed and quickness potentially saved the situation.

5. Remove any hurdle or obstacle intending to stop you from reaching your man of God in your search for God's solution. The Shunammite woman directly went to Mount Carmel, and caught Elisha by his feet (2Kgs 4:25-27). In times like these, it's time to head for the company of anointed believers, serious prayer meetings, crusades, and attempt anything Scriptural. For Hebrews

11:35, says, "by faith women received their dead raised back to life again".

6. Relate your situation in 'bitterness of soul' if you would (2Kgs 4:28). There's a difference between 'faithlessness' and 'bitterness of soul'. Here, she is plain and to the point, and that's the beauty of being in a relationship with God. Even the Psalmists called on the Lord, at times from the midst of their pains and distresses: *"I called on the Lord in distress, the Lord answered me and set me in a broad place" (Psalm 118:5)*. *"In my distress I called upon the Lord, and cried out to my God; He heard my voice from His temple, and my cry came before Him, even to His ears" (Psalms 18:6)*.

You can express and relate your fears and frustrations to God without being faithless. After all, it was the Shunammitte woman's faith that her son would rise again that drove her to the man of God. Faithlessness does not energise, but rather seizes someone from taking positive steps toward God. The pain and frustration of the Shunammitte woman were that, her miracle child had already given them great headlines in the 'dailies', and had brought good changes, including joy, and also readjustments in certain areas of their own family. And suddenly, he died. How could she explain that?

7. Refuse 'Gehazi', or any excuse from the man of God and get the Lord on your side (2Kgs 4:30). There are battles that only the Master can fix, so don't settle for anything other than the Master Himself. It is also crucial that you avoid the easy deception of Job 1:21 which says *"Naked I came from my mother's womb, and naked shall I return there. The Lord gave, and the Lord has taken away, blessed be the name of the Lord."* In

resurrecting your miracle, you need to be resolute in your desire for only one thing, 'resurrecting your miracle', and no other alternative. Otherwise faith will shut down, because you've given it an option and alternative.

8. Receive and embrace your miracle again (2Kgs 4:36). Many of us know how to ask or even stand in faith because of a need, but we often do not know how to receive as well. Learn to receive what you ask from God. Concerning this area, two things are crucial: maintain a good confession. Only say what you believe is true concerning the promises of God for receiving your miracle. Don't speak your fear or speak in fear, as it would only contradict and undo your hope and expectation. (cf. 2Cor. 4:13) Secondly, always expect to receive what you ask for, and be confident. One sign of being expectant is to begin to thank God for a desired outcome after you have prayed (cf. Eph. 5:20). In Psalm 50:23, we read, that *"whoever offers praise glorifies Me; and to him who orders his conduct aright, I will show the salvation of God"*.

9. Render glory, worship and honour to the Lord God for resurrecting your miracle, it's the work of God not man (2Kgs 4: 37; cf. Ps. 50:23; Eph. 5:19,20).

Final Words on Resurrecting Your Miracle

Resurrecting a miracle is not for the faint hearted. The Shunammitte woman troubled the prophet to the end. In 2Kings 4:36, Elisha looked worn out by the unwavering persistency of the woman. He tells Gehazi, *"call this Shunammite woman"*. That's the voice of a man worn out by a persistent mother. In effect, he says, tell that "crazy and *uneven* woman" (*Refer to meaning of Shunam*) to come over here. We all need to be 'crazy' and *uneven* about things in our lives that we feel so passionate about. Just don't let it go once you know God has given it to you. *It took conceiving faith to receive your miracle, and it will take persistent and irresistible faith to resurrect it. Pray and pray until you've gotten your result.*

A good way to see and to exercise that kind of persistency, and of course irresistible faith through prayers and deeds, is what the Lord Jesus Himself illustrated powerfully in Luke 18:1-8. I'll include the parable here for your study, encouragement and further action.

> *Then He spoke a parable to them, that men always ought to pray and not lose heart, ² saying: "There was in a certain city a judge who did not fear God nor regard man. ³ Now there was a widow in that city; and she came to him, saying, 'Get justice for me from my adversary.' ⁴ And he would not for a while; but afterward he said within himself, 'Though I do not fear God nor regard man, ⁵ yet because this widow troubles me I will avenge her, lest by her continual coming she weary me.'"⁶ Then the Lord said, "Hear what the unjust judge said. ⁷ And shall God not avenge His own elect who cry out day and night to Him, though He bears long with them? ⁸ I tell you that He will avenge them speedily. Nevertheless, when the Son of Man comes, will He really find faith on the earth?"*

The Lord Himself grant you every grace you need to conceive and to preserve all of your miracles from God. Whatever good thing that the Lord gave you as your portion and blessing, which the devil has stolen from you, be restored to you a sevenfold, in Jesus Name!

Chapter Nineteen

THE PERMANANCE OF GOD'S BLESSING: HOW I RECOVERED MY 'MIRACLE'

> *So David inquired of the LORD, saying, "Shall I pursue this troop? Shall I overtake them?" And He answered him, "Pursue, for you shall surely overtake them and without fail recover all." (1Sam.30:8)*

There are valuable lessons to learn from the Shunammite woman's story in second Kings 4:8 to 37. The story undoubtedly brings to light the process and power of what everyone seeks; miracles and, if they for some reason slipped out of our hands, how to get them back.

It is definitely no secret that almost every person in life will be faced with, even if not now, a desire to receive a miracle of a sort or may be confronted with how to resurrect a lost miracle. And both of these situations were true in the life of the Shunammite woman.

Interestingly, in Scriptures, the Shunammite woman's experience is not an isolated occurrence. Similar stories, with paralleled lows and highs exist in the New Testament, including the death and raising back to life of Lazarus. Also the son of the widow of the city of Nain, and of course Dorcas, the generous woman, whose works among fellow disciples of Christ were outstandingly noticeable.

The significance of all these stories regards the gravity of the immense sense of loss, and the subsequent restoration of both hope and the essence of life. It strongly emphasizes need for timely miracles in which God's awesome power becomes demonstrably visible within the overwhelming state of helplessness and hopelessness that people generally and unfortunately face.

Particularly, while it is true that many of us currently desire some miracles from God, in relation to our specific needs; whether of healing, deliverance or child birth and so forth, some who have received theirs, unfortunately could not keep them. For those who lost what they received, they might now be wishing and praying for a breakthrough for restoration. And the story of the Shunamite woman, therefore brings a fresh and crucial revelation to such desires, and ultimately, how to overcome the challenge of believing for a miracle and regaining that which was lost.

The blessings of God are permanent and God's desire for His people is that we will walk in great miracles, and at the same time be able to keep, and not lose what He puts in our lives as His blessings for us. Ecclesiastics 3:14 says, *"I know that whatever God does, it shall be forever"* but the thief, Satan's job is to *steal, kill and destroy"*, according to John 10:10a. So, *"for this purpose the Son of God was manifested, that He might destroy the works of the devil"* (1 John 3:8), and that we might have life, and have it more abundantly (John 10:10b). This is why I know that God wants us to recover all that the devil has stolen from us.

My 'Miracle': A Personal Testimony

As a young man, just coming out of college, I had barely finished my probation period on my very first job with a university, when a friend and I decided to go into partnership in business. We had all kinds of great ideas, which we believed held wonderful prospects for our future and partnership.

Our initial attempt was to run what we termed as an *executive* taxi business. The idea was to begin with one car and then increase our fleet as time went by and the business succeeded. In our own minds at the time, it was a great idea, almost new in the country, having special cars specifically on private hire basis, running from the major airport of the city to posh and lush hotels within the cities.

We could almost literally see our wealth and financial fortunes before us because of our big ideas. We simply believed that it would not be too long before we would not have to rise in the mornings to *push papers* for our employers. We were going to be the employers.

One night, as my colleague and I were heading for a meal in the company of another friend, we hired a taxi to take us to a restaurant on the outskirts of the city, where we lived. Along the way, we got into conversing with the taxi driver about the profitability of running a taxi and what it entails to have one. We briefed the driver about our intensions and, incidentally, the very taxi we hired was on sale privately. In fact, the driver was the owner, but he had plans to travel abroad if things went well.

So, our 'business heads' immediately kicked in and we asked the driver if we could buy his car. He agreed and promised to help us with the initial preparations for making the car more presentable and also finding us a creditable driver.

Until then, he was going to drive it to ensure things were in good order. His proposals sounded too good to be ignored. So much so that our friend, who had picked a lift with us asked if she could partner with us in our new joint venture. We refused, but, without wasting anymore time, we gave the driver our word, '*count your car already purchased, by tomorrow morning your money will be ready in cash*'. We exchanged mobile phone numbers and told him exactly where he could find us at work.

The following morning we got very busy. We knew exactly what to do because we spent a good part of our night brainstorming about how to raise the money for the car. A few months before, our university's bankers spoke to us members of staff and proposed to offer same-day loans, as long as we had letter of introduction from the university. They were willing to give members of staff ridiculous amounts, provided that staff's monthly salary could afford the loan's monthly repayments, including the interest.

It all sounded like a great giveaway from the bank, but what we didn't know was that the bank was willing to take all the initial risks just to win the entire business of the university and staff. Their offer, which would not last, was only a clever enticement for people like us, who were seeing only our profits and returns but were very oblivious to the small print. In the end it turned out that the bank's 'blithe generosity' would surprisingly "sting and bite like a adder" (cf Prov. 23:22). Majority of the staff, and top bosses in the end, included!

We got the car loan on a compound interest basis, probably over two or three years. Our intention was to pay it off as soon as possible, using portion of our salaries and income from the taxi runs. The interest rate on the loan was very high, and to complicate things it was calculated on a compound interest basis. I vaguely remember now, but I think we had to pay the interest first, before the principal amount, and in some cases we paid interest on interest, because the interest on the loan was originally calculated over the full term of the loan and added to the principal amount.

The funny aspect of all our bank transactions was, my 'business partner' was a qualified accountant, very good with figures, but we both walked blindly into the bank and allowed ourselves to be taken in by them. I suppose because we were more concerned about getting started in business than we were about banks 'plucking our eyes out'. Whatever the explanation was, one thing remained certain; that our eyes were still fully fixed on our profits and the prospect of a good future with financial freedom.

We bought the car with cash and then left it with the original owner and driver to prepare it for private hire, sticking to our initial business idea. By this time, the full amount of money we borrowed as a loan had been exhausted, and we had to plough into our personal funds to make the car decent enough to meet our specifications. All went well. Sometimes we had some misgivings about all the monies that were been requested for repair works on the car, but, overall, we thought we did well because we had, as much as possible, kept our eyes on the receipts for purchases of parts. Initial works on the car had taken more than we anticipated, but we were almost there!

How I Lost My 'Miracle'

With all the mechanical aspects now taken care of, we hired a driver on the recommendation of the original owner. Together they decided, as a way of recouping some of our personal expenses on the fixing of the car, they would attempt an overnight 'pick-and-drop' taxi service. That way, we expected to get some more money that we could use to finalise preparation for the original 'private hire' idea.

We welcomed their suggestion and the driver started immediately on the night of June 20th 2000. I expected to see the driver at least the next morning before leaving for work, but he did not show up. I managed to get to work as usual, looking forward to a great day. At about 9.30am, I had an intercom call advising to meet some visitors in the front office. I had no suspicion or horrible feelings of anything wrong, but I dashed quickly for the front office. Two men approached me, one of them looking terribly shocked and the other almost breathless, and they couldn't wait to tell me what had happened.

The two men were our newly hired driver and the gentleman whom we bought the car from, but who also recommended the driver. This gentleman, a good man, had quickly graduated into our friend over the short time since we met, sometimes referring to me as his brother, which was culturally acceptable. My 'brother' became the spokesman that hectic morning. He began by saying, *'the car has been stolen'*.

It was forcefully seized at about 4:30am at gunpoint by armed robbers who almost killed the driver during scuffles over the keys to the car and proceeds from the night's sales. In fact, he alleged that there was one bullet shot through the driver's door; the same bullet meant to kill the driver who later escaped unharmed. The driver had miraculously escaped, but we had just lost our *'miracle'*.

But all that was immaterial to me. I was only very glad that the driver was safe and alive. As if to shock them even more, my response was so calm and unusual under the circumstances. Without questioning them or suspecting any foul play from either my 'brother' or the driver, I reached out for money in my front pocket and then handed it over to them for taxi fare, to help them return to their homes. Later the case was reported to the police, and that was all I did after informing my 'business partner'.

He didn't seem to have any further issues with the circumstances involving the theft of our car, except that we both knew that we would have to continue paying the bank loan, from our meagre monthly wages. We had just lost our *'miracle'* of a car, forfeited our income, and our dream of becoming financially independent through our business partnership had now been literally dashed. It evaporated!

Furthermore, the fact that I handled things including the driver light-handedly, without subjecting him to police interrogation, seemed to suggest that some kind of collusion had taken place between me and the driver. Hence, the situation was at least viewed by some as a super scam to deprive my 'business partner' and friend.

The God of Restoration: How I Recovered My 'Miracle'

Weeks passed, and we had no further news about the stolen car, even though the police had said they would send radio messages right away to their colleagues around the country, to assist with the investigation and possible recovery of the car.

One day, I turned up at a student friend's house probably after church on a Sunday afternoon. We happened to be looking at some photographs and there, on one of the photographs, we had the car in the background before it was stolen. It looked good and somehow, for the first time, it actually dawned on me that the cad has been stolen and it didn't make sense why.

Incidentally, the same month, which was July, was a month of fast and prayer at the church we belonged to. We met nightly for at least an hour of prayer at the church, throughout the entire month. I became stirred to include the supernatural recovery of our stolen car on my list of prayer topics for that month, having seen the image of the car in the background of our photograph. I Left my student friend's house for home, but my desire to recoup the car continued to intensify.

I got home and began to listen to a sermon tape of the late great faith preacher, Archbishop Benson Idahosa, in which he challenged the Christian to take back whatever the devil has stolen from them and to stop succumbing to satanic lies about *'God gives and God takes!'* He disagreed that God would want to bless us and then take it back. 'No, it is the devil who steals from us what God has given to us', and it was wrong to quote Job 1:21 as a pretext for our unwillingness to resist the devil when he touches God's children.

I agreed fully with his concept and my anger against Satan intensified even more. I told myself that I was going to call the car forth, like Jesus did to Lazurus, for the rest of the days of fast and prayer in July.

I persisted and kept commanding the car to come back to us from wherever it had been taken to. About two weeks later, in the month of August, after the prayer and fasting month has ended, we received a police report that the car had been located almost a day's journey from the capital city where we resided.

The first person who received the report was the original owner of the car, the gentleman who sold it to us initially. He informed me and told me that some of the armed robbers, who previously seized the car at gun point, were actually in the car that morning and had been arrested when the car was recovered by the border police. The armed robbers, interestingly, had continued to use the same car for more armed robberies, terrorizing villages in their localities. The bad news was that the car was almost a wreck, although still mobile.

We quickly arranged and towed the recovered car back to our city. It was quite defaced, but I was very grateful to God who honours and answers prayers. God, through that incident showed me that, not only is He the *'recovery'* God, but also the God of 'supernatural restoration', who also defends and exonerates His people from those who accuse them falsely. So, we took the car to a garage and trusted God for it to be restored.

By the grace of God I got the car converted for private use, after I managed to reimburse my 'business partner' his interest in the car. I couldn't let go of the car, because it had become a crucial part of my spiritual journey, and a true symbol of my life's learning curve. My *Miracle* was not just recovered, it was restored and became my very first privately owned vehicle, with good memories that I will continue to cherish in my lifetime.

What has Satan stolen from you? Have you lost your 'miracle'? Are your blessings being threatened? God can restore them. Trust Him and call back what the enemy has stolen from you. Then, expect a supernatural breakthrough from God Almighty.

Closing

Having and Living the Triumphant Life is a Decision Away

"You shall know the truth, and the truth shall make you free" (John 8:32);" was Jesus' honest advice to the Jews, who believed in Him. Until now, His listeners had only assumed that they were free, being Abraham's descendants, and were not in bondage to anyone. To some extent, it seemed they were thinking more of a physical or political bondage. But in verse 34 of John 8, Jesus continued, *"Most assuredly, I say to you, whoever commits sin is a slave of sin."*

If you have been around Christians or have taken some interest in Christianity for a while, then you probably, have heard this quotation already; mostly from preachers or friends who are Christians. Over the years, it has almost become a ready-made answer to, when people ask us some of life's most important questions. There are even those who take the same quotation a little bit further to say, *"it is the truth you know and apply that will set you free."*

It all sounds great, and almost easy for anyone who might desire to do it without sweat; just knowing the truth and applying the truth. But, here is the difficulty regarding this statement about knowing the truth, which was much the same difficulty Pontius Pilate had with a similar statement from Jesus, as he questioned Him, just before His crucifixion.

When Jesus said, *"for this cause I was born, and for this cause I have come into the world, that I should bear witness to the truth. Everyone who is of the truth hears My voice"* (John 18:37, 38); Pilate then asked Jesus, *"What is truth?"*

"What is truth?" This was obviously a legitimate and key question, because of the significance attached to the question of *truth* in view of faith, life and our eternal destiny. Although Jesus chose not to answer Pilate's question, He had already defined the *truth* elsewhere, while speaking on other occasions.

For example, in John 14:6, Jesus referred to Himself as *"the way, the truth, and the life"*, and in John 17:17, during his prayer in Gethsemane, Jesus, in prayer, asked His Father to sanctify His disciples through His truth, saying, *"Your word is truth"*, obviously referring to the Word of God.

Also in John 1:14, we know that *"the Word became flesh and dwelt among us, and we beheld His glory, the glory as of the only begotten of the Father, full of grace and truth."* As the begotten of the Father, Jesus declared, *"therefore if the Son makes you free, you shall be free indeed" (John 8:36)*. Who then is Jesus? He is the *'living truth'*.

Now, for all who preach the *truth* and those who seek the *truth*, knowing the *truth* is of foremost importance. How else would they become free and also help others to become free? (see John 8:32). However, the question still remains, do you know the *truth*? What does the *truth* look like and when is truth really the *truth* that sets one free? That the Lord Jesus Himself is the *truth* is incontestable, but we must come into the knowledge and revelation of this *truth*.

That is why the question of knowing the *truth* is so unavoidably crucial, although it often gets complicated, especially thinking of it in the context of the mysteries of God. A good case in point is Pilate, who had Jesus, the *living truth*, standing before him but failed to recognise Him. Similarly, knowing the *truth* poses a challenge to those who might want to know it, simply through the letters of the

Scriptures, when indeed God's *truth* which sets people free is, by nature, the *mysteries of God*. (cf Matt. 13:11; Luke 8:10; 1Corinth. 4:1; 2:7; Romans 16:25; Eph. 3:4; Col. 1:26; 1Tim. 3:16; Rev. 10:7)

Clearly, there's a big difference between the letters of the Scriptures, and the Scriptures as the revealed *truth*, or the wisdom of God for setting God's people free. It takes the Holy Spirit, who leads all into the *truth*, to move us from the letters of the Scriptures into the revelation and *spirit* of the Scriptures, for the *truth* that we need to know. Otherwise, that all-important question of Pilate, "what is the truth?", will always hang unanswered. Like Pilate, the *truth* might be standing right before us, and we might still not see it, suggesting that such *truth* never comes by physical observation, but by spiritual revelation.

This is how the Holy Spirit helps us to achieve the spiritual revelation we require. He does it by lifting and converting the Scriptures, from the mere 'letters of the Scriptures' to *prophetic Scriptures (Rom. 16:26)*, and the *prophetic word of God* revealed and confirmed as *"light that shines in a dark place, until the day dawns and the morning star rises in our hearts"* (2Pet.1:19). This is how the *truth* is conveyed by the Holy Spirit of God, who is the Spirit of *truth*, in bringing people into the knowledge of the things they need to know, so as to set them free (John 16:13; John 14:26; Luke 12:12; 1Cor. 2:10). And, this *truth* is often conveyed as the *mysteries of God* or God's revealed wisdom to those who trust in Him.

Therefore, to be free and free indeed, one needs to first receive and establish an understanding of the mysteries of God, which is the *truth* that makes free. After receiving the Lord Jesus, who is the 'living truth' for our salvation, then we also need to ascertain for ourselves by the help of the Holy Spirit, the nature, power and purpose of the mysteries of God. This was what we attempted to accomplish in the very first part of this book, by mainly focusing on the life, blessings and inheritance, of those who believe in Jesus Christ, the Son of God.

Hopefully, by believers exposing and availing themselves to the *truth*, through having the proper understanding of the *mysteries of God's will* or His revealed wisdom, they can easily attain to God's quality of life, originally intended for all who believe in Him. This quality life, of course, is what I described as the *triumphant life*. A life from God that trusts in, and relies on Him completely, and therefore enjoys God's unlimited blessings with a promise of eternal life after physical death.

What about those who don't believe, or who haven't made any real commitment to God through the Lord Jesus Christ, who is the 'living' *truth*? First, they need 'God's kind of life'; the quality of life He offers to all who put their trust in Him. Thus, they can have and enjoy a full *triumphant life* from God, with His blessings of peace and unconditional love in this present troubled world. Additionally, they will also have eternal life spent with God after they die. They don't have to fear death.

Second, to begin with, they must know the *truth* in order to be set free from other issues that have held them bound, including Satan's agenda to destroy them.

How can you personally know, or come to the *truth* for a God given *triumphant life?* Pretty simple compared with what you might have heard elsewhere, or even what you've been reading so far. The Bible, the Word of God, says,

> **But <u>as many as received Him, to them He gave the right to become children of God, to those who believe in His name</u> (John 1:12).**

Here is the path you have to take: You need a person, Jesus, the Son of God, who is Himself "*the way, the truth and life*", bringing you surely into triumphant life and triumphant living (John 14:6). Only Jesus can set you free, and truly free (John 8:36). Not only will He give you His Spirit, who leads you into all that you need to know, He also helps you and gives you all the power you need, to make all the necessary changes and adjustments that you need, in order to come into God's quality life of triumph with a hope for a glorious future.

By coming to Jesus, you make His victory your very own, including victory over sin, suffering, and death. This works in the same way as when your favourite sports team wins a championship; their victory becomes equally your victory, because you belong to the team, or support that team.

Similarly, Jesus, as our champion has already gone ahead of us and won the victory, and bought us freedom from the punishment for our sins, including eternal sufferings in hell fire, in order for us to live in the love of God, and to spend eternal life in heaven with God after we die (Rom. 3:23; Rom. 6:23; John 3:16).

I will encourage you as you read this page; this is the right time you entrust your life and your future to God who wants to protect and to care for you in amazing ways. Here is your opportunity, and I gladly love to be a part of your new journey in Christ by you allowing me to pray with you right now!

How do you then connect to Jesus to find help for the forgiveness of all your sins, and to enjoy all He has promised including eternal life?

This is how it is. The Bible (the Word of God) says, "that if you shall confess with your mouth the Lord Jesus, and shall believe in your heart that God has raised Him from the dead, you shall be saved" (Romans 10:9). That means that, if you don't know Jesus, and have continued to walk in rebellion to His love and ways for you, then you must first recognise your need for Christ. Know that He died for you, forgiving you your sins, and taking away your guilt and punishment, so that you may live, and may receive the life He designed for you. Just as Jesus rose again, so also you too can have victory in every area of life, and you can keep rising to the top with

Christ Jesus. Most importantly, you will have eternal life with God, and heaven becomes your home after you physically die. If you receive Jesus in your heart and in loving relationship as your Lord and Saviour, you have no reason to fear being condemned to hell and everlasting punishment, because He has taken your punishment, and opened a new way for you to spend the rest of your life under God's grace, love, forgiveness and mercies (Rom. 6:23).

The truth is, that you can be forgiven all your sins, and God will not hold anything against you because Jesus His Son has already paid in full for your sins, together with all your guilt and shame and the eternal punishment that you should have had. For everything that you wrongly got yourself into, God wants to lift the weight off your shoulder and in exchange to give you His joy, peace, and a brand new life with a brand new start.

Just pray right now: Dear Jesus, I now believe and confess that you died for me and rose again in victory. I confess that I am a sinner. I have sinned against You, but I choose right now to give you my life and everything about me. Please forgive me and take away my guilt, shame and punishment for the bad things I have done. I need your love, peace, joy and blessings. Come Lord Jesus and be with me. Come into my heart and give me the assurance of your Holy Spirit. I vow to follow you for the rest of my life and to submit to You always. I love you and thank You, Jesus for receiving me right now. I believe my life has changed, and I will live to fulfil Your purpose for me, and my new life.

My dear Friend, you've just made the most important decision of your life. My particular prayer for you is that, the miracle you've always looked for has begun! May the Lord heal your body of any disease or sickness, and may His unlimited power of favour come upon you, right now, right where you are. God richly bless you! Amen. Now, please feel free to contact me for further help and information. We love to help where possible.

Epilogue

Having a Nice Day in a 'Nasty World'

I believe, with all my heart that God desires that every one of His children should have a nice-day, despite all the problems throughout our present world. By 'nice-day' I mean the individual's ability to be hopeful, happy, or joyful in what is God's wonderful gift to humanity called, day.

The literal meaning of *day*, of course, suggests and holds an awesome promise of life and goodness. *Day* is normally when we come alive. In the *day* we burst with energy, and the light of vitality break upon us. It's when we get going and head for life's many storehouses. We follow our dreams, and hope again. The *day* is God's treasure trove of opportunities, which He hands to us in the morning. We've got to get what we must have on that *day*. We cannot not have a nice-day, or else we allow ourselves to be robbed of another day's treasure. And, life begins to lengthen in shadows and creep in darkness, just allowing the *day* go by.

Even our Lord Jesus Christ was so excited about the potential, power and effectiveness of the *day*, that He said, "*I must work the works of Him who sent Me while it is day; the night is coming when no one can work.*" (John 9:4).

Similarly, the *day* is presented to be full of good expectations and hope, so much so that the psalmist says, "*…weeping may endure for a night, but joy comes in the morning*" (Psalms 30:5). It is almost as if, whatever good works the Lord will do for His people in the form of blessings and deliverance, would come in the *day* time. (see Ps. 42:8)

Unfortunately, many go through the *day* not looking forward to it, not even wishing that the *day* ever comes, simply because it seems to always bring to them nothing but unhappiness.

As I complete the writing of this book, I am fully aware that the entire world is in the middle of a dreadful credit crunch, and a global economic recession that has become a source of intense unhappiness for most people. Especially for the present generation, the effect is said to be unprecedented.

Cleary, it is no secret that the majority of us were caught unaware, and many will have to sadly endure the untold backlashes of the credit crunch. This of course is only one more scheme intended by Satan to instigate and to complicate the climate of unhappiness already prevalent in our world. In fact, considering the colossal damage the recession has already caused individuals and families, through extreme and unexpected financial losses and job cuts, our present world is now considered by many as a 'nasty world'.

Already, it used to be deemed by many as a world of 'survival of the fittest', a not so great description, but meant to describe the real roots of the inhumanity, intolerance and selfishness that had beguiled every fibre of our world and society, promoted largely by our own choices.

Even so, there are other things that we don't have control over. For example, not very long ago, the entire world was taken by storm over the damage and absolute devastation caused by the earthquake in Haiti and Japan. For the first time in recent history we saw, not only the countries involved brought to a stand still, but also their entire governments and their economic instruments grounded to a halt.

In some areas, we were told that important government buildings and palaces were broken and tens of government officials sadly died. Even the United Nations and other key relief agencies, apart from losing essential buildings, unfortunately suffered the loss of the lives of important personnel, and their mission in both countries were adversely affected. They could hardly coordinate aid distribution from the outset of the earthquake in Haiti, and there was absolute logistical chaos, to the extent that the search and rescue efforts for victims became almost impossible.

With countless numbers of bodies lining the streets, many were trucked away and simply dumped into open fields of mass graves. Millions of people around the world watched this sad spectacle of death and suffering broadcast on cable news channels.

Unfortunately, when things of such nature happen, we all tend to be affected in one way or the other. Personally, my worst experience with natural disaster is limited to flood and earth tremor, so I don't know what an earth quake feels like.

But, somehow, I know, life can sometimes feel like an 'earth quake' experience in some circumstances, and such experience has the potential to change the lives of its victims in many ways. Living in this world myself, I have had my own experience of some of the challenges, sufferings and contradictions that are all too prevalent to human beings.

In fact, a moment ago it knocked at my door. While one family member was phoning to tell us about their good news about the arrival of their new born baby, another, far away in another country without any immediate family support, phoned weeping obviously highly troubled, and literally crumpling under the sheer weight of sorrows and disappointments.

On the one hand, we had a birth of a new born baby, symbolising hope, and on the other hand, we had the abortion of hope, symbolised by disappointments, setbacks and sorrows. But, can we still be happy and find happiness in a world that only seems to be bleeding with contradictions? How do we go about having a 'nice-day' in a 'nasty world'? Is there hope for humanity?

First of all, there is nothing new. At least that's the testimony of the Bible. In fact, the Bible, speaking from the advantage of both hindsight and foresight, foretold and captured the problems of our world in terms that we now are all too familiar with. And the apostle Paul, without being negative, put it this way;

> *But know this, that in the last days perilous times will come: [2] For men will be lovers of themselves, lovers of money, boasters, proud, blasphemers, disobedient to parents, unthankful, unholy, [3] unloving, unforgiving, slanderers, without self-control, brutal, despisers of good, [4] traitors, headstrong, haughty, lovers of pleasure rather than lovers of God, [5] having a form of godliness but denying its power. And from such people turn away! (2 Timothy 3:1-5)*

The second thing is this. That, given the nature of things at the moment in our present world, it will be futile and totally fruitless to look to any form of human system, or organisations for any feasible and permanent solution, when in the first place, they were largely responsible for the woes of this world. Again, no human person, nor any human design, or device can give us the hope, the fulfilment, and happiness desperately needed for having a 'nice-day' as we desire.

Understandably, sometimes, we are told, the choice to be happy, to find fulfilment, and to have a 'nice-day' will always start with the individual, and the responsibility lies with them. In fact, it is said that we are not always responsible for what happens to us, but we are liable for how we respond to what happens to us. That, they refer to as 'the power of choice', and people are encouraged to choose their response in the circumstance.

However, many have used their very 'power of choice' to blame others, blame God, blame their backgrounds, get angry and cynical, and even resentful towards religion. Some too choose to resign, and do nothing. Whatever it is, one thing is true. This world will present us with diverse situations, and people will always respond differently, some in the negative and others in the positive.

Without judging the principle or morals of 'the power of choice', in relation to our happiness, fulfilment and having a nice-day, let's agree that anyone desiring any good change in their life and circumstances will have to take some important steps in realising their desired change.

For example, when Jesus spoke to people who were expecting some good changes in their circumstances, including those caught in the grip of unfavourable time, who seemed not only overwhelmed but also surprised at what they were seeing, hearing, or going through, He said something like this *"…but be of good cheer"*. I counted about eight times in the New Testament, and almost always, Jesus' words to people facing, or about to face perilous situation, were predictable; *'be of good cheer'* or simply put, *'be happy and wear a winning spirit!'*

Similarly, I want to say to readers, no doubt, there might be some things in life at the moment that might be a real challenge. For some it might be the loss of their homes, financial difficulties, marital situations, the crushing hands of sicknesses or family issues and so forth. However, it is possible, even through that, to *'be of good cheer'*, and to *'be happy and wear a winning spirit,* as Jesus commands.

Remember, an important part of your victory for change requires you personally taking some important steps. The power to take the right steps into the direction of your change for a 'nice-day', and the power that will make the same change possible, are contingent upon these truths,

> "*those who do wickedly against the covenant he shall corrupt with flattery; but the people who know their God shall be strong, and carry out great exploits" (Daniel 11:32).*

First, *know your God*, and the rest will definitely follow. The reason why you must first 'know your God' is that, all that we desire by way of happiness, peace and having nice-day, as you are aware, are nothing that this present world system, or our own strength can give us, no matter our best efforts,.

These are simply the *last days*, about which Paul attests; "*but know this, that in the last days perilous times will come" (2Tim. 3:1).* So, in view of this, only '*the people who know their God shall be strong, and carry out great exploits' (Daniel 11:32).* It will never be by any human might, but by the Spirit of God.

Second, after you have 'known your God', then go on and use your power of choice to 'Call to Him", as He has said, *"Call to Me, and I will answer you, and show you great and mighty things, which you do not know" (Jer. 33:3).*

Remember, the mighty things God wants to show you are things which generally elude this present world as it is, "things you do not know", in terms of your unrealised dreams and desires. These are the very things you desperately desire to experience, and to make a reality in your life, as the change you've been waiting for. So, if you are not yet experiencing personal fulfilment, happiness and a nice-day, which certainly this world and your own strength cannot give you, God says that, He can afford them, but first 'call to Him'. Pray.

Finally, "*be anxious for nothing, but in everything by prayer and supplication, with thanksgiving, let your requests be made known to God;*

and the peace of God, which surpasses all understanding, will guard your hearts and minds through Christ Jesus" (Philippians 4:6-7).

Also, it will be helpful to know, my friend that

> *"...we do not wrestle against flesh and blood, but against principalities, against powers, against the rulers of the darkness of this age, against spiritual hosts of wickedness in the heavenly places. ^{13} Therefore take up the whole armor of God, that you may be able to withstand in the evil day, and having done all, to stand.*

Jesus also taught us about getting our priorities right in the world of uncertainties like ours, in which we seek good changes for our happiness, personal fulfilment and for having a nice-day. He told the crowd of people who had gathered to listen to Him,

> *"Therefore do not worry, saying, 'What shall we eat?' or 'What shall we drink?' or 'What shall we wear?' ^{32} For after all these things the Gentiles seek. For your heavenly Father knows that you need all these things. ^{33} But seek first the kingdom of God and His righteousness, and all these things shall be added to you. ^{34} Therefore do not worry about tomorrow, for tomorrow will worry about its own things. Sufficient for the day is its own trouble (Mtt 6:31-34).*

I believe that Jesus' address and teaching on getting our priorities right is perfect advice for generations of the "last days", who seek to be happy and to continue to have a nice-day in a 'nasty world'.

Now, go on my friend, you can make it with the help of God, and you will come through by the grace of God Almighty, for *"weeping may endure for a night, but joy will come in the morning" (Psalms 30:5)*, and *"God will not allow your foot to be moved; He who keeps you will not slumber" (Psalm 121:3)*. Jesus will give you, and will keep you in

His *'perfect peace'* always, if you stay your mind on Him and trust in Him (Isaiah 26:3).

> *"looking unto Jesus, the author and finisher of our faith, who for the joy that was set before Him endured the cross, despising the shame, and has sat down at the right hand of the throne of God" (Hebrews 12:2).*
>
> *Seeing then that we have a great High Priest who has passed through the heavens, Jesus the Son of God, let us hold fast our confession. [15] For we do not have a High Priest who cannot sympathize with our weaknesses, but was in all points tempted as we are, yet without sin. [16] Let us therefore come boldly to the throne of grace, that we may obtain mercy and find grace to help in time of need (Hebrews 4:14-16).*

Regardless of how bleak things might seem at the moment, for those who 'know their God' and have their priorities right in relation to the kingdom of God, there is definitely hope for a happy and triumphant life, even in a world that seems so 'nasty' at times. There's no secret about the fact that God cares about us, and in His own words He says, *"Yes, I have loved you with an everlasting love, therefore with lovingkindness I have drawn you" (Jer. 31:3)*. Our hope in God shall not be disappointed and, if we remain faithful to Him, He shall strengthen our hearts and we shall always find happiness, fulfilment and a nice-day in Him (Ps 31:24).

> *... the whole earth is full of His glory! (Isa. 6:3).*

I will leave you with these soul lifting words from a wonderful hymn called, *My Hope is Built*, written by Edward Mote *(1797-1874)*.

1. My hope is built on nothing less
than Jesus' blood and righteousness.
I dare not trust the sweetest frame,

but wholly lean on Jesus' name.

Refrain:
On Christ the solid rock I stand,
all other ground is sinking sand;
all other ground is sinking sand.

2. When Darkness veils his lovely face,
I rest on his unchanging grace.
In every high and stormy gale,
my anchor holds within the veil.
(Refrain)

3. His oath, his covenant, his blood
supports me in the whelming flood.
When all around my soul gives way,
he then is all my hope and stay.
(Refrain)

4. When he shall come with trumpet sound,
O may I then in him be found!
Dressed in his righteousness alone,
faultless to stand before the throne!
(Refrain)

Encouraging___ Practical, Precise & Life-Changing.

"Walking in the Light of His Mysteries...": The Revelation of Jesus Christ

First of all, why is it of any significance that one should even think about the 'mysteries of God, or of Christ'? It is simply because, no one, is going to be like Jesus, unless they first receive a revelation of His person and principles or His Word. (cf. Acts 22:14,15, 18)

Nowhere is this fact made clearer than in the conversion experience, testimony, and the life of Paul, the Apostle. Here is an abstract of his testimony in which he argues in the defence of his apostleship, his call, and lifestyle, on the basis of the revelation and vision of Jesus:

> *"It is doubtless not profitable for me to boast. I will come to visions and revelations of the Lord: I know a man in Christ who fourteen years ago—whether in the body I do not know, or whether out of the body I do not know, God knows—such a one was caught up to the third heaven. And I know such a man—whether in the body or out of the body I do not know, God knows— how he was caught up into Paradise and heard inexpressible words, which it is not lawful for a man to utter." (2Cor. 12:1-4);*

Similarly, the dialogue between Paul and the Lord at the time of his conversion to Jesus, in Acts 9:1-10, reminds us about the need for Jesus to be revealed and, for us to receive a revelation of Him. In this regard, in *verse 5*, Paul asked a crucial question, which is doubtlessly, a question of revelation. He asked, *"Who are You, Lord?"* The Lord answered, *"I am Jesus, whom you are persecuting."*

Space will not permit to comment much on Moses and how he had God to first reveal Himself, before he could embark on his extremely critical ministry in Egypt, to deliver Israel from bondage. Like Paul, on 'Damascus Road', Moses initially encountered God at the 'Burning Bush', and God revealed Himself to him as, 'the God of his father' (Exod. 3:6). In verse 13, Moses asked a crucial question; *"Indeed, when I come to the children of Israel and say to them, 'The God of your fathers has sent me to you,' and they say to me, 'What is His name?' what shall I say to them?"* In other words, Moses was saying, "I cannot even begin to speak to your people, if I don't have a 'revelation' of You – I don't know You". Then, God revealed Himself to Moses as, *"I AM WHO I AM." And He said, "Thus you shall say to the children of Israel, 'I AM has sent me to you.'" Moreover God said to Moses, "Thus you shall say to the children of Israel: 'The Lord God of your fathers, the God of Abraham, the God of Isaac, and the God of Jacob, has sent me to you. This is My name forever, and this is My memorial to all generations.' (Exod. 3:14,15)*

The Lord Jesus, Himself, was quite keen on ensuring that His disciples had a true revelation of His person and teachings (principles). So, He asked them: *"Who do men say that I, the Son of Man, am?" So they said, "Some say John the Baptist, some Elijah, and others Jeremiah or one of the prophets." He said to them, "But who do you say that I am?" Simon Peter answered and said, "You are the Christ, the Son of the living God." Jesus answered and said to him, "Blessed are you, Simon Bar-Jonah, for flesh and blood has not revealed this to you, but My Father who is in heaven." (Matthew 16:13-17)*

John, the evangelist, apostle, and the "disciple whom Jesus loved", also put it this way: *"Beloved, now we are children of God; and it has not yet been revealed what we shall be, but we know that when He is revealed, we shall be like Him, for we shall see Him as He is." (1 John 3:2)* He continued in another place, saying, *"Love has been perfected among us in this: that we may have boldness in the day of judgment; because as He is, so are we in this world." (1 John 4:17)*. In other words, when we personally get to know Christ through revelation, for who and what He really is, then it would be easy for us to walk, talk, act, and do things like He did and does. We have to encounter Jesus in some ways, by the revelation of Himself, and that has to be settled in our spirit. Until then, we will walk, talk and act like mere mortals, although God 'expects great things to accompany our salvation' (Heb. 6:9).

The power of the above referenced passages lies in the fact that, you can only function according to the level of revelation currently available to you. Beyond that you are helpless and weak. The more 'we know Jesus', the more "we make it our aim to please Him" (2Cor.5:9), and to live out fully the power of Him who works through us.

1 John 3:9, Says, we have "the seed" (spiritual DNA) of Christ in us, and agrees with Acts 17:28,29; that "we are His offspring. In Him we live, move and have our being". But, again, the effectiveness of this truth about God's "seed" being in us relies on our revelation of Christ. We are only able to appreciate and appropriate the power of that "seed" if, Christ has first been revealed or made manifest in our spirit, to the extent that we see ourselves "as He is in this world". That does not mean that, any person can pose as the Lord Jesus. No, because there is only one Lord and Christ, who is the begotten of the Father. (1Cor. 8:6; 1Tim. 2:5; Acts 4:12). But we have His "seed", and we are "His offspring", who should walk in His love, grace, power and authority. (John 14:12-14; 15:4,7; 17:20-14; Matt. 18:18).

That's why this book and its title are so relevant "walking in the light of His Mysteries". The idea is to help people to go after the revelation of Christ and His truth through the power of the Spirit. The aim is to help believers to realise, appreciate and appropriate all that Christ has already placed in their path, through His finished work on the Cross. By this, hopefully people would not just see their potential, but would desire and try to walk in the grace and dominion that Christ has already released to them. More importantly, people would live and act like Christ in this world. That, 'the mysteries of God', as it is known, will become a revealed truth and wisdom for the people of Christ; enabling them to walk in victory continuously.

Actually, *"Walking in the Light of His Mysteries"* is an attempt to 'demystify' the mysteries of God, for the blessings that they contain to accrue to anyone, who will trust in the Lord Jesus Christ. It is meant to help believers to take positive steps in making 'the mysteries of God' an everyday life experience, leading to victory, godliness and fruitfulness. In 2 Peter1:3, 4, we read that, "His divine power has given to us all things that *pertain* to life and godliness," How? "Through the knowledge of Him who called us by glory and virtue, by which have been given to us exceedingly great and precious promises, that through these you may be partakers of the divine nature, having escaped the corruption *that is* in the world through lust."

The Author is no stranger to God's miracle power, and he also wants to affirm here that, miracles are possible even today. This book is an attempt to demonstrate, *why* and *how* miracles happen today; part of which includes personal testimonies. Expect a miracle!

About the Author

Pastor Didi and his wife, Dorothy, live and pastor in England, United Kingdom. They both love the Lord Jesus Christ passionately and are the founding pastors of an all-inclusive people-background church, Good Word Ministries, UK. Together, they continue to enjoy God's unlimited grace and favour at various levels and in different aspects of their ministries. A core area of their own purpose is reaching out in faith and obedience to assist people to realise the love of God in Christ, and to help them discover their God given purpose and potential. They believe that every one of God's children is loved and has unlimited potential to become the best that God intends for them.

Their first book, *Beyond Me, Doing the Impossible with the Purposes of God*, has already received wide acceptance and excellent praise from both Christians and non-Christians, and is set to be a leading book in Christian spirituality, faith, and motivation.

Pastors Didi and Dorothy are presently both directors of Aleph World Ltd, and Pastor Didi holds a BA (Hons) degree in Theology, and a Master of Philosophy (MPhil) degree in Religious Studies.

****

To Contact Good Word Ministries, UK, Please visit
www.goodwordchristiancentre.org.uk

Please include your prayer requests and comments when you write.

****

Acknowledgements

We are truly grateful to Miss Julie Stubbs, our special friend and sister in Christ, who volunteered to proofread the finished work of this revised edition, for errors. Thanks very much for your time and commitment in helping to make the necessary corrections.

Also, our ongoing gratitude and sincerest thanks go to all members of Good Word Ministries and our friends. Your friendship and support in various ways have been inspiring. You have all helped and have added greatly to our overall experience in one way or another. Together, we are fulfilling God's purposes, and thank you all!

END NOTES

[1] W. S. Mcbirnie, *The Search for the Twelve Apostles*, (Illinois: Tyndale House Publishers, 1973), TBN Edition, pp. 18-19

[2] *Remember she felt freed (vr..) and further in the text she is told by Jesus, 'be freed of...'.* Free in the first instance describing how she felt, in the greek it is *Iaoma*, which means to heal, cure, restore, to bodily health (Lk 5:17; 6:19; 22:51); to heal spiritually (mtt 13:15; Jn 12:40), In the passive, it means to be healed bodily (mtt 8:8, 13; 15:28; Mk 5:29; also to be healed spiritually (1Peter 2:24). *Free* referring to Jesus' command is the greek, *Hygies* meaning to be sound, healthy. Mainly taken by the NT to mean sound, whole and complete in health (mtt 12:13; 15:31; MK3:5, 34; lk 6:10; jn 5:4,6,11,14,15; 7:23; Acts 4:10) of sound speech or doctrine, wholesome, right (titus 2:8). Another word for Hygies, is Hygiaino; from Hygies, meaning sound, healthy. To be healthy, sound, physically well (Lk 5:31; 7:10; 3jn 2), signifying to be safe (Lk 15:27); metaphorically of persons to be sound in the faith, meaning firm, pure in respect of Christian doctrine (1Tim 1:10; 2tim 4:3)

[3] *By the way, some theologians, yes, theo-lo-geans, make interesting connection between Jairus' daughter who died at 12 and this woman who had issue of blood for 12 years. They believe, even though the text does not say so, that the spiritual significance in the little girl's story dovetailing with this woman's is to help us see the woman's actual condition which may have begun at 12yrs. That she may have suffered some irreparable tragedy leading to her dying spiritually speaking at 12yr. As a result she would have been stroke real deeply to cause her untold inner sufferings, pains, unforgiveness, depression and the like. In a way Jesus gave her life back symbolically by the raising of Jairus' daughter from the dead. However, this woman who was now older than 12, still had that 'little girl' (her childhood) in her crying to be set free. Sounds like a deep revelation, but the text does not make such connection anyway.*

[4] Watches Of Night

The Jews, like the Greeks and Romans, divided the night into military watches instead of hours, each watch representing the period for which sentinels or pickets remained on duty. The proper Jewish reckoning recognized only three such watches, entitled the first or "beginning of the watches," (Lamentations 2:19) the middle watch, (Judges 7:19) and the morning watch. (Exodus 14:24; 1 Samuel 11:11) These would last respectively from sunset to 10 P.M.; from 10 P.M. to 2 A.M.; and from 2 A.M. to sunrise. After the establishment of the Roman supremacy, the number of watches was increased to four, which were described either according to their numerical order, as in the case of the "fourth watch," (Matthew 14:25) or by the terms "even," "midnight," "cock-crowing" and "morning." (Mark 13:35) These terminated respectively at 9 P.M., midnight, 3 A.M. and 6 A.M.

[5] The Apostolic Fathers, *The Fragments of Papias*, p. 315. p318, has it that *Justus drank the poison of snake in the Name of Christ when put to the test by unbelievers and was protected from all harm*

⁶ The literal meaning of Bartimaeus is, "son of Timaeus". Mark translates the name into Greek. Bartimaeus has a double meaning; first being Greek meaning, "Great, Worthy, Priced (ransomed), or honourable man"; and second, the Hebrew meaning being, "heir or son of unclean, abominable, impure." In Jewish tradition and theology, people easily assume that blindness was a form of curse of punishment from God. (see John 9:20-34). There is ambiguity about the meaning of the name in Hebrew / Aramaic, but generally, the first translation is consider the strongest, and is widely accepted and supported.

Thank God for ambiguity. First it makes us humble, and helps us to see our own inadequacies. Second, God uses ambiguity as a teaching opportunity; to help us to appreciate that things are not always as they appear, in black and white. Third, usually, what is considered unclean in one culture could be seen honourable in another culture, and never be a slave to your culture or lead by your culture, but by God's Word and wisdom alone." Then Peter opened his mouth, and said, of a truth I perceive that God is no respecter of persons: But in every nation he that feareth him, and worketh righteousness, is accepted with him." (Acts 10:35KJV). Read Acts 10:9ff

⁷ In *The Intellectual Tradition of the West, Vol.1,* 1967. page 50-56
⁸ Ibib. P.51

⁹ Ibid. p.46 & 48

www.ingramcontent.com/pod-product-compliance
Lightning Source LLC
Chambersburg PA
CBHW032025290426
44110CB00012B/667